Top Team Planning

a study of the power of
individual motivation
in management

Top Team Planning

*a study of the power of
individual motivation
in management*

PAMELA RAMSDEN

A HALSTED PRESS BOOK

JOHN WILEY & SONS
New York

English language edition, except U.S.A
Published by
Associated Business Programmes Ltd.
17 Buckingham Gate London SW1

Published in U.S.A. by
Halsted Press, a Division
of John Wiley & Sons, Inc.,
New York

First published 1973

This book has been printed in Great Britain
by The Anchor Press Ltd., and bound by
Wm. Brendon & Son Ltd., both of Tiptree, Essex

ISBN 0 470-70770-4

Library of Congress   72-7882

Contents

PART III: USING THE ACTION PROFILE

PART IV: RESULTS

List of Action Profiles, Tables, Charts, Figures and Photographic Section

ACTION PROFILES

TABLES

CHARTS

FIGURES

PHOTOGRAPHIC SECTION

Acknowledgements

I would like to extend my sincere thanks to Warren Lamb, Vincent Nolan, and Professor William Guth for their concentrated advice on the typescript; to Michael Baynes, Robert Jones, Professor John Morris and Richard Hayes for their useful comments; to John and Ian Marks for their financial assistance and encouragement; and to Derek Drage for his innovative photographs.

I wish to thank also, all our clients who have so kindly granted permission for case studies to be based upon their companies.

Foreword

Creativity and risk taking are in the long run essentials to business survival. On the other hand, ill-advised risk taking and wrongly applied creativity can do grave damage. To the extent that this is so, soundly applied management judgement is at the heart of business, and management is the key resource at a company's disposal.

A means or system therefore which permits the analysis and evaluation of personal management talents is of important interest to business leaders. Pamela Ramsden's book deals with the problem of planning management ability, a more difficult and more important problem than planning any of the company's other resources.

The technique which Miss Ramsden describes, with clarity and in great detail, is one which recognises the importance of individual motivation in management behaviour. The method is to delineate a manager's Action Profile and by this means match the manager's potential to the demands of a job or management task. In this way it is possible not only to improve the manager's performance, but to assist him develop his potential.

The methods outlined by Miss Ramsden have been put to the practical test by the firm of management consultants, Warren Lamb Associates, with which she is professionally connected. My company, among many others, have commissioned them to assist in our Top Team planning. Their work gave me, as I am sure this innovative book will give many others, a much wider perspective concerning the use of a manager's ability, and perhaps more importantly a greater insight into achieving greater understanding and spontaneous co-operation within the management team.

P C BOON
Managing Director (Export)
Hoover Limited

Preface

This book is an explanation of a systematic way of describing managers'
behaviour. It includes a framework of management activity comprising 12
factors organized around a three stage sequence of activity. Managers are
assessed against this framework of management activity and for each manager
a pattern of behaviour is deduced, known as the Action Profile.

This approach to the description of managerial behaviour has been successfully applied in the study of senior management teams. Known as Top Team
Planning, this form of study encompasses a direct approach to the investigation of senior managers as individuals, and then as members of a management team. It leads to a plan for the development of a balanced team able
to create a business climate well matched and adapted to the broader industrial and commercial environment within which it functions. The Top Team
Planning approach has been developed gradually over the last ten years and
now the founder of the Action Profile method of assessment, Warren Lamb,
and I are fully employed upon this work.

The Action Profile method of assessment has a long history. Warren Lamb
pioneered the technique and in his function as a management consultant his
work has been highly respected by clients, some of whom have used his
services continuously for as long as 15 years. Amongst the academic
behavioural scientists, however, the basis of this work has, in the past, found
little understanding, (a) because up till now it has not been expressed in the
context of a theoretical framework placing it in perspective with other
behavioural approaches, and (b) because it was simply before its time. The
assessment method, as mentioned before, is grounded in the study of non-
verbal behaviour, an area very little studied until the last decade.

Construction of the Action Profile of a person requires highly detailed
observation of minute variations in non-verbal behaviour. The ability to
make the observations requires long and intensive training. Until recently,
struggling on his own as a one man band consultant, Warren Lamb found
neither the time nor resources to train another consultant. He has trained a
very dedicated psychiatrist in New York who now has her own group of
trainees, but they are working in psychoanalysis, not management.

As a psychologist I was originally employed by a long-standing client of Warren Lamb's to further the research into the Action Profile. I showed such interest and degree of aptitude that I became trained in observation whilst carrying on the research. Up till this time even many of Warren Lamb's most loyal clients had been sceptical of the scientific basis of his assessment methods. Every one recognized that he showed evidence of enormous perception, but it seemed most sensible to leave it at that. However, now that a second practitioner is fully trained in making the observations and constructing the Action Profile, there is beginning to be greater acceptance of the underlying theory and system on which the assessment is based.

In the course of my research I found it necessary to develop a theory of behaviour which would place Warren Lamb's findings in context with other schools of thought. I found for instance that it formed a logical link between personality and motivation theory. I have written this book in order:

(a) to recount the history and origin of the action profile method of assessment;

(b) to outline case histories of companies who have used the Action Profile approach in the planning of managerial resources; and

(c) to incorporate all our findings into the beginning of a comprehensive theory of behaviour.

This book is directed mainly toward the practical manager and, to this end, the theoretical framework is substantially illustrated by case histories and accounts of actual Top Team Planning assignments in companies. However, as managers have often expressed a need for greater knowledge of the theoretical underpinnings of this method of assessment, the theory is developed in some depth. Many have said that the observation system and analysis of non-verbal behaviour is difficult to understand, but it is recommended that a little effort and concentration be given, for it is the foundation stone of the whole system.

It must be recognized that this is an account of work in progress. Although the Action Profile concepts have been researched, tested and used enough to provide a valuable and practicable tool in management, there is still a great deal to be learned, both in theory and practice. So to the practical manager we can say—this is the stage the Action Profile theory and technique has reached and this is how it can be used. To the behavioural researcher we can say—this is the progress made in a new and interesting area of research. It isn't complete by any means but is behavioural research ever complete?

The following account of the application of the principles of the action profile assessment to Top Team Planning is based largely upon my personal experience within British manufacturing companies. May I point out, however, that whilst all the case histories are based upon actual situations, all the names and identifying features are fictitious.

Because this book is written as an account particularly of work using the action profile method with top management, the emphasis throughout is on senior managers. This is not only because a major part of our work is with senior managers, but also because behaviour of managers at top level is less studied than the behaviour of managers at other levels. It is perfectly explicable in terms of the position of power held by top managers, but for the progress of management science it is a great weakness. Having said that, and although the emphasis is upon senior managers, the principles and practice of the action profile approach apply also to managers and management teams at middle and junior levels.

Finally, I would like to offer a warning to the reader. As a practising consultant, highly committed to a particular behavioural approach, I cannot claim impartiality, but I have endeavoured throughout to present a realistic and objective picture.

Pamela Ramsden

PART I

The Problem and a Tool

CHAPTER 1

The Manager as a Cause of Events

At the head of every company there is a group of men who are responsible for the survival of that company. They set the basic policy and the major decisions are taken by them. They have to pit themselves against the giant forces of commerce and industry, the corrosion by competition, the lure of attractive but false markets, and catastrophies of the economic and political climate. They have to fight constantly against a myriad of external circumstances of often unknown magnitude and certainty. It is managers versus the business environment in which they function, and this amounts almost to a fight for survival. But is this really so? Are managers really so much the defenders coping with external factors over which they have little or no direct control?

If a company is put out of business by competition, is it really the whole truth of the matter to explain the phenomenon in terms of the efficiency, sales acumen, lucky new products, etc., etc., of the competitor company? In fact does it have any real bearing on the situation at all? If a company is destroyed over time by gradual socio-economic changes, is the answer really to be found in an account of the nature of those changes? If a company enters an unproductive market, will it really throw any light on the problem to recount how and why and to what extent the market was unsuitable? All managers would recognize that in each case there is another side to the story. Part of an explanation of any event such as the ones described above would always be in terms of the mistakes and failings of the management of the company concerned and of course particularly the top management. However, the explanation in terms of the various external events will always be more precise, accurate and comprehensive than any of the explanations in terms of the failings of the managers. This is simply because it is easier to talk about external events. They are more amenable to quantification and precise definition. Managerial behaviour on the other hand is a very elusive phenomenon to actually pin down systematically in order to give a rational and consistent explanation of an event as momentous and complex as, for instance, the slow decline of a former lion of industry. And yet it is in the behaviour of managers that the real explanation will always lie.

It is possible to go so far as to say that there are no real mishaps in management, only managers who cause them or cannot cope with them. A company doesn't decline because there is no longer a demand for its products. It declines because managers didn't recognize the trend. A company in a fast moving consumer industry doesn't get into difficulties because the competition is too tough. It gets into difficulties because its managers are not quick and opportunist enough to compete effectively. Most managers would probably agree with this—that at the centre of any problem in management there will be the strengths and limitations of individual managers and groups of managers.

But managers are also responsible for the successes that occur in business. Most successful managers would attribute a great deal of their success to ability but always they will admit to an element of luck. There is, of course, no such thing as luck, only combinations of circumstances and factors which cannot be analysed. So far the factor which has most successfully defied analysis is the manager himself. Managers achieve success because they actually create a particular business climate around themselves which happens to match the broader industrial–commercial climate. Most managers would agree that it is they who cause the rise and fall of companies through their ability and inability to react to external pressures. But how many realize that they actually create those pressures themselves?

Managers do not just react to circumstances, they create them. If a manager asserts with conviction that there are absolutely no alternatives to a particular unsatisfactory course of action and that there is no recourse but to persevere with it, it is not because there really are no alternatives but because he has created a climate where alternatives do not exist, but obstacles with which he can persevere certainly do. Another manager will claim with equal conviction that there are always alternatives and there is no point in persevering with any one particular course of action, particularly if you run into obstacles. He will create a climate where there are really no obstacles at all, just thousands of alternatives. Another manager will create a world full of prospects, targets and visions of the future. Another will see things in terms of issues and straight facts. Another will see only the need for quality, standards and principles.

In other words there are no absolute realities, only those which individual managers create in their own environment.

Because each individual manager creates the business climate within which he works, a combination of managers creates, in an infinitely more complex way, the total business environment within which a company functions. The degree to which any individual manager affects the total company business climate will, of course, vary according to the power of his personality and his position within the company.

The term 'business climate', as has already been suggested, refers to the climate in which a company conducts its business. However, it is not only a climate governed by factors external to a company but one which is actually created by the company itself. Business climate, in the sense used here, is akin to the concept of company style. Company style, however, is a term used more commonly to refer to a company's characteristic way of reacting to circumstances and the kind of internal environment it generates. A company might, for instance, consider its style to be individualistic and competitive. The managers all act in a highly individualistic way and compete fiercely against each other.

If you extend this, the managers will not only compete with each other, but with the rest of the business world as well. They will not just react to events competitively, but will be constantly looking for opportunities to seize more quickly than the next man, whoever he might be, and even if there is no next man. They will be keen to be the first to take advantage of the slightest new possibility, and even if no real advantage is to be gained at all. Hence they are creating a particular business climate for themselves and their company in which to function. Obviously, the distinction between company style and business climate is a small one and more a matter of emphasis than a true difference. But the difference in emphasis is important because it highlights the necessity for studying managers rather than management.

The total business climate within which a company functions, therefore, is created ultimately by the combination of the individual styles of its managers. However, they combine at many different levels and in different sized units. A manager and a subordinate is one such unit for instance. In combination they create a different business climate around their particular function than each would on his own. A much larger unit would be a division within a company or a department, or any other clearly defined section within the company. A particularly important unit is the management team, and especially the 'top team'.

A top management team is a highly potent force in the creation of business climates. If one risk-taking competitive opportunist can create a few opportunities, how many more can a whole team of them create! A top team always develops a distinctive character or style which tends to perpetuate itself. As a result a particular business climate is created which is also perpetuated.

A management team is not just a mixture of personalities. It is not just people who get together because they have a job to do and co-operation is needed to get it done. No member works in isolation, each is affected by the others. Certain characteristics in time become dominant. Odd men out get left out. The style of a management team and the business climate it consequently creates (except where environmental accidents such as takeovers occur) may change perhaps, but only very slowly. Once the style develops it tends to perpetuate itself. Members within a team cannot see this. They are too closely involved and have no standard of comparison. No-one asks whether the team style and the business climate it has created is the right one.

Sometimes the style of the top team and the business climate it creates may be quite wrong for the present situation of the company. It may be one sided and biased in the wrong direction. There may be men on the fringes of the top team with just the right balancing characteristics but going unrecognized. Individuals may be structured into the team in such a way that such balancing characteristics as they have are prevented from coming to the surface. The top executive may not recognize the very men who have the most valuable contribution to make, for their particular strengths are not in line with the predominant team character. And so the situation continues and a particular business climate is created and preserved. If it is in line with the broader industrial and commercial climate the company will succeed, if not it will fail.

If managers do in fact react not only to circumstances according to their abilities and failings, but also actually create the business climate within which they function, it would seem imperative to study and analyse the behavioural characteristics which contribute to this process. But of course, managerial behaviour, like any other behaviour, is often complex and contradictory. Consider for instance the behaviour of three managers. Two are managing directors and one a works director. All are encountering problems of varying magnitude and in each case the difficulty is due largely to the behaviour of the manager himself and the kind of business climate he personally creates around himself. In each case the key to the problem is in the behaviour described below.

Mr. J. Lexington

Concern at the lack of initiative shown by his senior executives led Mr. Lexington to commission a study of his people, primarily with the aim of gaining advice as to how he could best induce his subordinates to contribute more. He wondered whether it was just on the basis of his personal assessment and in comparison to himself that they appeared lacking in initiative, or whether they really were of low calibre. The study of his executive team revealed them to be, with perhaps one or two mild exceptions, exceedingly capable managers. Yet all admitted that they felt unable to compete with Mr. Lexington's brilliant display at meetings and brilliant performance overall and all admitted that they found it difficult to contribute. In contrast to many other companies studied in this way, this seemed an unusual attitude. It was as if the executives felt there was every opportunity to contribute and that they were positively invited to do so, yet were unable to comply. None of them ever complained of Mr. Lexington's approach; on the contrary, all were outspoken in their praise and appreciation of his brilliance. None thought that he hampered their ability to contribute in any way and most thought that he was highly capable of developing and fostering their managerial potential.

Mr. Lexington's company is a medium small-sized company in the toy industry. Goods are distributed through wholesale and retail outlets. He is mainly in competition with giant corporations and is achieving considerable success.

Mr. Lexington himself is a short, dark, stocky man of Mediterranean descent. One is immediately aware of his terrific restless energy. He has a darting quickness in everything he does. He speaks with enormous speed and fluency. He pours out a continuous stream of racing ideas. He asks ten questions at once and hardly pauses to wait for an answer to any of them. He is highly conscious of the impression he is making. He makes enormous claims about his intellectual brilliance, his desire for power and sense of uniqueness. He states outright that he is a star performer, that it is due to his brilliance alone that his company has become profitable and that he is unparalleled in the realm of strategic planning and policy formulation. Everything he says sounds highly convincing. He is the type who could make a convincing case for almost anything and you would at first believe him. He takes a delight in showing off his admittedly very efficient recall memory. He will 'test' you on various obscure points of general knowledge and take great delight in displaying his knowledge of the right answers. He is constantly flinging out challenges of one kind or another. He may make an enormously bold declaration of some kind but will not carry the point through to its logical end, or defend it against consistent opposition.

In dealing with people he can practise a subtle and often conscious tactic of manipulation. He may play one person off against another for instance and perhaps unwittingly promote conflict between them. It is rather like army tactics. He sows seeds of dissent amongst his opposition and so weakens their position, thus further enhancing his own power. In a discussion, such tactics can obviously be very disconcerting and no doubt achieve their purpose. He seems instinctively to regard other people as opposition. He cannot really allow people to co-operate with him at his own level. Any such attempt he immediately sees as competition, yet at the same time he was forever complaining of his lonely position, and need for contribution at his own level.

Mr. Lexington is behaving in such a way as to both invite and reject his colleagues' initiative at one and the same time. There is a considerable conflict in his attitude. He is a capable manager, dedicated to his company, yet he is behaving in such a way as to reduce his own and his colleagues' effectiveness. How can the elements in his management style contributing to this problem be isolated and systematically described?

Mr. E. Irving

Mr. Irving commands great loyalty from his subordinates and a great sense of comradeship is evident amongst them. They often refer to themselves as 'Irving men'. There is a great feeling of unity in the face of 'adversity' amongst the team. The main adversity which they all felt themselves to be facing in their role as a production team, was lack of co-operation and understanding from the sales people. Mr. Irving felt this to be a fact of life, a burden to be battled against, fumed at, remonstrated about, but endured. He never once considered that some of the misunderstanding could stem from his side or that he could take steps from his side to reduce the problem.

Mr. Irving is the General Works Manager of a medium sized engineering firm, Fellows Acre Ltd. He worked his way up from the shop floor to a position on the Board. He has never had any formal engineering or management training. He has a remarkable man-to-man, matter-of-fact manner. He is a strange mixture of sophistication and roughness. He strides into the room with a forcefulness strangely overlaid by a casual, almost slouching, bearing. There is a nonchalant, lackadaisical air about him, belied by his obviously deep concern and feeling about everything he does. It is as if he seeks to ease his terrific involvement with an outward show of unconcern. He throws himself into everything he does, with powerful intensity.

He easily becomes vociferous about certain points to the extent of thumping the table. In the face of problems he displays enormously angry frustration. He fumes and froths, remonstrates and struggles unceasingly against the bondage of circumstances over which he feels he has no control . . . such as the demands of the sales department. He lapses into streams of vociferous ramble. The angrier he gets and the more frustrated, the more involved and confused become his dissertations. He swears unashamedly, but is otherwise faultlessly polite with the same air of casualness.

Mr. Irving has a problem and to some extent it is due to his own way of acting in carrying out a management responsibility. But how exactly is it due to him and how can his behaviour be described systematically to throw some light on the problem?

Mr. T. Myer

Mr. Myer is the Managing Director of a subsidiary of an American owned international company. Mr. Myer's company, Kale and Co. Ltd., had been taken over just prior to his appointment there. It had been a traditional family-owned company run in an almost feudal manner. Mr. Myer's brief was to rejuvenate the company using the existing people so far as possible and render it profitable by means of up to date scientific management methods, a task he was to find bafflingly difficult.

Mr. Myer was born of a poor family. As a youth he used to caddy at golf for business executives. Listening to them talk he became enthralled with the world of management and business. He was determined to become a manager. He studied accountancy and joined the group for which he still works. At a comparatively young age he was a Managing Director. He has managed subsidiaries in various places all over the world, building two up from scratch, in each case very successfully. At the age of 35 he was tackling his third major assignment—the rehabilitation of a company.

He is a quiet, studious, intense man, who seems older than his years. He is totally unassuming and totally wrapped up in his work. He works incredible hours with little apparent strain. He is exceedingly humble in seeking advice and almost painfully concerned to do the best for his subordinates. One can see that he suffers at causing others distress. He has established an informal relationship with his subordinates, to the extent that he wanders about speaking to all and sundry by their christian names, yet in his nature there is something inherently formal. He feels at a distance. He can speak interminably about his people problems and always with the same mixture of sympathy and concern and frustration at their shortcomings.

He is always preoccupied with results. He never fails to report in detail by how much sales and production are up and down. Yet even whilst recognizing his managers' shortcomings in ability to reach projected targets, he cannot bear for a man to be prematurely condemned. He took advice on his own strengths and weaknesses with the greatest humility, perception and self knowledge. He has no qualms at his group chief reading the report submitted on his style of management. There is nothing defensive about him. He rarely defends himself against advice or criticism.

As mentioned before, Mr. Myer's most difficult task was to convert a group of subordinates, used to an antique patriarchal form of leadership, into a democratically organized team of progressive hard-headed managers. A veritable revolution in outlook had to be incurred. A complete re-education in business principles had to take place. Throughout it all morale had to be kept up, a difficult task, but then Myer had dealt with difficult tasks before.

Mr. Myer, in two years, had made some progress. He had opened a new factory and increased production but not enough. Nor had he made the expected profits. Overall he had enormous problems with management at all levels and particularly the top management team. He seemed constantly to come up against an amazing degree of self delusion. The men persisted in believing that they were highly successful, despite all evidence to the contrary. One by one many of the old team had to go. After struggling with this situation for eighteen months, Myer had made little real impression upon the situation. He was becoming burdened by its apparent immutability and was beginning to show signs of stress.

To a considerable extent the difficulties being encountered in this situation were due to Mr. Myer's personal way of getting things done. But how can the relevant factors stemming from Mr. Myer's personal style be isolated and described?

There is nothing extraordinary about these examples of managerial behaviour. It is not altogether unknown for an intelligent, sophisticated managing director like Mr. Lexington to have difficulty in drawing from his managers and encouraging them to take most of the burden off his shoulders. It is not all that unusual for a highly capable Production or Works Director like Mr. Irving to encounter problems with the sales people, or for a previously highly successful manager like Mr. Myer to suddenly appear to fail in what seems to be a fairly similar situation to those previously handled. What is extraordinary is that such behaviour is not studied systematically. The characteristics within managers that cause such behaviour are not studied, but it is such characteristics that create the business climates within which companies function and upon which companies rise and fall.

Lexington isn't just an autocrat who deliberately destroys his subordinates' ability to take initiative (although it could appear that way). He is a manager with certain inbuilt characteristics which both make him behave toward his subordinates in a certain way and cause him, with them, to create a certain business climate. Irving isn't just an over-earnest, ham-fisted pusher. Because of his inbuilt characteristics he positively requires certain conditions to exist within his environment. He isn't just determined, he requires obstacles against which he can pit his determination. If there are none he will create them and along with them a whole business climate will exist. Myer cannot just be written off as a puzzling failure, one of the management mishaps. He is a man with certain inbuilt characteristics which cause him to build a certain climate around himself. He ran into problems because the climate he personally tried to create was just too far removed from the business climate already existing around the company.

We are not just talking about managers' quirks and mannerisms, or even just about managers' personalities. We are talking about the stuff of management—more than that, the stuff of the whole industrial and commercial fabric. Somehow we have to break down behaviour like that of Lexington, Irving and Myer and turn it into information that can actually be used.

Of course no manager would deny that it is important to study managerial behaviour, and particularly that of top managers. It is necessary to study the behaviour of top managers first not only because they are the final decision makers, but also because changes effected at lower levels can so often be negated by conservatism at the top.

There are, however, two very potent reasons why the behaviour of top managers is not very often studied in a systematic and comprehensive way. Firstly, most of the techniques for studying the behaviour of managers are inadequate to some degree. Secondly, the senior ranks of management are in a very good position to hold themselves sacrosanct against any intrusion into their domain. It would be foolish not to recognize the very human truth that there will always be a political situation to some extent and this will always militate against a fresh look being taken at behavioural trends at top level even though there may be reliable and relevant methods for doing so.

To expand upon the first point, consider the various forms of personality assessment and behavioural study applicable to managerial behaviour. The various methods fall into two broad categories, assessment for selection and group training of one kind and another.

1. *Assessment for Selection*

  (i) Psychological testing and interviewing

  By 'psychological testing' is meant the use of objective tests of various kinds, to measure level and kind of mental ability plus (sometimes) personality factors. The combination of psychological testing and personal interview is one of the most widely used methods. It is said to have the advantages of allowing the psychologist to apply his professional skills and common sense to all the information available to him, allowing him to take the 'whole' person into account. The disadvantages, however, are that the accuracy of this technique is rarely verified rigorously and depends largely upon the personal experience and ability of the psychologist. The accuracy and relevance of the descriptions produced are often questionable particularly in terms of whether or not they relate to success or failure on a job. This is particularly true of predictions made about leadership potential, or interpersonal skills.[1]

  (ii) Graphology

  This method is fairly widely used for assessment of senior managers particularly in Europe. It is difficult, however, to discover any evidence that it is a particularly relevant or highly practicable approach to the study of significant behavioural factors in management, except as an adjunct to other methods.

  (iii) Intelligence testing

  This is usually used as an adjunct to other methods of aptitude and personality assessment. Intelligence is recognized to bear some relevance to managerial ability but it is nowhere near the whole story. David McClelland, author of the 'Achieving Society' commented recently that the most important research needs at the moment are some way of measuring competence as opposed to intelligence testing. He considers that the testing movement is in a rut and has been in it for 40 years '. . . the only way out is by getting some other tests that measure the ability to behave "intelligently" in life situations'.[2]

  (iv) The Straight Interview

  The interview is still the most widely used method of assessment for appointment of managers at all levels. It can hardly be called a method of studying behaviour but as a selection technique it is certainly not the least reliable method. The consensus of opinion about interviewing at present is that there are 'good' interviewers and 'bad' interviewers. The 'good' interviewers are as accurate in their judgements as objective personality tests in certain areas[3], the 'bad' interviewers are worse than useless.

(v) Group Dynamics

This method requires a group of candidates to co-operate in tackling a task, such as building a model village or making a construction of some kind. The candidates are assessed according to their observed performance. This is a valuable approach in that it is stimulating full scale behaviour, and interaction or group behaviour.

Problems are, however, that the composition of any particular group will strongly influence the behaviour of any individual (he may behave quite differently in another group). It may be difficult to make the tasks really representative of particular managerial situations and judgements will ultimately depend on the perceptivity or non-perceptivity of the observers.

2. *Group Training*

The training situation provides a more comprehensive setting for learning about managers' behaviour. At least it usually allows more time and variety of situation than the selection situation.

(i) T Group Training

The use of T Group Training techniques for the study of behaviour at senior level is still fairly uncommon but becoming more widespread. It involves the bringing together of a small group for the purpose of studying the participants' own behaviour. Each member of the group attempts to learn about the effects his behaviour has on others.[4] This technique is probably more applicable to the investigation of dynamic management behaviour at senior levels than any so far mentioned. However, there are problems associated with this kind of approach.

(a) It is based upon study of the interaction of one particular group. Hence findings on the behaviour of an individual manager which may be valid within that group may not be valid for other groups or other types of interaction.

(b) The success of such training will depend upon the ability of the leader. It is certainly a valuable sensitizing device but a rather hit and miss one, unless the trainer is highly perceptive.

(c) There is no comprehensive and systematic framework of behaviour which can put the behaviour of individual managers in context or allow them to see it in relation to a broader managerial environment.[5]

(ii) Management Grid[6]

This is a system of classifying managerial behaviour which is also well suited to the treatment of senior managers. It involves a simple dichotomy between people orientation and production orientation. The ideal is the '9/9' man who is both highly people and production oriented. In its clarity and simplicity it provides a useful categorizing tool for muddled thoughts about managerial behaviour.

Again, however, it is nowhere near comprehensive and again it is reliant upon a particular group composition as judgements are made by members of a group of one another. It is a worthwhile exercise, but does not provide a comprehensive framework for describing managerial behaviour.

(iii) Team Training

This is a development of group training methods which stresses that for such training to be relevant it must concentrate upon an already existing group and be centred around practical functions which at least are similar to tasks with which the group is normally concerned.[7] This is obviously a useful vehicle for the study of managerial behaviour for although behaviour will be studied only in terms of one group composition at least it is a real group and hence the lessons learnt during training can be carried over into everyday functioning.

There still remains, however, the problem of observation and feedback of the behaviour to the participants which is reliant for accuracy and relevance upon the sensitivity of the participants and the group trainer. There is still a need for a systematic and comprehensive framework into which the behaviour observed can be categorized to allow determination of what is relevant to managerial effectiveness and what is not and in what way.

(iv) Training in Interactive Skills (DIS)[8]

This is the most recent and sophisticated technique so far developed in small-group training. It is based upon a systematic appraisal of all the earlier methods and attempts to eradicate their failings. It is built upon the principle that in order to achieve behavioural change, people have to change themselves on the basis of objectively measured and systematic feedback. It also attempts to relate behaviour modification closely to what is acceptable according to a particular organizational climate or value system. The organizational climate of a company is defined by identifying all the behaviours which are considered by the managers as necessary for effectiveness. This is a highly systematic and practicable method of studying managerial interaction behaviour.

It escapes the weakness in Management Grid, T Group Training and Team Training of reliance upon unsystematic feedback based upon unreliable observation, by ensuring thorough training of observers and constant inter-observer reliability checks. The behavioural observation must be dependent to some extent upon the particular group composition but this has been controlled to some extent by changing the composition of groups. It is valuable that the behavioural categories chosen for close attention are tied in with the organizational climate of the particular company.

Despite all the advantages of this method, however, there is still one major area of weakness. There is no comprehensive framework of managerial behaviour against which the behaviours valued by one particular company can be compared. Thus there is no way of telling how the business climate created by any one company compares with that of other companies, or whether, for example, it is severely one sided, producing a destructive climate. In addition there is still no basis for a commonly understood 'language' of managerial behaviour.

All these methods have been designed to suit different purposes but they are all methods designed for the study of managers and they are representative of the kinds of methods that are available for the study of senior managers. The assessment methods apply of course to all levels of management but most of the training work is done at middle and junior level. There are, however, one or two practitioners who specialize in training work with senior managers. One for instance uses a T Group type of approach with 'top teams' which has the advantages and disadvantages of the T Group method as with any other level of managers. Another uses concentrated simulated experience, 'compressed experience', which is thoroughly recorded with videotape and microphones. The results of the observed 'compressed experience' are fed back to the managers in a depth interview where an attempt is made to trace childhood causes of the behaviour observed. It would depend upon one's theoretical orientation, whether one thought such an approach was suited to the study of managerial behaviour or not.

The above is not intended to be a thorough investigation of all the methods of personality assessment and behavioural study available to managers, but a general survey in order to crystallize a few key points. Despite their various advantages, not one of the above methods possesses all of the following necessary characteristics:

(i) A systematic, comprehensive and relevant framework for describing managerial behaviour.

(ii) A method of observing behaviour which is not totally dependent upon inferential classification made by observers varying in sensitivity on the basis of inadequately defined behavioural categories.

(iii) A method of observing behaviour which is not conditioned by a particular situation or group composition.

If these criteria are fulfilled then there is a greater likelihood of achieving a method of studying behaviour which is relevant to what managers actually do and capable of adaptation to different kinds of managerial functions and situations. There will be a basis for a commonly understood language of managerial behaviour and hence the possibility of greater clarity in the understanding of a so far very confused area of human behaviour. In addition, there will be a tool which can be used in the study not only of individual managerial behaviour but also group and team behaviour and finally the behavioural weighting or business climate created by a whole company. Lastly it should be a relatively reliable tool.

It can be claimed that the action profile method of studying managerial behaviour, described in this book, does fulfil the above criteria, at least to a greater extent than any of the other available methods.

(i) It is based upon a systematic framework which has proved to be both comprehensive and highly relevant to managerial behaviour. This has come about largely because it has been based upon twenty years' study of managers. Before the framework now in operation was crystallized approximately 5,000 assessments were made using individual job specifications. From consideration of the requirements for a vast number of different management functions, twelve basic factors were isolated.

(ii) The raw observation data upon which inferences are made (only at a later stage), according to the above framework, is non-verbal behaviour. Instances of non-verbal or movement behaviour are simply recorded without any interpretation. It would be absurd to claim that the personal attributes, mood, etc., of the individual observer does not intrude at all, but it is enormously reduced.

All of the methods of personality assessment and behavioural study described previously are heavily dependent upon observation. Even psychological testing is usually substantiated by interviewing and other forms of observational situations. Whether it is recognized or not, a very large degree of the interpretation made of behaviour observed whether it be in an interview, T Group, Management Grid, Team Training, or Interactive Skills Training is based upon non-verbal data. Any observer who has tried to categorize behaviour operationally will be aware of this. Verbal data can be highly misleading. It is possible for instance to say the words 'what do you mean' and **behave** as if you are: seeking more information, absolutely amazed, flatly contradicting, insulted, concerned for the other person's sanity or offering a challenge. All these nuances in meaning are achieved through non-verbal, or movement accompaniment to the words. The action profile approach recognizes the importance of non-verbal data in behavioural observation and uses it in a systematic and disciplined way.

(iii) Managers are observed individually in a normal interview situation. Because of the framework around which the assessment is constructed, predictions can be made, concerning a manager's behaviour in any management situation and in any group situation provided the other members of the group have also been studied individually.

These are obviously very big claims to make for a relatively unknown method of studying behaviour. However, they can be substantiated, as the rest of the book will reveal. This is not to say that the action profile method of studying behaviour is anywhere near perfect, but it is already a valuable tool in behavioural study and can be developed to give much greater service.

Before any of the applications of the action profile method can be described including how the behaviour of Lexington, Irving and Myer can be explained and classified in a meaningful and useful way, it is necessary first to outline the framework of management action around which the system is organized.

CHAPTER 2

The Framework of Management Action

Consider the following descriptions by managers of colleagues' characteristic ways of working.

> 'He has a great sense of perspective and certainly an overall appreciation of the company and is always going to do this that and the other, but he never seems to actually do anything much.'
>
> (He apparently starts off the action process well with a broad examination of the situation and seems to form some intentions but peters out toward the end of the process.)
>
> 'He's like a bulldog when he gets his teeth into something. He certainly never lets up, but he pushes it too far. He's so convinced his way is right he won't listen to other people's suggestions.'
>
> (He certainly gets past first base and is pretty resolute in getting at least something done. However, maybe if he started off more carefully and considered all the alternatives first he would get there quicker.)
>
> 'He's a great opportunist, but a slippery one—never perseveres with any one thing. You never know where he's going to jump next but he sure gets things moving.'
>
> (He seems to get to the action alright but does little else. It seems he doesn't follow the process through from the conception of a single idea to its fruition, but rather seizes on anything and everything so long as it gives the promise of action.)

If you look at managerial action as a sequence of stages from the first conception of an idea, or recognition of a need through to the final implementation of a plan of action based on that idea or need, you will see that each of the above descriptions are referring to such a sequence but with varying emphasis upon the various stages, as pointed out in the comments in brackets.

Study of (now) approximately 8,000 managers has indicated that every manager will concentrate more activity into certain stages in the sequence of action and will correspondingly neglect others. This is an inbuilt pattern of behaviour and remains constant regardless of the demands of a particular job or situation.

If the manager is able to act in accordance with this spontaneous pattern he will be effective and satisfied. If he is prevented he will be ineffective and unsatisfied. Because of the satisfaction gained from acting in accord with the pattern, the tendency to emphasize a certain stage of action is known as an action motivation. It is because managers cannot help but act according to their action motivations, particularly where they have considerable freedom of action as do top managers, that they cannot avoid creating a certain kind of business climate or environment around themselves.

Although it is true that it is managers who through the expression of their action motivations create the environment in which they operate, the potential of any individual manager to make a personal impression will vary according to the power of his personality. Even then, although one powerful leader may have a bigger impact upon his environment than ordinary mortals, still no one person can create a business climate totally on his own. Thus any single manager will to varying degrees be subject to pressures arising external to himself. Not that any of these pressures will be capable of objective definition. Even something as straightforward as a job description will depend upon the nature of the climate which a company has created. The climate created by the managers will even determine whether some functions exist or not, let alone how they are defined.

In studying any one manager according to the action profile method of assessment there are basically two areas of study.

1 The situation into which the manager is going or is already established (the climate created by the managers already there).
2 The manager himself (the climate he is likely to create).

Thus, according to this distinction, on the one hand you have the situation which will require certain emphases in terms of the stages of action. On the other hand you have the individual manager with his inbuilt readiness to give emphasis to certain stages in the sequence of action. The situational factors are known as the *Action Requirements for Management*. The individual factors as already mentioned are known as *Action Motivations* and the patterning of these factors as the *Action Profile*. The sequence of action is considered a three stage sequence consisting of *Attention — Intention — Commitment*.

THE THREE STAGES OF ACTION

1 *Attention*

A manager to some degree gives attention to the situation in which he finds himself. He researches, questions, surveys, probes, analyses to varying degrees. If he does not give attention at all, then his decisions are made blindly.

2 *Intention*

Having given attention the manager forms an intention. He resolves on a course of action. He makes up his mind with a certain degree of determination, conviction and forthrightness. If he does not form an intention there is no solid basis for implementing his decisions.

3 *Commitment*

The manager commits himself to his intention. He is prepared to make a decision and act on it. He is prepared to start off the process of implementation. This is the logical end stage of the process.

Managers are activating this three stage process at all different levels and over different time spans throughout their entire activity. The whole process may be gone through in seconds as in an everyday situation where it is imperative that action is implemented immediately. If you are driving a car and see another car swerving out from a side street you will go through the attention — intention — commitment process within seconds. If, however, you are engaged upon a lengthy research project the process will be very much more protracted.

The three stage action sequence—Attention — Intention — Commitment, is the basic framework, but for practical working purposes the action motivations can be further subdivided.

Chart 1, page 34, shows the total Framework of Management Action containing the twelve action motivations.

THE TWELVE ACTION MOTIVATIONS

To each of the three phases of the action sequence there are two aspects. Energy can be exerted in two ways. To get something done you can either apply direct effort or assert yourself in such a way as to make things happen or you can, by keeping everything in perspective or balance, so arrange things and events that the job just gets done. One is a direct application of energy, the other indirect in the sense that results are achieved through the structuring and arranging of the situation.

Considering just the first stage, the giving of attention; you can ASSERT yourself to give attention. You can actively probe and question and search in order to find out something, or you can give attention by getting all the sources of information into context or PERSPECTIVE. In this sense you are not busily probing a defined area, but are gaining an awareness of the range of areas that are relevant to be probed.

In the ATTENTION giving stage, the application of direct energy or ASSERTION is called INVESTIGATING. In *investigating* a manager actively seeks out information. He first of all defines, categorizes an area of information and within that defined area he ferrets, probes, delves.

B

ACTION MOTIVATIONS	ACTION SEQUENCE	INTERACTION MOTIVATIONS

THE DECISION MAKING PROCESS IN ACTION

ATTENDING

1. INVESTIGATING — defining, categorizing, fact finding, establishing method, defining standards and principle; teasing out information within a defined area.

2. EXPLORING — having awareness of scope of information; looking for alternative possibilities and ways of approach; looking for alternative reasons; questioning assumptions.

7. COMMUNICATING — establishing and maintaining reciprocal communication; approachability; imparting and inviting knowledge and information; harmonizing, including, sympathizing; sharing own process of investigating and exploring.

INTENDING

3. DETERMINING — having firmness of purpose; determination, persistence against difficult odds; resistance to pressure, strong conviction.

4. CONFRONTING — crystallizing issues, establishing importance, challenging; realistic recognition of immediate needs; forthright acceptance of hard facts.

8. PRESENTING — maintaining confidence, making a positive demonstration, declaring intentions, influencing, persuading, emphasizing, insisting, resisting; sharing own process of determining and confronting

COMMITTING

5. DECIDING — having sense of timing; starting off a process of implementation at the appropriate moment; decisiveness in order of time priorities; seizing opportunities; flexible on the spot programming

6. ANTICIPATING — looking ahead, farsightedness, foreseeing consequences of action; evaluating practicalities; constant anticipation of future developments; systematic future programming.

9. OPERATING — on the spot organising of people; creating sense of urgency or slowing down of pace, spurring people on or delaying activity with awareness of objectives; controlling the action; sharing own process of deciding and anticipating.

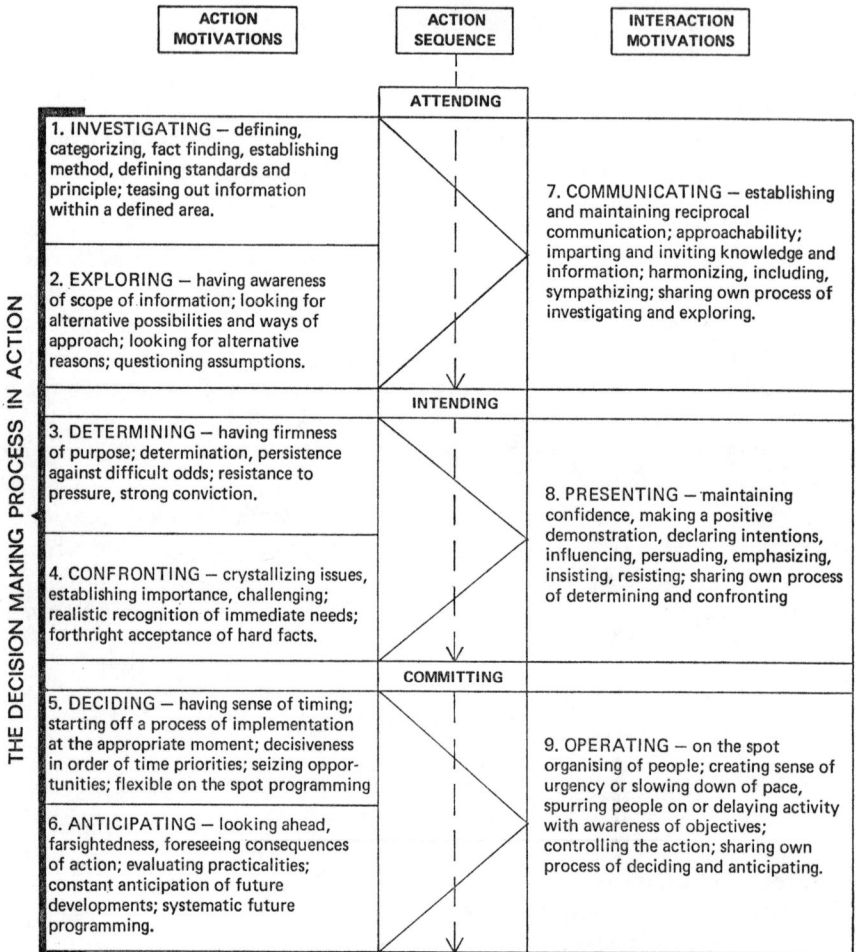

BEGINNING THE PROCESS OF IMPLEMENTATION

TOTAL POTENTIAL ACTIVITY MEASURE

10. DYNAMISM — initiative in promoting action; drive in terms of exertion.

11. ADAPTABILITY — embracing constant process of change; readiness to change own position, customs, attitudes to fit in with a new situation.

12. IDENTIFYING — of self with the organisation and its aims, traditions, methods, environment, personalities, with sense of participation.

Chart 1

The *investigation* may be only as thorough and detailed as the requirements demand if the motivation is moderate. *Investigation* taken to an extreme (where the motivation is very strong), however, may lead to immersion in a narrow area that is out of all proportion to the requirements. Applied to a reasonable extent it leads to careful definition of underlying principles, the setting of standards, thoroughness in establishing systems and methods and an analytical appreciation of information. A manager motivated to *investigate* will always be concerned to define things precisely and aware of the basic principles behind any course of action.

The application of indirect energy or gaining of PERSPECTIVE is called *exploring*. In this activity the manager is more a receptor of information than an active seeker. He is aware of information on a much broader range. This enables him to have an awareness of alternatives, various possibilities, and motivates him to look for alternative explanations and different ways of approach. *Exploring* is completely without definition. As soon as an area is defined for more detailed attention then *exploring* has stopped and *investigating* has begun. *Exploring* enables a manager to structure the information he receives and put it into perspective with other knowledge and experience.

Exploring is being receptive to information, not only from the area of immediate interest, but from all over. It is sometimes the basis of creativity in that it leads to the readiness to question accepted facts and fundamental assumptions. As a result new ideas and different ways of approaching old problems arise. If the motivation is very strong it leads to constant distraction with all kinds of 'other' alternatives and possibilities. If very weak there is a narrow concentration of attention upon a limited area.

In the INTENTION forming stage the direct ASSERTION of energy is called DETERMINING. The maintaining of an intention requires a determination and persistence to a greater or lesser extent. Perhaps even more importantly it requires a sense of self conviction. It is the urge to get to grips with a job. It is the desire to resolve upon a course of action and to maintain that resolution firmly against considerable odds. In the extreme it leads to an indomitable mission—like sense of purpose. Employed to a moderate degree it enables a person to stick at a job long enough to get it done even in the face of serious obstacles and adverse pressures. If completely lacking in spontaneous motivation it leads to flexibility amounting to an almost complete absence of purpose.

The gaining of PERSPECTIVE is called CONFRONTING. It is a very different kind of perspective from that gained via *exploring*. Whilst *exploring* leads to an endless ocean—like perspective, *confronting* gives a black and white wall-like perspective—a stark realism. Just as it sounds it means the confronting of a situation, whatever it may be. It means the need to face up to demands straightforwardly and without evasion, accepting the hard facts of the matter. It leads to the forthright establishing of needs, the desire to 'have it straight'. Primarily it is the readiness to establish an order of importance and to evaluate things accordingly. This leads to readiness to crystallize issues out of a collection of facts or ideas. When a fact or idea is built up in importance or made into an issue it becomes an arguable matter. There is then the possibility of 'for' and 'against' and consequently a clearer basis for action is formed. As a result there is often a provocative, challenging aspect to *confrontation*. A great *confronter* may actually seek out challenging situations in order to exercise his ability to face up to a challenge.

The two ways of applying energy in the COMMITMENT stage are called:

DECIDING : (ASSERTION)
and ANTICIPATING : (PERSPECTIVE)

DECIDING is firstly making commitments, which result in definite action. People who are naturally very strong in *deciding* motivation are always ready with a committed yes/no answer. They see a situation in terms of a series of go/no go choices. Others who give *deciding* less emphasis will never really commit themselves to action unless pushed to do so. There is a large time element in the *deciding* process. *Deciding* is the timing of the implementation of decisions appropriately. Often it is better to wait than to act immediately. The application of this time sense enables a skilful ordering and reordering of time priorities and leads to effective on the spot programming.

A strong *decider* just has a feel for the right moment. He is opportunist because he can immediately see an opportunity and is poised to seize it. His heightened sense of timing will give him a sense for the moment by moment sequencing of events and a sense for the most propitious moment for any action, hence a facility in any situation where keen tactics are required.

ANTICIPATING is the process of looking ahead not only immediately, but also in the long term. It is keeping events in a time perspective, an intuitive awareness that past events are leading to certain future events. It is constantly foreseeing the consequences and implications of any proposed action or course of action. It is looking ahead, seeing the future as a sequence of actions, consequence upon consequence all leading to a particular end point. A strong *anticipator* is always quick to evaluate the practicalities of a proposition. 'If we do this then that will occur which will lead to such and such. . . .' *Anticipating* is the inbuilt need to always have a target or objective in mind be it short or long term. In the extreme it is crystal ball gazing. If completely lacking it would render a person vulnerable to being always taken by surprise by the turn of events.

A major part of a manager's job is dealing with people. We are talking about how a manager interacts with or relates to his people in a way to produce constructive action. This is not dealing primarily with how he 'gets on' with people in the sense of being friendly, or easy to get on with, though this does come into it. A man who promotes conflict may often also promote a lot of constructive action. In this sense (i.e. promoting constructive action) there are basically three modes of interaction. These are once again based on the three stage sequence of action. The three modes of INTERACTION are:

COMMUNICATING

PRESENTING

OPERATING

COMMUNICATING in this sense is not just getting the message across, it is relating to another person in such a way as to promote action of the *investigating* and *exploring* categories. It is as if the two people *investigate* and *explore* the situation together.

This kind of interaction leads to consideration of facts, figures, all kinds of information. It encourages the contribution and discussion of ideas. Participants in such a relationship will feel they are really being given attention, that their ideas are genuinely being listened to and heeded. The atmosphere will be of sharing ideas and information. It is essentially a mutual, reciprocal process. No-one will feel left out.

A natural *communicator* in a group situation instinctively takes a harmonizing, including and sympathizing role. *Communicating* is the ideal type of interaction for true education as distinct from the instruction on specific skills. The participants are drawn out and encouraged to contribute in their own way.

PRESENTING is a manner of relating that promotes action of the *determining* and *confronting* nature. It is as it sounds, relating in a manner of presentation and demonstration. In this kind of relationship participants take a stand on issues. They virtually make a display of what they have to offer.

Matters will be dealt with forthrightly and straightforwardly. It results in everyone knowing where they stand and what is required of them. Such a relationship is not teacherlike in a true educational sense, but is ideally suited for clear demonstration of specific material or skills. It results in the clarifying of issues, the delineation of needs and resolution upon what the course of action should be.

A natural *presenter* can be highly persuasive. In a group he tends to take on the role of influencing, emphasizing and insisting. He actually makes other people feel more determined about and more aware of the importance of a particular issue than they were before, because he is constantly wanting to share his own *determination* and *confrontation* with them.

OPERATING is the sharing of the activities of *deciding* and *anticipating*. It is the type of relationship conducive to the straight organizational activity of getting people's activities scheduled and programmed, and targets set.

It is simply sorting out who should do what when. Decisions are taken, plans projected, likely outcomes anticipated. Participants in such a relationship are being committed to action. It is as if all the information has been gathered, the needs and direction for action have been established. Now is the time to swing into action, to get things moving. There may be an air of competitiveness about it. Participants are keenly aware of the pressure of time and there may be a sense of urgency. People are not educated or instructed, just organized and programmed into action.

A strong *operator* will control the pace of activity, engendering in others his own sense of urgency or calm and the same awareness of the ultimate end or objective of the activity.

In these three descriptions, of course, extremes are given. Relationships are rarely so clearly of one type or another. They will nearly always be some combination of the three and even sometimes with other elements intruding.

Interaction Modes between Two People

To clarify further what is meant by an interaction mode, consider first the simplest group—of two people. If neither is a *communicator* for instance (no matter how much of the ingredients *investigating* and *exploring* are shown by either) it is certain that the research-like survey, review, analysis, definition, developing of ideas and associated activities will not happen as a result, or integral part of the interaction, but rather as a separate adjunct to it.

An apt analogy is that of people swimming under and above water. When under the water they are acting alone, without contact, when above they are in contact and the activity is carried out jointly. There is opportunity for a 'building process'. Each person can benefit from the other's contribution and build on it, so that the net result is greater, or at least quite different from the situation when each is acting alone. Where an interaction capacity is not evident, it is as if the person is always under water whilst carrying out the component activities. If, for instance, a man is strongly *investigatory* and *exploratory*, but not a *communicator*, then he carries out his *investigations* and *explorations* as if under water, hence always alone. There is no opportunity for anyone else to participate in the process or build upon his ideas. The results of the 'under water' *investigation* and *exploration* may be reported to them, and they may then comment, but this is a different process.

To carry the analogy further, supposing this man, call him N.C. (for non *communicator*) were to be working closely with a person who was a *communicator* (call him C.) and also highly *investigatory* and *exploratory*. N.C. would periodically emerge from his under-water investigations or be called up from them and would report them to C. who would immediately want to build on them in a process of joint co-operation. Hence he would comment in such a way as to invite a like response. N.C. would, however, not respond to the invitation, instead he would figuratively submerge in order to consider C.'s contribution and continue the *investigation* further on his own.

This might be apparent behaviourally in a number of ways. N.C. may appear disinterested, even bored, perhaps just vague or distracted, but, however it is shown, C. will 'feel' whether he recognizes it or not that N.C. is just not 'with him'. It may leave C. feeling any number of emotions in fact, from mild

The Framework of Management Action   39

surprise and frustration through to a deep feeling of rejection, but of course he would not know why he felt like this nor would he be able to justify it. More often he would not even admit to such feelings. Such a sequence of interaction could even happen in minutes and could look like an ordinary conversation, with both c. and n.c. appearing perfectly friendly and co-operative, which they would be. Careful analysis would show, however, that the sequence was somewhat disjointed and that ideas were not followed or developed in a smoothflowing organic way.

Consider on the same analogy a very straight-forward interaction mode between two people P1 and P2. Both are *presenters* and predominantly strong in the components of *determining* and *confronting*. P1, however, is stronger in *investigating* whilst P2 is stronger in *anticipating*.

Let us take one isolated issue which will simplify the situation for illustration purposes. P1 and P2 are both Managing Directors of relatively independent subsidiaries of a large internationally owned group. A suggestion has come from the group personnel adviser that a new salaries scheme should be put into operation. Both P1 and P2 submerge for a short time to give attention to the idea. P1 gives himself time to *investigate* and finds that he has evidence that the system is an importation and would not suit the British mentality. He remembers that he tried a similar system and it did not work. In addition he has just put in a computer system to deal with salaries according to the old type system. P2 is not so probing in his attention, but he nevertheless emerges with the feeling that he too is against the idea. After giving attention 'underwater' both men now emerge and interaction takes place. Both are beginning to form the intention to try and stop the new scheme being introduced.

Their interaction consists of the mutual reinforcing of this intention, facing up to the situation as they see it; that they must confront the board with their intention. The results of P1's *investigations* are 'reported' and serve not as a building, attention-giving process, but as fuel for the *intention* fire. They each reinforce the *determination* in the other to smash the plan, and they end up a force to be reckoned with.

For the actual planning of the implementation their intention, the timing of the action and *anticipation* of the results and implications (*operating*), they will go 'underwater' again. They will then emerge to make a *presentation* each of his own particular plan. P1 surfaces *determined* to go straight to the board and present their case. P2, however, has *anticipated* that the Group Managing Director is to be present at the next board meeting and he has already expressed doubts as to both P1's and P2's performance. Thus when P1 and P2 emerge to 'report' on their singly considered ideas on the course of action (their substitute for *operating*) the interaction becomes a confrontation on the basis of different intentions. However, P1 is grudgingly sensitive to P2's warning and allows himself to be persuaded into delaying until an occasion when the Group Managing Director would not be present.

Once agreement has been reached the interaction serves to refuel the intention fire once again. Although the timing of the implementation of the plan has been changed, the interaction has still resulted in a building up of *determined* intention to *confront* the problem which is now greater in each man than would have been had the interaction not taken place.

From looking only at the action and interaction motivations, one could say confidently that the interaction of these two men would result in a building of resolve, the straightforward determining of immediate needs, the urge to get to grips with the situation, to confront the action, to act firmly on the basis primarily of here and now considerations.

So far the first nine of the action motivations for management have been described, including the basic six action motivations, three concerned with the ASSERTION of effort and three to do with the gaining of PERSPECTIVE according to the three stage action sequence. It has been seen that each pair of assertion and perspective components according to one of the stages of action combine to form one of the three INTER-ACTION modes. This leads us on to the tenth action motivation, *dynamism.*

Dynamism

Every person has a typical overall level of activity or *dynamism.* This is a non-specific measure of total energy or drive. It is predominantly evident in the readiness to initiate action of all kinds. Most of us have met some people of whom we would say something like 'he has terrific go'. This is the man with a high level of *dynamism.* This does not mean such a man is necessarily effective. It will depend on other factors, such as the particular form his high energy level takes, his level of intelligence and technical skill and how his job is structured whether his energy is utilized to the best advantage.

A *dynamic* but unintelligent manager for instance may be deadly—a bit like a high powered car with an idiot for a driver.

Adaptability

In this world of change, some managers are spontaneously *adaptable.* By *adaptability* is meant the readiness to change even one's most basic attitudes to fit in with a changed situation. An ideally *adaptable* person could go to live with a primitive tribe and actually adopt the life style of the 'savages'. Such people are rare. In the management world, a moderate degree of *adaptability* will ensure the tolerance of change, better still the encouragement of change. An *adaptable* manager is not simply one who is versatile in the sense of being able to take on many different jobs with basically the same attitudes. An *adaptable* manager will change himself to fit the new situation, not endeavour to change the situation to fit him.

Identification

Much of the most important interaction that takes place in a company is that which occurs spontaneously and informally. This does not happen just accidentally or to the same extent with different groups of people. It will depend on how many of the people have the capacity to really participate in the activities of others. Often the ability to generate enthusiasm and participation in others goes along with it. It is the quality that makes for a closely welded team. It is the readiness to become really involved with the company, the job and all that goes with it. A person possessing this capacity to a high degree may not of absolute necessity become strongly identified with any particular company, however, it may depend on his appreciation of the company and whether he feels he can sympathise with its philosophy, policy, value system, image, etc.

This participatory quality obviously has a great effect on the nature of interaction, but it is not the same as the three categories of relating, *communicating, presenting* and *operating* that were discussed earlier. It can play a part in any one or any combination of these types of interacting, but does not of itself constitute a relationship that is productive of constructive action. It makes for an easy spontaneous 'all in this together' atmosphere. Such an atmosphere does not necessarily promote constructive action. On the contrary much useful action is the product of conflict. A high level of *identification* combined with an effective activation of one or a combination of the three interaction categories will, however, make for the most fruitful, productive type of interaction in terms of the action produced.

This completes the description of the 12 factors related to different ways in which people are motivated to act in a management context. They correspond to the twelve action requirements for management which is the yardstick against which individual managers are assessed.

In conclusion it may be well to clarify the nature of the behaviour that is being described when referring to action motivations. It has been stated that it is readiness to take action that is referred to. It is necessary to emphasize that it is an inbuilt or spontaneous readiness to take action that is being described, as distinct from the use of consciously controlled methods or techniques. To take the action requirement *exploring* as an example; a manager who lacks a natural *exploratory* approach, who is just not spontaneously aware of the scope of possibilities and alternatives available to him, in dealing with any particular situation, may, having become aware of this limitation, be very concerned to initiate procedures say of market research or 'brainstorming' to counteract this limitation. On the other hand the man who is naturally *exploratory* and is confident in his ability to just come up with ideas and alternatives, who is never stuck for a way out of a problem, will tend to take this for granted and be less likely to institute formalized procedures of review or survey.

How do action motivations relate to intellectual abilities?

The activity of *deciding* as it is defined here is an interesting case in point. The process of 'decision making' is a much discussed phenomenon in management theory and practice. It is usually treated as a wholly intellectual activity. Making a decision is seen as gathering and analysing data, selecting choices and choosing one of them. All this can be done in a cloistered back room, far away from the day to day turmoils of practical management.

The *deciding* process described here is not an intellectually based activity. It is action based. It is what a manager does when he is subject to the pressures of any normal management situation and there is not always the time or the inclination to sit down and work things out coolly and clinically. *Deciding* in the action sense is not just having it in mind that such and such is the best thing to do, but the readiness to initiate the actual process of implementation, and to choose the right moment, or time span in which to do it.

This is why it also involves the ability and readiness to act opportunistly. Opportunism is the readiness to initiate a process of implementation in perhaps a split second which has to be the right moment otherwise the opportunity is lost. To extend this idea further, it can involve a whole series of time oriented manœuvres or a sequence of tactics.

The *deciding* activity is being stressed here because it is a process of great concern to managers and because it has come to be treated by management theorists so much in terms of intellectual activity.

Whilst acting according to his own particular action motivations a manager is, of course, employing his intellectual skills at the same time. There is a constant intermingling of the two processes. A highly intelligent manager motivated to *investigate* will probably come up with more valuable observations than a very unintelligent manager who is just as motivated to *investigate*.

However, the highly intelligent manager who is *not* spontaneously motivated to *investigate* will simply avoid such activity altogether so far as he can and in this respect he will be less effective than a less intelligent manager who *is* motivated to *investigate*.

The action motivations affect the workings of brain power not directly but indirectly by governing the type of activity to which the brain power will be directed. Even if it were possible to literally tie an intelligent *non-investigator* to an *investigatory* task for an extended time he would probably prove fairly ineffective. All the damaging effects of dissatisfaction, boredom, frustration would have full sway. It could almost be suggested that a less intelligent manager who was motivated to *investigate* would be more effective.

What often happens in normal management situations where you cannot actually tie managers to a particular clearly defined task, and where of course tasks are not always clearly defined anyway, is that the manager just does what he is motivated to do regardless even if he calls it something else. And if he is successful he will be allowed to go on doing it. If by some sad blow of fate a manager is constrained in a job for which he is not action motivated and this does happen to varying degrees, depressingly often, then all the concomitants of dissatisfaction and frustration have full sway and the manager is, to some extent, ineffective.

Although as mentioned before there is a constant intermingling of intellectual and action motivation process, it is nevertheless important to make the distinction. Study of the effect of action motivation factors upon managers' performance has shown that they comprise a highly spontaneous and compelling form of behaviour. Intellectually acquired skills and techniques are usually used as curbs against the action motivations where they are inappropriate and stopgaps where they are not present.

So, although undoubtedly a manager should cover his limitations in spontaneous behaviour by acquiring intellectual skills and techniques it is certain that in any normal managerial situation, with its customary complexity, the spontaneous inbuilt action motivation will prove by far the most effective and flexible instrument. This is, of course, why it is so useful to ascertain the distribution of these inbuilt action emphases within each manager's distinctive individual approach to management.

THE ACTION PROFILE

No two managers are the same. No two managers have precisely the same mental or technical abilities. Similarly no two managers have the same action motivations. Every manager has his own pattern of action motivation or action profile.

Consider, to begin with, patterns according to just the first six action requirements, in relation to the three stage sequence of action.

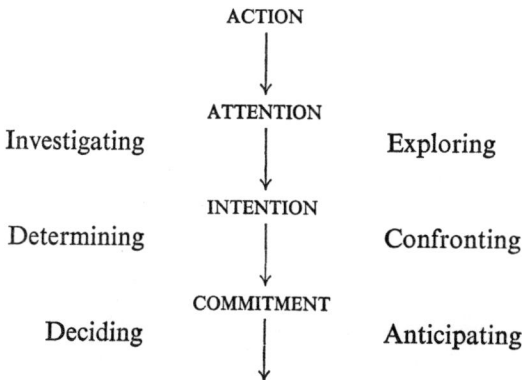

It looks on the surface as if it would be a good thing for one person to perform all these activities equally. Experience with 8,000 managers has shown, however, that people never do. They always put more emphasis, more activity, into one, two or three of them. Each person has an action pattern or profile, and this makes a large contribution to his individual style of management. Here are some examples of different action profiles. Supposing a manager has a certain level of *dynamism* which can be shown as follows:

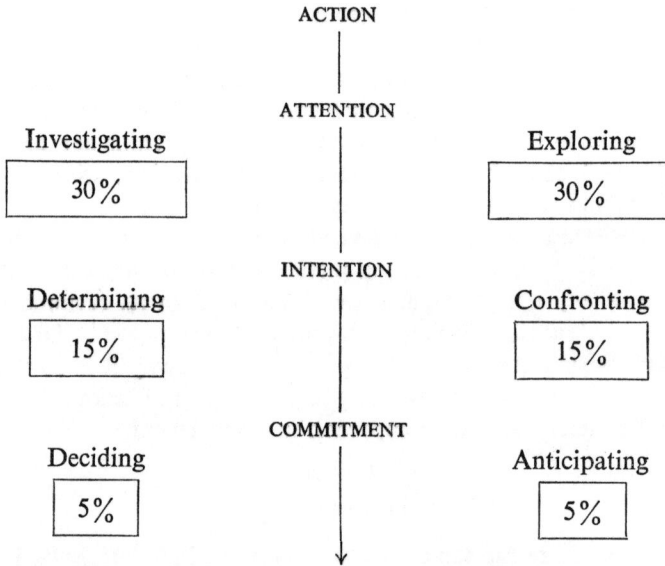

ACTION

ATTENTION

Investigating	Exploring
30%	30%

INTENTION

Determining	Confronting
15%	15%

COMMITMENT

Deciding	Anticipating
5%	5%

This man will be truly research minded. He will always be motivated to give full attention to the situation. He will be totally unable to make a decision until he feels he has all the necessary information at his finger tips—and all the necessary information will mean a lot of information for him. He will of his own volition want to look for information, to research, survey, dig up facts. He will in addition be naturally receptive to any miscellaneous information. He will be open to ideas and will always question whether the established way is the right way. He will never be considered a decisive man of action. He will rarely of his own accord take a decision. Other people will have to force decisions out of him. He is a good man for going back to first principles and establishing the basis of any operation. He is likely to be a good policy maker and standard setter. He is better seen as an adviser than as a 'doer'. Such people are useful in a management team. They offer the results of their research. They never conform to the conventional picture of a 'go ahead', 'with it' man of action. They are vulnerable to being wrongly structured even perhaps into a position where they are required to keep things moving, to constantly make 'on the spot' decisions. In such a position this man would be wasted, under considerable strain and considerably under-motivated.

Here is another pattern:

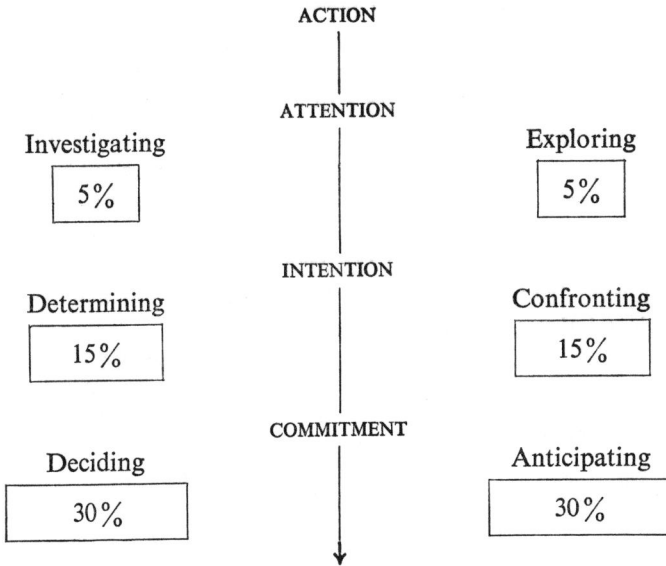

This manager is obviously very different. He is indeed a decisive man of action—competitive and opportunist. He will, however, take his decisions on the basis of hints or clues, the information that is staring him in the face, rather than on any thoroughly researched appreciation or awareness of the total situation. He is inclined to act blindly, but he does get to the implementation stage and this is very necessary for a manager. If in a position where he can initiate action and get things going, he will make mistakes if there is no system for feeding him all the relevant information. If constrained by the nature of his job or by his technical expertise, or educational discipline; e.g.: of research scientist, engineer, laboratory technician, or whatever, and hence required to exercise predominantly faculties of an attention oriented nature and surprisingly this can happen, such a man will once again be wasted, liable to stress and under-motivated. He will simply be applying a learned intellectual skill without any true vocational interest in the job.

Two very straightforward patterns have been given, just based on the first six action motivations. As you can see these already give a lot of information about a manager, particularly with respect to how his job should be structured and indeed what kind of job it should be.

Experience with a very large number of managers has indicated that the action profile is a predominant factor in determining behaviour. When a manager's action profile is revealed to him he nearly always recognizes that this is the source of a very fundamental pattern of motivation for him. Many report endeavours to control and modify their basic action profile by various intellectual techniques. This it seems can result in a certain degree of compensation in behaviour, particularly in well experienced situations. However, in the long run and when under any degree of pressure the basic action profile seems to emerge as a chief determiner of behaviour.

Patterns of action capacities are rarely as straightforward in real life as the ones described here, and there are still six more action motivations to be considered. However, at this stage only an indication is being given of how styles of management can differ radically and how important in this respect is a consideration of how a manager's total action capacity or *dynamism* is patterned.

To give a clearer illustration of the amount and type of information that can be deduced from the action profile, some real life managers will be described in relation to their action profiles.

CHAPTER 3

The Action Profile in Action

In Chapter 2 some imaginary styles of management were described. They were considerably oversimplified examples. Now let us take another look at the three managers described in Chapter 1 and see how their behaviour is tied in with their particular action profile. These examples are all drawn from actual Top Team Planning assignments.

EXAMPLE 1: MR. J. LEXINGTON

To remind you he is the Managing Director of a medium sized company in the toy industry, which includes the manufacture of consumer goods distributed through wholesale and retail outlets. He is mainly in competition with giant corporations but has nevertheless, over the last few years, successfully turned a loss into a profit.

His action profile is shown on page 48.

Explanation of the Action Profile Chart

The presentation of the action profile used for Mr. Lexington is a standard presentation which will be used throughout the book.

The key on the left hand side shows the three stages of action with the corresponding assertion and perspective factors, i.e. the first six action motivations. The column headed '% of total activity' indicates the emphasis in percentage terms given to each of the six action motivations. Mr. Lexington, for instance, concentrates 22 per cent of his activity in *investigating,* 18 per cent in *exploring,* 5 per cent in *determining,* etc.

The potential interaction activity corresponds to the extent of the component activities. Mr. Lexington's *communicating* activity could correspond to the 22 per cent and 18 per cent of *investigating* and *exploring* but it doesn't as he is not capable of *communicating* at all. The actual extent of the interaction activity in each case is indicated by the shading. Mr. Lexington is obviously a strong *presenter* using to the maximum the *determining* and *confronting* components.

Dynamism, Adaptability and *Identifying* are quantified according to a four-

		% of total activity	Extent of Interaction activity	
ATTENTION	Investigating	22		Communicating
	Exploring	18		
INTENTION	Determining	5		Presenting
	Confronting	25		
COMMITMENT	Deciding	22		Operating
	Anticipating	8		
Dynamism			3·9	
Adaptability			2·0	
Identifying			3·9	

Action Profile 1   MR. J. LEXINGTON

point scale. A score of 0·0 indicates a complete absence of the activity, whereas a score of 3·9 will show maximum activity.

On seeing Mr. Lexington's profile without having even met the man, some extremely interesting points would be immediately apparent.

1 The great predominance of the *confronting* factor without the matching *determining* factor.
2 The predominant *deciding* factor without the matching *anticipating* factor.
3 The strong *identification* factor with a relatively weak coverage of the interaction factors.

4 The strength on *presenting* with a weakness on *determining* albeit
  a strength on *confronting*.

5 The very strong degree of drive or *dynamism*.

If you refer back to Chapter 2 to the description of the twelve action motivations, you will see with reference to point 1 that *confronting* refers to the
need to face up to demands, straightforwardly without evasion. You may note
the word need was used. This is because in all of these factors we are speaking
of inner motivation to take action. This means that people positively need to
take action in this particular way. Thus a person who shows the *confrontation*
motivation very strongly is not just capable of facing up to an issue when it
arises, he feels practically compelled to face up to issues. This means he will
make issues himself or create challenges with which he can deal. This may
lead, for instance, to the practice of making rather hefty claims because this
automatically creates the challenge of having to defend those claims.

Where this occurs without sufficient *determining* energy to back it up,
however, a difficult situation can arise. The constant battling against self
imposed challenges must obviously require a good deal of plain 'guts',
determination and persistence. It requires a sense of conviction and self
purpose. Imagine how it would feel to be continuously under challenge, under
battle fire so to speak, knowing within yourself that you don't really have
sufficient self *determination* to fight your way through. It sounds amazing,
yet it can happen and happens to Mr. Lexington all the time. It must lead
to some strange behaviour, you would think, and it certainly does.

With reference to point 2, a similar mismatching occurs with the *deciding*
and *anticipating* factors. Mr. Lexington is motivated to act in a *decisive*
way. He has an inbuilt sense of timing. He is exceedingly quick on the
uptake and readily opportunist. This is not balanced, however, with a sense
of perspective as to the timing of events. His sense of timing is strictly a
here and now affair. He can seize the right moment today but will not predict
how his action will influence the future. It is an effort for him to project
forward. He isn't 'tuned' so to speak to an awareness of trends or a natural
appreciation of where events are leading.

This is particularly interesting in Mr. Lexington's case because he does all
his forward planning in a strictly intellectual way. He displays what appears
at first sight to be a perfect strategic plan, meticulously and precisely worked
out according to a management-by-objectives system. However perfect it
looked, however, one could predict that it would be a relatively rigid and
formal instrument, not flexibly in tune with the changing environment.

On reading the strategic plan one notices that it is written very predominantly with the present situation in mind. There is practically no attempt
made to predict future developments or trends in the market. In fact the word
trend is mostly mentioned with reference to performance over past years;
i.e. strictly historically. Such predictions as are made about future trends in

the market consist of newspaper statements made by competitors of appreciation of trends in their own situation. There is no sign of a personal prediction of future developments. It is interesting to note too that whilst at the beginning of the plan it was stated that it was intended to follow the Mbo theory of making a company set down a comprehensive one year plan, followed by a five year plan; at the end of the plan it is asserted that it is a waste of time to follow the procedure of so many companies who prepare detailed plans for five years ahead, as no company could or should be so static in its thinking.

Such a statement is not, however, an infallible indication of a lack of *anticipation* for many spontaneous *anticipators* would never feel the need to write down a detailed forward plan. Forward thinking for such a person happens so much as a matter of course. If required, however, a strongly *anticipatory* manager could detail five years ahead, confident that although perhaps not strictly accurate, such a document could be meaningful. For Mr. Lexington, however, the reasons against it are different. Firstly, he would find it almost meaningless to try and think so far ahead, and secondly, would find such a detailed forward plan a very difficult instrument with which to work.

In all, Mr. Lexington's strategic plan is a brilliant presentation of the present situation with a highly imaginative and resourceful outline on how it should be dealt with.

In point 3 it was pointed out that Mr. Lexington shows evidence of a very strong *identificatory* or participatory factor with a relatively weak coverage of the interaction factors. This is another rather problematical combination. As explained in Chapter 2, *Identification* is that quality which causes a person to emanate a participatory readiness which is felt by others. It makes for an easy 'all in this together' atmosphere and obviously has a great effect on the nature of interaction. However, it is not the same as the three categories of interaction, *communicating, presenting* and *operating*. They are modes of relating specifically in the sense of promoting constructive action of one sort or another. Now Mr. Lexington, having the participatory quality, unconsciously invites people to relate to and co-operate with him. However, as he actually relates only in a way to promote constructive action of the *determining* and *confronting* type, there is a kind of contradiction.

This is aggravated even more by the fact as mentioned in point 5, that he is strong in the *presenting* type of relationship but with a weakness on *determining*, which is an integral part and product of the *presenting* type of relationship.

A final point to make is that Mr. Lexington is an extremely dynamic man. He has terrific drive, a great capacity for action.

After the discussion of all the points above, you might wonder how the man manages to function successfully at all. But of course he does. However, the points mentioned are a large determining factor in much of his behaviour.

It was mentioned in the earlier description that Mr. Lexington seemed to behave in such a way as to both invite and prevent initiative from the members of his team. They in their turn felt impelled and encouraged to contribute, yet at the same time unable to do so. It was concluded that the cause for this strange kind of stalemate lay partly in the patterning of the interaction aspects within the team itself (overall, they, like their Managing Director, were very weak in this area) but also just as much due to the personality of the Managing Director himself.

He genuinely felt a need to invite co-operation and participation from his colleagues yet could not help but respond to any attempt at co-operation as if it were a challenge to his position. He responded to any such 'challenge' with such power, quick-wittedness, forcefulness and clarity of *presentation* that it would require terrific ability to counter him. The executives gradually ceased to make the effort.

Mr. Lexington sounds a very complex person. But of course people are complex. Few are as obviously and flamboyantly complex as Mr. Lexington, yet most people express at least a degree of contradiction in the way they behave.

Let us go back to Mr. Lexington's action profile and the five points made about it and see if they can provide some further insight into his behaviour.

Firstly he is well motivated to give attention to *investigate* and *explore*. Hence he is truly an ideas man. So he really does have a basis for the claims he makes.

Secondly, he is a great showman due to his strength in *presenting*. He makes a brilliant *presentation* consisting of ample bold *confrontation* but little *determining* effort to back it up. This enables him to present his ideas brilliantly. However, due to the lack of 'power' to back up his punch [limited *determining*] he must feel a constant insecurity. He rarely feels enormously convinced of the point of view he is so provocatively upholding. He must resort to quick-witted tactics to prevent people from really taking up his challenge or contesting his *presentation*. He delights in the challenge but he must win. He couldn't tolerate a battle in an entrenched position. Hence he must always be one step ahead of his colleagues and never really allow them to contest him. Because of his strength in *deciding* he is well able to deal with people in this way.

It may seem rather odd that the battle-like aspect of his type of relating is so much stressed. If you refer back to the interaction part of the profile you will see that he is strong in a *presenting* type of relationship but not the *communicating* type, which is the kind that promotes action of the simply *exploring* and *investigating* kind. In this type of relationship it is quite possible to just *explore* ideas with no thought as to what should be done with them. In such a context the contribution of an *exploratory* suggestion could never be considered a statement of intention and hence a challengeable issue. However, if one party is predisposed to relate in a *presentation* context he is just motivated to view all suggestions as challengeable issues rather than simple *explorations*. This is, of course, what Mr. Lexington does and why his milder colleagues finally give up making suggestions.

A third pertinent factor derived from the action profile is Mr. Lexington's combination of high *identification* with relatively low interaction skills. This explains the executives' feeling that they are constantly invited to contribute but in fact they are unable to do so. It explains too Mr. Lexington's nagging frustration and distress at his executives' reluctance to show initiative and challenge him on his own ground.

Again, as mentioned before, there is the mismatching between the *deciding* and *anticipatory* factors. The keen awareness of timing resulting in a sense of opportunism gives Mr. Lexington much of his competitive spirit. It also gives him his tactical facility and his ability to manipulate events and people. However, he doesn't really consider the consequences of his action due to his limited *anticipatory* motivation. He just doesn't foresee that constant manipulation of people could in time lead to defensiveness and wariness in any form of co-operation.

Finally, there is his great drive and energy to be considered. He is highly motivated simply to do things. He must act, he must be busy, he must achieve. This is obviously a strong factor in his achieving success—he can simply cope with more than most other people, but it does make it very difficult to keep pace with him.

A rather negative picture of this undoubtedly highly successful Managing Director has been presented. Let us look at the more positive side.

1 He is highly motivated to *investigate* and *explore*. This means he is always well equipped with sufficient information. He could never act blindly. He will be aware of the whole range of possibilities open to him, hence always a source of ideas.
2 He is highly motivated to *confront*. So he will see any situation which faces him with great clarity. This promises courage in the sense that he will never evade action that is obviously needed, definiteness in the sense that he will never procrastinate, confidence in the sense that he will always know where he stands even if everyone else is vague as to their position.
3 He is not motivated to *determine*. This results in a considerable flexibility. He will never persist too long at a thing. He will always find a new avenue of approach. There is nothing overbearing about him. He will be clear in what he expects of others but won't follow it up with persistence.
4 He is strongly motivated to *decide*. This means he will experience always an unavoidable sense of personal commitment. He cannot confront a situation without feeling that he may be obliged to do something about it.
5 He is not motivated to *anticipate*. He is strictly a man of the present. He is an opportunist exploiter of current circumstances, rather than a far-sighted planner for the future.

6 He is motivated to promote the *presentation* type of relationship, rather than the *communication* or *operation* type.

This means he is much more concerned to *present* the situation to people rather than to establish true reciprocal *communication*. He makes it very clear where he stands, and people will always know where they stand with him. Although observant, he quickly commits himself on the position of the people with whom he is dealing. He sums people up observantly and probably with some astuteness.

7 Strength on *Dynamism*.

As a Managing Director, this causes him to be a life force in the company. He is eminently capable of coping with a heavy weight of responsibility in terms of sheer exertion.

8 Limitation on *Adaptability*, except in certain circumstances.

He can be *adaptable* to some degree in any changed situation where great strength, *determination* or resolution is not required. He is highly versatile in seizing opportunities, but not *adaptable* in the sense of preparing for significant changes in order to work towards a completely new strategy.

9 Strength in *Identification*.

This means he is outstanding in degree of *identification* with the work situation. His loyalty, devotion, participation are likely to be felt by all those associated with him. It means to those who accept his leadership that there is a participatory zest about getting on with the job and personal loyalty for him.

Such then is the analysis of a 'style' of management according to the action profile. This man was achieving success really due to his own individual drive and ability. His executives backed him up, yet were really unable to work closely with him. It will be interesting to see if he can maintain his record of success.

An analysis of his company situation can show how well suited Mr. Lexington is with his particular action profile to this particular environment.

When he first took on the managing directorship the company was unprofitable and in competition with mammoth corporations. Mr. Lexington is:

1 Motivated by the prospect of a strong challenge.

This is the first prerequisite to his taking on the job at all. The job presented itself as an exciting challenge to Mr. Lexington. How could he resist?

2 Motivated by competition.

This is the second prerequisite. Nothing could have been more congenial to him than the thought of beating huge organizations at their own game. He recognized clearly that he had a major attribute in the smallness of his company, enabling rapid and flexible manœuvring against the slower moving giants.

3 Motivated to look for new ways of approach.

He is ideally suited to get a stagnating company back into circulation. He took initiative in a great many new and original ways; for example, in the publicizing and promotion of his products—ranging from clever packaging to books concealing advertisements for his own products.

4 Motivated to take an enormous amount of initiative.

He delights in driving himself, delights in success and being seen to be successful. He is a specialist star performer and he likes it that way, despite the sometimes unfortunate repercussions.

EXAMPLE 2: MR. E. IRVING

As mentioned before, Mr. Irving is the General Works Manager of a medium sized engineering firm, Fellows Acre Ltd. He worked his way up from the shop floor to a position on the Board. He has never had any formal engineering or management training. Discussions with him took place on several occasions during and after a Top Team Planning assignment performed for his company. A formal assessment of him was only performed after a second stage of the work had been commissioned. His company is separated geographically with sections in Bristol, Manchester and Nottingham.

Mr. Irving's action profile is reproduced on the opposite page.

Looking at the action profile, several interesting points stand out.

1 Exceptionally strong *identification* in combination with a good coverage of interaction factors and high *dynamism*.
2 The great predominance of the *determining* and *anticipating* factors.
3 The limitation on the interaction factor *presenting* with a very strong *determining* factor but weak *confronting* factor.

With reference to point 1, this combination results in him being what is known as a 'contaminator'.* This means he has enormous personal influence over people. He has a 'presence' which is felt all through the works. If he is in a bad mood people will just sense it. He creates followers, hence the term 'Irving Men'. How is this derived from the combination of factors mentioned above?

1 Extremely high *identification*, i.e. he 'involves' people to a high degree. They can never feel detached from him.
2 High *dynamism*, i.e. the involvement is reinforced with great energy and force.
3 Strong interaction ability: he conveys his feelings. He can be understood. People feel they know him.

* The concept is discussed in full in Warren Lamb's *Posture and Gesture*, Duckworth 1956.

		% of total activity	Extent of Interaction activity	
INTENTION	Investigating	14		Communicating
	Exploring	8		
INTENTION	Determining	24		Presenting
	Confronting	10		
COMMITMENT	Deciding	20		Operating
	Anticipating	24		
Dynamism			3·5	
Adaptability			1·5	
Identifying			3·9	

Action Profile 2 MR. E. IRVING

This is obviously a very significant factor in his style of management. It means he cannot help but create this kind of team partisanship and sense of camaraderie. Neither can he help but establish a very personalized style of leadership. No man could be tolerated in his team who did not harmonize with him. This leads him to build a team with a strongly unified character biased in the direction of his own personality. Indeed, as it will be pointed out in Chapter 14, looking at the members of the team, there is a truly remarkable bias toward strengths in *determining*, *anticipating* and *operating*, precisely the most outstanding features in Mr. Irving's own action profile.

Considering Mr. Irving's approach to the problem of lack of co-operation and understanding from the sales side, mentioned in the previous description of Mr. Irving, points 2 and 3 are significant. He is primarily motivated to express *determination* and to always project ahead toward an *anticipated* goal. He will simply put up with any amount of frustration as if he considers that simply by persisting in the same way he will get to his target. He sees his objective simply as 'to get the stuff made'—usually in the face of all obstacles 'deliberately' set up by the sales people. He is strangely narrow minded in his appreciation of this objective. Although he appreciates that sales must have their own conditions, he doesn't see that a process of re- conciliation of their needs with his own production problems can be an integral part of the achieving of his own objective. One answer, it would seem, would be to deliberately educate the sales people in production problems, or create certain stipulations clearly stated to guide the sales people's demands. These possibilities never seemed to occur to Mr. Irving. He is a capable intelligent manager. Is it not strange that he persists in an unsatisfactory mode of approach?

It can be explained by the dominance of the *determining* and *anticipating* factors over the 'attention' giving factors. Although Mr. Irving is motivated to some extent to gain a fair appreciation of the situation and to some extent to *explore* new possibilities, the *determining* factor takes over so easily that he tends to become entrenched in a particular attitude. He sees his objective clearly and is highly motivated to want to get to grips with any problems in the way of his path toward that objective. Once he is entrenched in battle with some impediment he wants to persist way beyond the endurance of many other relatively determined men. He expresses great frustration but he is excellently equipped to cope with it. Just as the last manager, Mr. Lexington, seemed almost to seek challenges, so Mr. Irving appears literally to seek hardships. It isn't surprising. It is a facet of human nature that we feel most comfortable in situations with which we can best cope.

Another facet of the production versus sales problem is the fact that Mr. Irving has a board position and the chief promulgator of difficulties from the sales end is the Managing Director. Why is it that Mr. Irving cannot gain sufficient understanding from the Managing Director? One reason could be that the Managing Director is young, relatively inexperienced as a Managing Director and particularly fascinated with the whole sales area. However, there is another contributing factor, again stemming from Mr. Irving's action profile.

In point 3, it was mentioned that although Mr. Irving is so strong on *determining* and not completely lacking in *confronting*, which are the com- ponents of the *presenting* type of relationship, he is in fact weak in *presenting*. Owing to his strong *determining* motivation he has very strong intentions, but the demonstration of those intentions in interaction with others is positively dismal. In trying to express his intention to persist with the sales/ production problem, he becomes wound up in a veritable maze of fantastically earnest verbiage. One can hardly disentangle a single clear concept from it. Whilst Mr. Irving is *communicating*, i.e. simply sharing information and ideas, he is perfectly understandable. So too when organizing and programming people and events [*operating*] he is superbly clear and concise. But whenever he is expressing resolution or intention he seems to lose all clarity and coherence.

These are concrete illustrations of how the action profile can be seen to act as an influence on behaviour within a specific area. A more general summary of Mr. Irving's management style as derived from the action profile is as follows:

Emphasis on Determining (24 per cent of energy going into this area)

He works as though it were a first priority to come to grips with some positive task or project and to persist purposefully towards a positive result. He is so motivated to apply a *determined* highly resolved approach that even if there wasn't anything particularly important to do he would still find something to fasten onto. This feature imbues him with a great sense of purpose. He cannot abide anything trivial and it is important to him that he can express a firm sense of purpose and an emphatically expressed *determination* to achieve it.

Equal emphasis on Anticipating (24 per cent energy exerted in this way)

He is also outstanding in his exercise of *anticipation*. He is naturally far-sighted and spontaneously looks ahead as to the likely effects of any action he takes. It is, however, of a later and secondary rating in his work application and there may be a danger that he allows himself to get stuck on matters on which he feels he should persist so that he does not take opportunities which he is nevertheless able to foresee. There is perhaps a form of conflict in that he cannot bring himself to let anything go, and yet at the same time he constantly recognizes opportunities. Such a conflict must be in the nature of the situation but to a degree it may also be self-inflicted.

Lack of Readiness to Explore (only 8 per cent)

One factor which exacerbates this conflict is that he cannot help but assert effort to get things done, even though results might be better achieved simply through preparing the conditions or allowing things to fall naturally into place. He makes a virtue of hard work to the extent that he may often work harder than is necessary in the circumstances. The tendency toward over assertiveness may be restrictive in preventing a more relaxed *exploratory* approach to alternative possibilities for getting work done. He comes to grips purposefully with the most obviously demanding tasks in a way which may almost be precipitate, in that more initial review and survey could possibly reveal whether the task should be done at all or the possibility of alternative methods.

Moderate Strength in Communicating

The ease and facility with which he is able to establish *communication* is fairly unusual for a man of such *determination* and drive. He is eminently approachable, invites consultation and probably invites others to seek his advice. When they do so, however, he is likely to respond not so much in an open, *exploratory* manner, but rather to imbue people with his own brand of action-oriented application. This may lead to over emphasizing, perhaps even dramatizing, aspects of the work situation which seem to him particularly challenging. As mentioned above, this is also an area where more initial surveying and reviewing of the relevant factors, and particularly the context in which activities are taking place, would be valuable.

High Dynamism (Score 3·9) and High Identification (Score 3·9)

He is highly dynamic in the overall quantitative sense of preparedness to act with vigour and this is linked to a participatory immersion in the work situation. He cannot help but live and breathe the work environment, although in any easy flowing way, without necessarily showing any feeling of burden as a result. When constructively applied it does mean that he has a great power for generating activity in other people.

EXAMPLE 3: MR. T. MYER

To recapitulate: Mr. Myer is the Managing Director of a subsidiary of an American owned international company. Mr. Myer's company, Kale and Co. Ltd., had been taken over just prior to his appointment there. It had been a traditional, family owned company run in an almost feudal manner. Mr. Myer's brief was to renovate the company using the existing people so far as possible and render it profitable by means of up to date scientific management methods. The situation was that Mr. Myer was having great difficulty in getting the existing managers to adapt to the new conditions and indeed was having difficulty overall in getting the company back into a profitable condition.

His action profile is on the opposite page.

Interesting Features

1 Highly developed *commitment* area backed up by strong *determining factor*.
2 Greatest interaction strength is *communicating* the components of which (*investigating* and *exploring*) are relatively the weaker areas.
3 Lack of *adaptability*.
4 Lack in the *identification* factor.
5 Extreme weakness in the *confronting* area.

		% of total activity	Extent of Interaction activity	
ATTENTION	Investigating	10		Communicating
	Exploring	12		
INTENTION	Determining	20		Presenting
	Confronting	8		
COMMITMENT	Deciding	25		Operating
	Anticipating	25		
Dynamism			3·0	
Adaptability			0·0	
Identifying			0·5	

Action Profile 3 MR. T. MYER

This was a typical example of a man in a position for which, by virtue of his motivational pattern, he was unsuited. It was an entirely new situation, both to the parent company and to Mr. Myer. Before this experience they could hardly have believed such antiquated business methods could exist. This situation then required a highly *adaptable* man; a man that would really give full attention to the new situation and gain a full appreciation of the facts before any thought of taking action.

Mr. Myer is, however, motivated to do just the opposite (point 3). As mentioned in point 1, the *determining* and 'commitment' areas are very highly developed, compared to the 'attention' areas. Mr. Myer is motivated to generate a fast moving system. The great predominance of motivation toward *anticipating* means that he always works in terms of a projected prospect, which he pursues with *determination* but without making it obvious to other people what the most immediate needs are (lack in *presenting*).

As mentioned in point 2, the strongest interaction area is *communicating* whereas the components of *communicating, investigating* and *exploring* are the weakest. Hence as Myer initiates a *communicative* interaction, the CONTENT (mostly commitment oriented) will be in conflict with the MODE of interaction, i.e. his 'manner' is such as to invite exploratory consideration but in fact he is already committed. Therefore, whilst he is apparently seeking other executives' ideas, they will feel defeated, because they sense that he has already made up his mind and committed himself to a course of action.

A further feature aggravating Mr. Myer's inability to get his top team to face up to immediate demands derives from his weakness in *presenting*. He cannot relate to people in such a way as to promote *determining* and *confronting* activity. He rather engenders the seeing of a prospect with the result that the executives share in the vision of the prospect but fail to face up to the needs of the present in order to reach that prospect.

The lack in *identification* (point 4) is interesting because it means that Mr. Myer cannot enthuse a team with his own sense of purpose. It is difficult for them to feel that they can really participate in the action with him. They must always see him as a lone leader—one who leads them to success rather than involves them in a corporate effort. It is a strange contradiction in the man's personality, and a very significant factor in his style of management, particularly in this situation.

Prior to this 'English exercise' he has been immediately successful in getting a new organization moving. However, the situations were significantly different. In each case he was backed up by an already sophisticated, efficient and highly motivated team. He didn't have to face them up to the obvious immediate needs or enthuse them with a sense of purpose.

In the English company Mr. Myer was just temperamentally unable to fulfil this essential requirement. Hence they suffered and so did he. His action profile just didn't match the requirements of the situation.

> Any manager, however capable and experienced, will perform below top efficiency if his action profile does not match the action requirements of the situation.

This applies in varying degrees depending upon the basic strength of the action profile. Some managers will never actually fail even though they may perform under par in certain wrong situations. Other managers may fail completely if they are wrongly placed. The difference is in the underlying strength of the action profile.

In this account, therefore, it is the weaker aspects of Mr. Myer's management style that have been highlighted. In a more favourable environment, one which drew on his strengths rather than his weaknesses, he would appear almost as a different man. The following strengths would have opportunity to shine:

Ability to see a prospect (Strength in *anticipating* 25 per cent)

He is exceptional in his *anticipatory* faculty. Because of the way it is applied in combination with other features he cannot help, whatever the work situation, but highlight what he sees to be the prospects. He does this quickly, spontaneously and with a perceptive flair. It is only partly related, however, to his own *investigation* and analysis. He acts as though under self-imposed pressure to read more into the facts of the situation than may be immediately apparent.

Ability to take decisions (Strength in *deciding* 25 per cent)

He is never afraid to commit himself and does so with precision. He acts as though he would fail in his job if he did not frequently take *decisions,* each one related to the other in a precisely programmed manner. He would probably feel he was failing in his job if he did not frequently take important *decisions,* even though a case could be made out for a period of review without undertaking commitments. This makes him incapable (without a special conscious effort) of making a review leading to one or two major commitments. Rather he makes a succession of commitments, possibly leading to a major one, but in a succession of stages. His manner is to keep things moving, as though there is never time to pause and reflect.

Communicability (Strength in *communicating*)

He is extremely approachable, disposed to want to understand people and be understood by them. No-one is ever likely to feel that he has failed in giving them attention. He will be truly felt to be sympathetic and concerned to recognize the individual position.

Demanding intent (Strength in *communicating,* concentration of activity into the 'commitment' stage [50 per cent] and strength in *determining* [20 per cent])

His attractiveness as someone to *communicate* with, plus his *decisive* pushing things along, plus the enigmatic aloofness, makes him a demanding person to work for. Subordinates are likely to feel, for example, that much is being expected of them without having been shown the way, although the freedom of *communication* would suggest that a way is being indicated. This can, of course, provide a high degree of motivation but only for those who can work out the way for themselves.

Sustained assertiveness (Strength in *determination* 20 per cent and strength in *dynamism* score 3·0)

He is assertive to get things done even at the cost of disturbing the structure. This is not obvious because he does not demonstrate intensity. There is a quietness about his assertion, however, which is disarming, and which is probably never suspected to hold the threat of *dynamic* action which it does. In general, it makes him concerned to act even though the conditions may not be right; earnestly anxious to take forthright action with colleagues without first preparing the conditions; predisposed to catch people unawares with some strenuous demand; again exhilarating for those who can cope with it, disastrous for those that cannot.

In conclusion it can be said that he is a man who shines when running a well set up, well known situation. He can keep an efficient business running at peak efficiency and can improve efficiency in a situation where he has well tried experience to draw upon—and in particular where he can use his considerable financial expertise to best advantage. This expertise, in combination with his *determination* and back up help from the American group, enabled him to win through on this assignment. Undoubtedly he learned a great deal, so although it was not a situation to make the most of his strengths, at least it was a valuable development experience. However, it is interesting to note that Mr. Myer could only benefit from this experience if placed in a situation almost exactly similar. For although he has learned how to handle a backward British management team, he still hasn't changed the underlying action dispositions as governed by the action profile. In another new situation (i.e. COMPLETELY untried) he would still want to run before he could walk. He still would not give enough attention to the new situation in order to find out how the place really ticked. Probably he would apply maxims learned in the Kale and Co. situation and put himself in the position of having to learn by bitter experience all over again!

PART II

The Action Profile: Theory and Measurement

CHAPTER 4

The Nature of the Action Profile

A CONSTANT AND INDIVIDUAL FEATURE IN THE PERSON

Reassessments conducted at intervals of between five and eighteen years indicate that the action profile is a constant feature in the manager's make-up. Often people say, 'But how can you claim the action profile is constant when people change according to who they are with; when they are different in different situations and according to the degree of pressure they are under?'

The answer is simply that people may appear to change but, with respect to the action pattern, no actual change takes place. It is only that different situations draw upon different aspects of the action pattern. If a motivation is not there to begin with, then nothing on earth can make it appear. If an action motivation is very strong then it will appear whatever the situation. If this motivation is patently inappropriate the person may try to repress it —but probably not too successfully or for too long. So he will either just continue to cope with the situation inefficiently or he will opt out, or be opted out!

If an action motivation is moderately strong, then it may well be given greater or lesser emphasis according to the demands of various situations, and providing the changed emphasis is not required for too long. Indeed if a person moves into a situation where a moderately evident motivation is suddenly required much more than ever before then this may cause a real change. The motivation may actually increase, but never beyond the next strongest, so that the pattern or relative weightings within the pattern still remains constant. For instance, if a person were predominantly strong in *confronting* but moderately strong in *anticipating* and were to move into some kind of a forward planning position where he was required mainly to project ahead, predict trends, etc., then there would be a good possibility that his *anticipatory* motivation would grow slightly. However, it would never grow beyond the *confronting* strength.

One of the most potent environmental factors in bringing out different aspects of people's action pattern is the people environment. In one group a person will take one role, in another he may even take what appears to be the opposite. A clear example of this happened during two group training

C

courses. One man attended both, so it was seen quite clearly the different effects that each group had upon his behaviour. Here is the action profile of the person in question, Mr. M. Shirley.

		% of total activity	Extent of Interaction activity
ATTENTION	Investigating	21	Communicating
	Exploring	8	
INTENTION	Determining	22	Presenting
	Confronting	5	
COMMITMENT	Deciding	23	Operating
	Anticipating	21	

Action Profile 4   MR. M. SHIRLEY

As can be seen his greatest strength is in *deciding* but he is almost as strong in *investigating* and *anticipating*. His strongest interaction mode is *operating,* but he is also able to respond in a *communicational* climate.

The first group in which he was involved was overall strongest in the 'attention' area, strong in *communicating, investigating* and *exploring,* but weak in the 'commitment' area, *operating, deciding* and *anticipating.* In this group he clearly took the role of the decision maker. He initiated an *operational* mode of relating and displayed no sign at all of *investigating* or *exploring* (at least during the half hour group exercise in which he was observed).

The second group in which he was observed was uniformly strong in *communicating,* but very weak in one of the components; i.e. *investigating.* Its strongest mode of relating as a group was *operating.* In this group Shirley played a completely different role. Because of the marked weakness in the other members of the group in *investigating,* he stood out as the strongest *investigator* of them all. He was overshadowed in *operational* facility. He appeared to become an *investigator* par excellence. He instinctively felt the lack of *investigatory* application and he felt ill at ease going on to make decisions on the basis of what he felt in this situation to be ill-defined premises. He constantly sought to bring the others back to square one for further *investigation* and definition.

This caused enormous irritation amongst some of the other members of the group (for to them further *investigation* seemed unnecessary and time wasting) but he continued to do it. Many of them expressed considerable surprise at this behaviour in him. They had never worked in this particular grouping before and had only observed him individually, or in combination with others. It was the great weight of motivation away from *investigating* within this particular group that caused him to display so much concern with *investigatory* activity. However, although Shirley's *investigatory* activity stood out in comparison to the others and in fact he did give it greater emphasis for short periods; over the entire course his pattern still revealed itself as constant.

If it is true that the action profile represents a part of the person which is a highly 'individual' and 'constant' determiner of behaviour, just what part of the person is it?

THE ACTION PROFILE AS PERSONALITY AND MOTIVATION

A theory is being proposed here that the behaviour described in what is called the 'action profile' is a cross between what is commonly known as personality characteristics and a particular aspect of what is known as motivation.

When it is considered that something about a person is individual and relatively constant it is usually said to be his personality, his character or his temperament or, often in management, his style. When, on the other hand, it is considered that something about a person is relatively transitory it is called mood or feeling or attitude. Therefore because the action profile is a constant and individual determiner of behaviour it is properly seen as coming under the heading of personality.

However, the term personality characteristic is usually used to describe a sort of permanent condition in the person. If you are extrovert, for instance, then you just *are* that way and that's that. Because you *are* a certain way you behave in a certain way. The action profile in a sense also describes what you are (i.e. because it is constant and individual) but it incorporates in addition a further dimension.

Behaving in accordance with the action profile is not simply a fact of life (as for an extrovert behaving extrovertly) it is also a satisfying and need fulfilling activity. If you are strongly *investigatory*, then you do not just act in an *investigatory* way, you want, need, are satisfied when you are able to investigate and frustrated and unsatisfied when prevented from doing so. This is why the action emphases are called 'motivations'. Motivation refers to a state which persons are in when they are pursuing something, the achievement of which will give them satisfaction. There are many different kinds of motivations of course but they all fall into two distinct classes:

> 1 Universal or common to everyone at some stage.
> 2 Individual or specific to each person.

The action profile as a complete pattern of motivation obviously belongs to the second class, for as is constantly emphasized it is a highly individual pattern and no two people are identical in this respect. To clarify the situation with reference to motivation in general, consider a summary of present thinking on motivation to see how the action profile concept fits into other theories.

PRESENT THINKING ON MOTIVATION

Early concepts of motivation

It was thought that men were primarily motivated by having their basic needs satisfied—e.g. food, shelter, security, etc. This led to the manipulation of monetary reward—various incentive schemes and fringe benefits, etc. In addition a lot of attention was paid to working and group conditions—physical environment, rest periods, group composition. All these factors are conditions which are external to the person concerned. The emphasis was on external motivation and the fulfilment of basic universal needs. Therefore the characteristics of this attitude toward motivation are:

> i Satisfaction of basic needs known as deficit needs
> ii External motivation

Recent concepts of motivation

These are based largely on the work of an American behavioural scientist, Abraham Maslow. According to Maslow's concept of a heirarchy of needs, a very compelling form of motivation comes from within. Man is essentially a self motivated animal.

The Hierarchy of Needs[9]

> ● *need for self actualization*
> ● need for esteem
> ● need for belongingness and love
> ● safety needs
> ● physiological needs

There is a fundamental difference between the lower four needs and the top one. The lower four are called 'deficit' needs. This is because they are motivational only in their absence. As soon as any one of these needs is satisfied the person is no longer motivated to take action. If a person is satiated, he no longer seeks food. Hunger is motivational only for a hungry man.

According to Malow even such a sophisticated need such as for esteem (from self and others) is a deficit need. If a man has self respect and feels he is esteemed by others he no longer strives to earn esteem and respect. Only the highest level need for self actualization is of a different order. Maslow calls this a 'growth' need as it is continuously motivational.

Self actualization sounds very high flown, but really it has just to do with the satisfaction one gets from doing something purely and simply for the sake of it. The person who reaches the point of continuous self actualization has necessarily satisfied all the deficit needs, and is able to integrate his interests, talents, and abilities to the point that he works toward becoming what he must become. This sounds a bit idealistic—more suited to dedicated musicians and artists than business managers. However, the motivational effect of a self actualization process can be found in any field. Whenever a person gets himself into that certain niche, where he can fully utilize his talents and hence finds satisfaction in achieving goals simply for the sake of it, then he is self actualizing.

Motivation—Hygiene Theory

Frederick Herzberg[10] saw the practical value of Maslow's theory for industry. He developed his own motivation hygiene theory. This draws a distinction between job 'satisfiers' and 'dissatisfiers'. They were found to derive from two different classes of experience. Those things which caused a worker to be 'dissatisfied' with his job were all to do with the environment surrounding it, e.g.: working conditions, salary, status, job security. To equate this with Maslow's theory, these are all 'deficit' needs.

The mere satisfaction of these needs is not the best way to motivate a man to perform better on the job for the following reasons:

1 It is very difficult to link the satisfaction of deficit needs with excellence of performance in a really relevant and meaningful way. At certain job levels, level of performance can be directly related to rate of reward as with piece work and selling on commission for instance. But this cannot apply to all types of work. For most managerial functions, for instance, a direct and quantifiable measure of performance is very difficult to attain. Thus such a direct link between reward and effectiveness becomes more and more difficult to make.

2 Once a deficit need has been satisfied it no longer provides real motivation. Conditions have to be really bad before a man will work at top efficiency just to ensure he gets his pay, or keeps his job. If his pay comes in regularly on moderate performance, why should he try harder?

Job Enrichment

The work led by Herzberg on various kinds of job enrichment is an attempt at dealing with motivation problems at a completely different level. The aim is to attempt to bring a man's 'self motivating' capacity to bear. This is done by so structuring the job that the man can gain satisfaction on the basis of the work alone. The job itself becomes his primary source of motivation.

This is not to say, however, that deficit needs are unimportant or can be ignored. On the contrary these needs must in fact be seen to before the self motivational aspects can be cultivated. Whilst the satisfaction of deficit needs does not provide continuous motivation, a state of dissatisfaction can be an impediment to the establishment of a continuous motivational situation. So there are two essential stages in the provision of continuous motivation:

1 Satisfy dissatisfiers or deficit needs, e.g. needs for food, sex, shelter, security, love, esteem.

2 Provide 'satisfiers' or opportunity for the satisfaction of growth needs.

This approach has caused conflict and argument, some staunch advocates, some stern critics. The theory of motivation behind it, however, is a very valuable one.

The characteristics of the more recent outlook on motivation can be summarized as:

1 Giving scope to the need for self actualization.
2 Internal motivation.

SELF MOTIVATION AND SENIOR MANAGERS

Work on motivation in industry has mainly been confined to the work force. Little attention has been given as yet to the more complex problem of motivation with respect to managers, certainly not at senior levels. The more recent attitude to motivation is particularly relevant when considering the motivation of senior managers. A senior management function allows for a relatively large degree of freedom of action. The manager to a large extent makes his job his own, and does it his own way. There is a great deal of room for self expression. In such a position, if a man is to be really effective he must be internally motivated.

How can the conditions capable of promoting optimal self motivation for a manager be defined?

The basic need motivations are common to everyone. We all need food, sex, shelter, love and self respect. But beyond that, where a person works for the sake of it, that driving force is entirely individual. No two people are driven by exactly the same things, and no two people gain exactly the same kind of satisfaction from the same situation. What is it that makes one man a desk pounding, disciplining, morale boosting company doctor wanting to tackle run-down low-morale outfits, while another is happiest keeping an already efficient outfit running smoothly? Why does one man want to instal standard systems all over the place, while another can't be bothered to systematize his own filing cabinet, but is in his element in a complex new situation requiring a completely new set of attitudes and methods? Why does one man measure satisfaction in terms of his ability to tactically outwit everyone, whilst another only gains satisfaction from establishing an open, participative environment where everyone understands one another?

The theory submitted here is that, in management perhaps more than any other field, it is the full expression of a man's action profile which gives him the greatest sense of self fulfilment, hence the greatest degree of self motivation on the job.

To refer back to the distinctions made earlier. Behaviour can be determined by characteristics in a person which are either constant or transitory, individual or universal. The following table shows how the various ways of describing aspects of the person which are considered to affect behaviour, can be categorized in this way.

Features in the person that determine behaviour and how they are measured or described

	Relatively Constant Features		Relatively Transitory Features	
	How described	How measured	How described	How measured
Individual	Personality Character Temperament Style (in management)	Personality tests Interviews Simulated experiences	Emotions Feelings Moods	Perception Intuition Various psychological tests
	Internal motivation	Action Profile	Attitudes	Attitude surveys and tests
	Intelligence	IQ and aptitude tests		
Universal	External motivation (up to a certain level)	Many and various From personal judgement to remuneration surveys		

Table 1

This shows clearly where the action profile fits in. It is concerned with a part of the person which is an individual and relatively constant determiner of behaviour just as 'personality', 'character' and 'temperament' are.

However, the kind of behaviour determined by the action profile characteristics is fairly specific, It is 'self motivated' behaviour, where a person is acting for the sake of it, for the satisfaction he gains from just doing whatever it is.

It must be recognized, of course, that the action profile is only a manager's potential for self motivation on the job. Just because every manager has an action profile doesn't mean that he is necessarily entirely self motivated. There may be constraints springing from the nature of the job, or the company or the manager himself which militate against a manager acting straightforwardly according to the dictates of his action profile. In such a case the manager may pretend to act differently or even genuinely attempt to *be* different in terms of the areas of action he emphasizes.

A manager who gives little emphasis to *deciding*, for instance, on perceiving that opportunism, a fast pace, instant decisions, etc., are valued in a particular management context, may attempt to force himself into this type of behaviour. At best he will appear over anxious, at worst ridiculous and in any event he won't be able to keep it up without serious damage to himself and his company. But again, of course, regrettably this sometimes happens.

A manager who cannot for one reason or another behave simply in accordance with the dictates of his action motivations without pretences, stop gaps, and defences of one sort or another may, of course, seek a more satisfying environment outside the work situation. Hence his work will become simply a routine performance, where he is dependent primarily upon external sources of motivation such as his need for security to keep him going. Once the basic needs are reasonably satisfied then his effort ceases and he is working far below optimum performance.

If we are to assume that most managers and particularly senior managers have reached that level where they have to be primarily internally motivated, then it is obviously a benefit to be able to define and measure those motivating forces and, of course, the action profile gives this definition and measure.

Before going on to describe how the information on these internal motivating forces contained in the action profile can be used in management, it is appropriate to describe how the action profile is measured. This is where the going gets difficult and considerable concentration is required. It is recommended that managers endeavour to gain at least an idea of the theory and practice underlying the evaluation of the action profile presented in the next section. However, for those who find they really cannot, or do not have time to study it, the rest of the book does hang together without the next section and does not presuppose a knowledge of the evaluation technique.

CHAPTER 5

Measurement of the Action Motivations

The action profile assessment seems like an ordinary meeting or interview. But how can one get a detailed and reasonably objective assessment from an ordinary interview? The answer is by making disciplined use of all the data that can be derived from an interview, particularly the non-verbal content. The operative word here is disciplined, because there is plenty of evidence that managers do already make use of the non verbal content of an interview though often they hardly realize it themselves, and the discipline to which they subject such information is highly open to question.

The evidence is that managers have, despite the development of objective testing methods, clung persistently to the interview as a method of assessment. It is as if they feel they can put more 'trust' in first hand contact. Even if they do make use of some other more 'objective' form of assessment, such as personality and IQ testing, it would be true to say that most employers will still for some reason want to check the findings of the tests against their own 'feel' of the man. Thus interviews still take place.

Because of this the interview as an assessment tool has been widely studied. It was necessary to find out just how accurate and reliable this method was. Were first hand judgements really so good? The consensus of opinion now seems pretty well settled. In some cases 'yes', in some cases 'no'. Some people are good interviewers and make highly accurate judgements. Some people are not. It appears that good interviewers are as good in judging people as available objective tests on some dimensions such as motivation and interpersonal skills[3] (Argyle p. 135).

What is it then that characterizes a good interviewer? An explanation of this phenomena has as yet not been found. No-one has, as yet, attempted to delineate either the nature of the special talent that makes a good judge of people or that data on which this more accurate judgement is based. There has been considerable study into the mechanics by which people do make judgements of others, but no attempt to differentiate between the more and less accurate judgers.

For example, one theory is that we assign people to categories, e.g. of sex, age, nationality, class, based upon inferences from particular physical cues, such as grey hair and wrinkles (for age), accent and clothes (for class), facial features (for race). We then infer certain personality characteristics, based upon a stereotype of the particular category; e.g. all Jewish people are shrewd, all people wearing glasses or having high foreheads are more intelligent, dependable, industrious and so on.

Another theory about how inferences from bodily appearance and speech to personality are made was suggested by Secord (1958).[11] He considered that analogy or metaphor may be involved. For example, a person with coarse skin is seen as coarse. Inferences may be based on functional qualities—a girl with full lips is seen as highly sexed. There may be generalization from the personalities of people who have been known in the past.

We are all susceptible to a greater or lesser degree to these kinds of processes. Yet there is evidence that they result in inaccurate judgements. Stereotypes, such as that all Jewish people are shrewd, are such over-simplifications as to make for as many exceptions to the rule as agreements. Some experiments have shown the lack of accuracy quantitatively—for example Brunswik (1945)[12] found that judgements of IQ correlated 0·25 with the height of the person; i.e. there was a tendency to consider a person more or less intelligent according to his height, but that actual IQ correlated only 0·10.

So we have some knowledge as to how some unreliable judgements are made, but virtually nothing is known about how the more accurate judgements are made. Does the more accurate judger have a special sixth sense, acute intuition, or what? Before becoming involved in the possibility of a sixth sense let us concentrate on what can be achieved with the ordinary five senses. Consider the wealth of data that is available from a person and that can be perceived by the five senses. Admittedly in our society and certainly in the context of an interview of some kind, the exercise of taste, smell and touch is somewhat constrained—not entirely though. We do shake hands, and we do often make use of our sense of smell. However, let us concentrate mainly on the use of information gained via sight and hearing.

Most obvious of course is words. We hear what the other person says. It is well recognized that the verbal impression given by a person of his situation, his characteristics, strengths and so on, will be subject to bias. However sincere and honest a person is he cannot escape this element of subjectivity. Therefore to rely on what a person says for any form of judgement must be fraught with uncertainty. What is left? The tone of voice, the way in which a person speaks is indeed a factor, but as yet difficult to analyse.

Apart from that there is only a human body which has certain proportions and features and is clothed in a certain way. Static or fixed things such as the size of facial features, colour of hair, physique and style of dress can also be ruled out as reliable indications of personality or character. They may well inform you about racial origin, perhaps even social class with some accuracy, but certainly not personality—or more to the point, how a person will approach a particular job, or whether he will succeed or not in a certain work environment.

What remains then for a so-called 'good' interviewer to use as a basis for his perceptions which are at least (if not more) as accurate as objective personality tests?

A likely theory is that good judgers detect certain elements from amongst the enormous array of data projected by an individual, that are constant, and are a reliable index of certain aspects of that person's personality.

Having subtracted all those things which are fixed and static such as dress, physique, colour of hair, what is left? There is still an enormously complex area of behaviour evident during any interaction or meeting which has not so far been taken into account. This is so-called non-verbal communication.* Over the last decade there has been a great surge of interest in non-verbal expression. The elements of non-verbal expression are being gradually established. Such things as frequency and duration of eye contact, preferred distance from others, preferred posture, typical gestures, and so on, have been isolated and studied, the aim being to discover what significance they have and how such things are interpreted.

Researchers have, for instance, carried out studies to determine the relative impact of verbal and non-verbal cues. Argyle *et al.* (1969)[13] found that in the interpretation of dominant and submissive attitudes, non-verbal cues were the most important. Mehrabian and Ferris (1967)[14] came up with the following equation. Perceived attitude $= \cdot007 + 0\cdot38$ tone and $0\cdot55$ face; i.e. $0\cdot97$ of the impression formed of the person transmitting the attitude was formed on the basis of non-verbal data. Probably the percentage would vary according to the nature of the interaction and the nature of the inference about the person being made.

Most of the researchers are looking for cultural similarities in non-verbal expressions. R. Birdwhistell[15], for instance, in his incredibly detailed and painstaking analysis, looks for interpretations of clusters of homogeneous responses which convey a meaning according to a specific social context. To him it is like a highly complex language, the interaction taking place at many different levels—as in verbal language: words, sentences, paragraphs. The tiniest flicker of a facial muscle is like a word. This is combined with other movements into whole sentences and paragraphs. This complex language is understood perfectly only by people of the same social origin, less accurately even by people of the same nationality.

This is one way in which non-verbal expression can be studied: it is a language as complex as verbal language, as specific to one's upbringing and background and learnt in childhood, in a similar way. Birdwhistell relates a

* The word communication is used here in the general sense, not the special definition as used in the twelve action motivations.

beautifully illustrative anecdote about the non-verbal message systems within his own family:

> '... my mother was an expert in untalk—she could emit a silence so loud as to drown out the scuffle of feet, the whish of corduroy trousers, and even the grind of my father's power machinery to which he retreated when, as he said, "Your mother's getting uneasy."
>
> 'My mother took great pride in her role of gracious hostess. She would say firmly, "No matter how much I disagree with a guest I never allow an unchristian word to cross my lips, I just smile." Well, my mother's thin-lipped smile, which could be confined to her mouth when accompanied by an audible input of air through her tightened nostrils, required no words—Christian or otherwise—to reveal her attitude. My mother was a sniffer, a great sniffer. She could be heard for three rooms across the house. And, to paraphrase Mark Twain, her sniff had power; she could sniff a fly off the wall at 30 feet.' [15]

Here the researcher is studying commonly understood systems of behaviour within one culture. He is seeing how all non-verbal factors contribute to the total interaction system within a defined social setting. Most of the study of non-verbal expression being carried out today is of this nature. A few exploiters have jumped on the bandwagon and published books purporting to let you into the secret of translating other people's so-called 'secret' non-verbal expression. Such works are basically superficial and they convey a fundamental error. There is nothing 'secret' about non-verbal expression. There is already a common understanding between people in terms of non-verbal expression—and there always has been. It is nothing new. Human beings no doubt interacted very effectively non-verbally before language was invented.

Some of us, however, are much more sensitive to this non-verbal expression than others. It requires a facility for observation and a sensitivity to detail. It may also require simply the opportunity to observe. People still speak of 'women's intuition'. It is often found that this is used in connection with judgements of people. It may well be that women in the past and to some extent now, take a less vociferously active part in social interactions than men. Particularly, of course, when husbands are discussing matters of business. It is the men who are totally involved. The women can remain detached enough to observe. Hence they can more objectively observe the subtle non-verbal elements in the interaction.

So far the most obvious interpretation of the term 'non-verbal communication' has been referred to; i.e. as the expression of attitudes and emotions, the moment by moment changes in feeling and attitude, an expression similar in nature to a language. In this respect a single movement or constellation of movements may have a concise meaning depending upon the context within which it is experienced. For instance, raised brows are often interpreted as surprise, half raised brows as worry, single raised brow as disbelief and so on

(Harrison 1965).[16] But, of course, in face to face contact, we do not only convey what we feel or what we think but also what we are. We are all capable of making quite hefty inferences about another person's character or personality perhaps as a result of only a relatively short meeting. Remarks such as 'gosh he looked a bit snooty' or 'I bet he's a go-ahead sort of chap' are pretty common. It is sometimes possible to sit in whilst managers are interviewing prospective employees. Afterwards, of course, there is a discussion on the relative merits of the person. On one occasion there was a candidate who on qualification, record, experience, and response to the interviewer's questions, was well suited to the job. The interviewer, however, couldn't get away from his 'feeling' that the man was 'superior'. On these grounds he was prepared to discount the candidate.

He was questioned as to the precise reason for this 'feeling' of his. Was it anything the candidate said? Was it anything he did? Was it the way he dressed? None of these seemed to be the answer. Finally it appeared it had been his 'manner'—not *what* he did or said, but somehow the *way* in which he did it. On questioning the manager as to the precise nature of this 'manner', no clarification could be gained. During the interview detailed observations of the candidate's verbal and non-verbal expression had been noted. It had been noticed that he had a persistent mannerism of raising his head and squinting down his nose. On further questioning of the manager it was established that it was this mannerism which had created the impression that the candidate was 'superior'. It had also been noted that this movement happened as if it was just a habit, an unfortunate unconscious expression of nervousness, in no way an expression of anything constant within the man's behavioural pattern, or indicating a constant personality feature. On this explanation the candidate was accepted and did in fact turn out not in the least superior, and highly effective.

This is a perfect example of an inaccurate interpretation of an element in a person's non-verbal behaviour. A bodily expression which could be recognized to be transitory was interpreted (albeit virtually unconsciously) as an indication of a constant feature of the man's personality.

How can accurate interpretation of the same data be made? How can the constant features in non-verbal expression be separated out from those of a transitory nature? For obviously the so-called 'good' judge of people must be particularly sensitive not only to the complex array of non-verbal expression, but also to some degree able to differentiate elements which are an indication of transitory emotion or mood and those which are an indication of an enduring aspect of the person.

CONSTANCY IN INDIVIDUAL PATTERNS OF NON-VERBAL EXPRESSION

First consider whether there are constant and enduring elements in a person's pattern of non-verbal expression, at all. The infinite variety of movement capabilities of the human body is put to use in two ways. First we use the movement capacities of the body for instrumental or functional purposes. We carry things, lift things, brush things, smooth things, open things, manœuvre things, etc. . . . We also move ourselves from one place to another, in a great variety of ways. We run, stroll, stride, leap, strut, rush, hurry and so on. There isn't a single mechanical instrument which can perform such a vast array of functions as the human body. It took engineers generations to construct a fork lift truck with such smooth deceleration that it could handle delicate loads. The human hand has been handling objects of the greatest fragility for centuries. We can vary our movement in the subtlest of ways. Imagine if you tried to comb your hair with the same type of movement as you use to clean your teeth!

The other way in which the enormous variety of movement capacity of the human body is used, is as a vehicle of expression. When we exert force in order to hammer a nail, we are using our bodies as an instrument; when we exert force in order to thump the table to emphasize a point, we are using our bodies as a vehicle of expression.

Perhaps it is easier at first to consider characteristic ways of performing various functions with the body. Walking is an obvious instrumental use of the body. Most of us have been in the position of being able to recognize a person by his or her walk. Sports often bring out very clearly people's idiosyncratic ways of moving. A good example is a tennis service. A person will always have a style particular to himself and no two people are ever quite the same.

To a certain extent, indeed the quality of a movement is governed by its purpose. However, not entirely. There will be differences to varying degrees in the movement qualities people use in performing even exactly the same functional action. Writing is a perfect example. The letters actually trace the structural and qualitative aspects of the writing action. The variations are enormous, so much so that graphologists have been able to make a whole study of the phenomenon. There are thousands of other such examples. Think of all the different ways people blow their noses, for instance, or the ways people smoke cigarettes. Thus it would seem there are personal and individual ways of moving even within the restraints of a particular practical function.

People also have characteristic and individual ways of bodily expression. The 'sniff' of R. Birdwhistell's mother is an example. If you imagine her doing it, you will not only hear the sound but you will imagine how her body moves as she does it. Perhaps she drew herself up and tossed her head as she sniffed—all an integral part of the total expression of the disapproving attitude. I remember a particularly unfortunate teacher. She would often lose control over the class. After tolerating an incredible amount of disruption she would finally reach a state of explosion. Just before the eruption there was always an invariable warning sign. The skin on her forehead would creep eerily backwards, causing her eyes to bulge out of her head in an expression of total exasperation. The class would recognize this sign and there would be a silent expectancy as the inevitable hysteria gathered momentum. Such marked idiosyncrasies in bodily expression stick in the mind, but we all have them to varying degrees.

It would be difficult to interpret such expressions in terms of enduring personality traits. In the case of the teacher the movement was rather an expression of emotion. It is non-verbal behavioural elements of a slightly different nature that can be selected out as indications of certain personality features.

> *There is a difference between* **what** *one does with the body and* **how** *one does it.*

The managing director moved through the door, went towards the chair and sat down.

The managing director crept through the door, edged towards the chair and shrank down onto it.

The managing director rushed through the door, strode toward the chair and threw himself down.

The first description tells *what* the managing director did. The next two give different descriptions of *how* he might have done it. The visual pictures engendered are vastly different. We can make little inference about the managing director from the first. From the second and third we can imagine what he might be like, what mood he was in and so on. Words descriptive of bodily movement can often give such a vivid indication of mood or character that they can give an odd picture such as in the second description. To speak of a managing director 'creeping' through a door 'edging' toward a chair and 'shrinking' onto it gives a picture of his personality or mood which is so different from the expected picture of a managing director, that it sounds odd. It seems much more normal to speak of a managing director 'rushing', 'striding' and 'throwing' himself into a chair, because it creates the kind of personality we might expect in a managing director. Our language is rich with words descriptive of how movements are performed. We can describe the differences in *quality* of movement by using colourful descriptive words, but can we pinpoint the variation in the mechanics of the movement which results in such differences?

THE MECHANICS OF MOVEMENT QUALITY

To obtain the many rich and varied qualities of movement that we do (without even realizing it mostly) we vary the intensity and combination of what are known as movement elements. There are movement elements of basically two different kinds, effort and shaping.

Effort

In terms of the effort or assertion quality of a movement we can vary the
focus with which it is done, the degree of pressure, the timing and the degree
of control or kind of flow with which it is done. Each of these elements of
variation can be considered a continuum, with a neutral area between each
extreme. The four effort-elements with their polarities or extremes are as
follows:

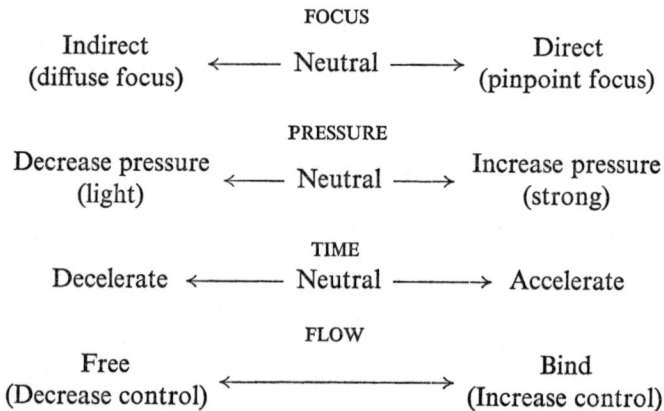

FOCUS

Indirect   ←——— Neutral ———→   Direct
(diffuse focus)   (pinpoint focus)

PRESSURE

Decrease pressure   ←——— Neutral ———→   Increase pressure
(light)   (strong)

TIME

Decelerate   ←——— Neutral ———→   Accelerate

FLOW

Free   ←————————→   Bind
(Decrease control)   (Increase control)

EXAMPLES OF EFFORT ELEMENTS—FUNCTIONAL
AND NON-FUNCTIONAL MOVEMENT

Directing and Indirecting

To give an example of what is meant by direct and indirect focus in the way
a movement is performed, consider firstly some straightforward functional
movements. Directing in movement is the process of making a straight
pathway through space to a particular point. Cutting a piece of meat on a
plate for instance will require you to make a series of directing movements.
Opening a letter with a letter knife requires directing movement as would
placing a pen in a pen holder. Indirecting in movement is the process of
making diffuse or wandering pathways through space encompassing a series
of foci. A functional movement which requires indirecting movements might
be spooning whipped cream out of a dish. Waving an ink written document
in the air to dry it would be done most effectively with indirecting movements,
although it could be done with directing movements in which case it would
look a bit as if you were cleaning a window with it. Opening and shutting
an umbrella requires directing movements. The curving motions when
cleaning the windscreen of a car will require indirecting movements.

Examples of directing and indirecting in non-functional or expressional

THE ELEMENTS OF MOVEMENT BEHAVIOUR SHOWING THE BASIC DIMENSIONS OF VARIATION

Photographs by Derek Drage

1. Gesture: At the beginning the face is fairly motionless. It gradually adopts a smiling expression which then fades. Only the mouth moves. The rest of the body remains totally uninvolved. An isolated *gesture* smile such as this is usually to be seen when people are merely being 'polite'. There is no sincere pleasure being expressed. *Gesture* movement can easily be faked. (see pp. 88–90)

2. Posture Gesture Merging (PGM): Here the smile begins as an isolated mouth gesture but soon the whole body is involved, i.e. the gesture movement has merged into posture movement. It is an integrated movement sequence employing the same qualities of movement all the way through. Whenever *posture gesture merging* (PGM) movement such as this occurs it is fairly plain that a genuine feeling is being expressed. In addition such movement is always performed in a way that is extremely individual and characteristic of the person. P.G.M. Movement *cannot* be faked! (see pp. 88–90)

3. P.G.M. Indirecting effort: Starting from a pinpoint focus (direct) rest position, a curving (indirect) head gesture leads the body into an indirecting movement, i.e. a convoluting movement with a wandering focus which ends naturally in a slightly twisted 'indirect' rest position. Indirecting-directing movements are often seen in expressions of query or interest. (see pp. 80–1)

4. P.G.M. Directing effort: A direct hand gesture leads the body into a directing movement, i.e. with a sharp pinpoint focus. The fourth picture shows the beginning of recovery into a relatively neutral position. If indirecting-directing movement is truly done with gesture merging into posture it will indicate that *attention* is being given and *investigation* is taking place. (see pp. 80–1, 102, 33–5)

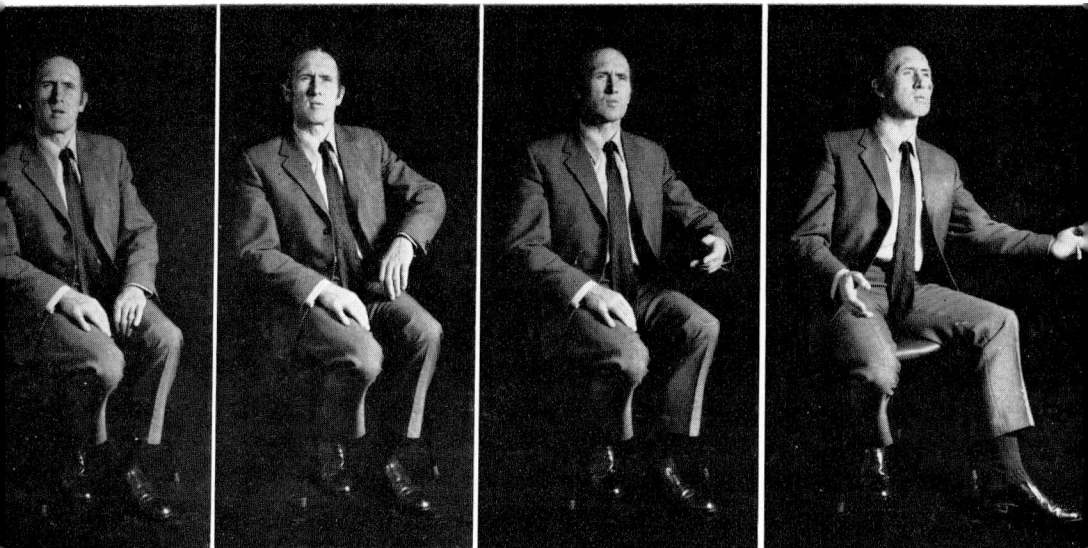

5. P.G.M. Spreading, shaping: From a relatively enclosed rest position, a spreading shoulder gesture leads into a postural spreading movement. See how the chest curves round as if the shoulders want to meet the back. (see p. 85)

6. P.G.M. Enclosing, shaping: Beginning in a spread rest position, this time an enclosing foot gesture leads the enclosing postural movement. The chest curves in a convex fashion, so that the shoulders move as if wanting to meet in front. High frequency of the spreading enclosing dimension of shaping in the PGM movement pattern indicates motivation to give *exploratory attention* (see pp. 85, 102, 35)

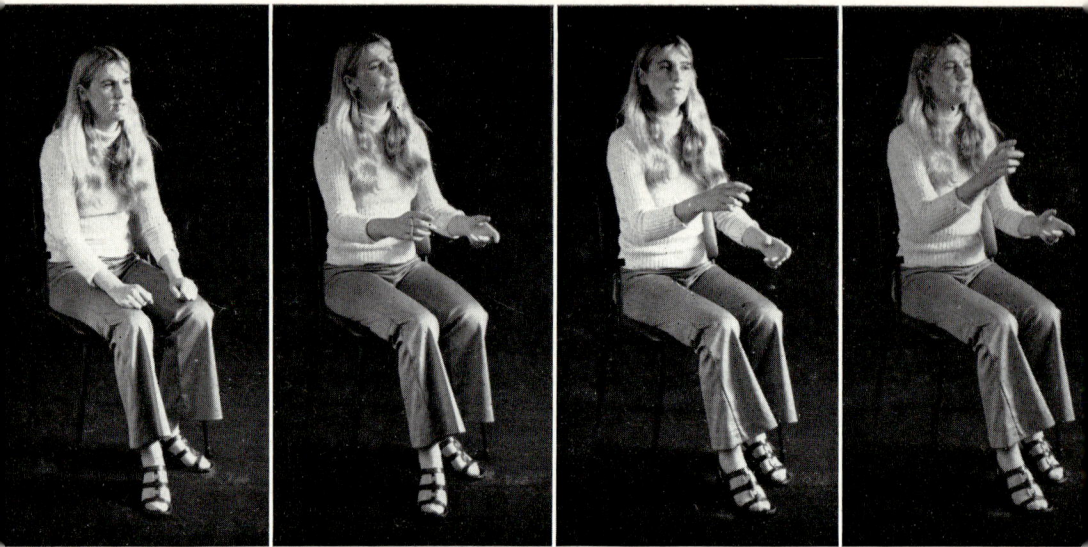

7. P.G.M. Decreasing Pressure effort: From a relatively neutral rest position a light trunk gesture (one can gesture with any part of the body) leads head, hands and rest of body into postural movement of decreasing pressure, i.e. having a light quality. High frequency of increasing-decreasing pressure in the PGM pattern indicates strong *determining* motivation. (see pp. 81, 102, 35)

8. P.G.M. Increasing Pressure effort: A strong hand gesture leads the body from a relatively neutral rest position into a postural movement of increasing pressure, i.e. having a firm or strong quality. P.G.M. increasing pressure is often seen in expressions of resolution and firmness of purpose (see p. 81).

Compare this demonstration of increasing pressure (Figure 8) with the beginning position of the figure 7 above. This was also supposed to demonstrate increased pressure as a contrast to the decreasing pressure in the rest of the sequence. It is patently obvious, however, that the performer (author) despite being a highly trained

9. P.G.M. Rising, shaping: From a descended rest position a rising leg gesture leads into a postural rising movement which in the fourth picture begins to descend again. Note the sideways curve which is the essence of rising-descending shaping. The rising-descending dimension of shaping is often seen in expressions of provocation or challenge. (see p. 86)

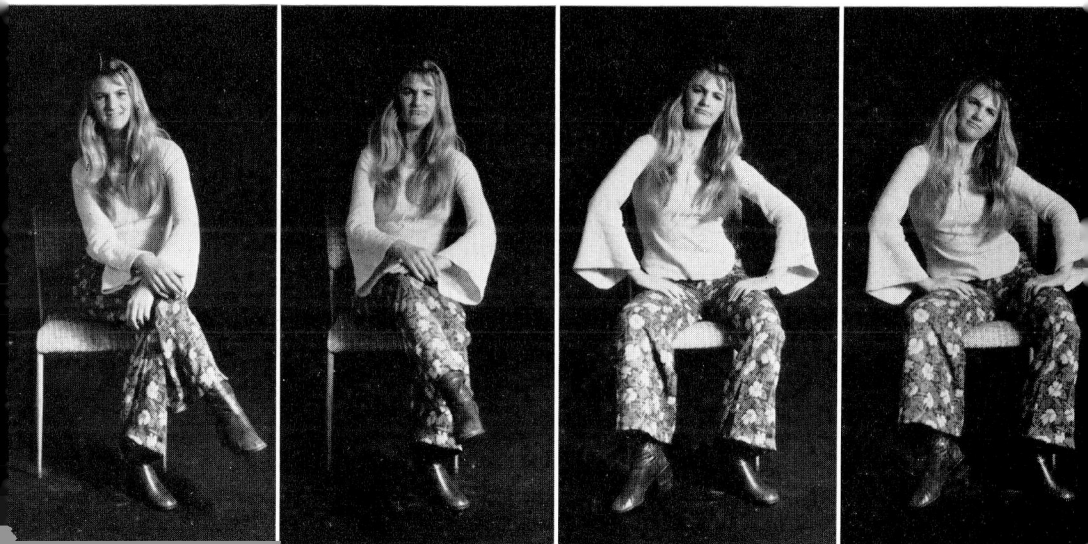

10. P.G.M. Descending, shaping: A slightly descending leg gesture leads the body from a risen position into a postural descending movement. Again note the sideways curve. High frequency of rising-descending shaping in the P.G.M. pattern shows a strong motivation to *confront* (see pp. 86, 102, 35–6)

specialist in both the observation and performance of movement has not succeeded in executing PGM increasing pressure. This is because increasing pressure is not part of her natural P.G.M. movement pattern! Remember P.G.M. movement cannot be performed to order, not even by 'experts'.

11. P.G.M. Decelerating effort: Decelerating hand gestures are leading the body in a series of decelerating postural movements. The decelerating quality might be seen in someone who was calming another down. It is difficult to see in a photograph but before each deceleration comes a very slight acceleration. The accelerating-decelerating dimension will be evident whenever a person is in control of the 'pace' of activity; his own or others'. (see p. 81)

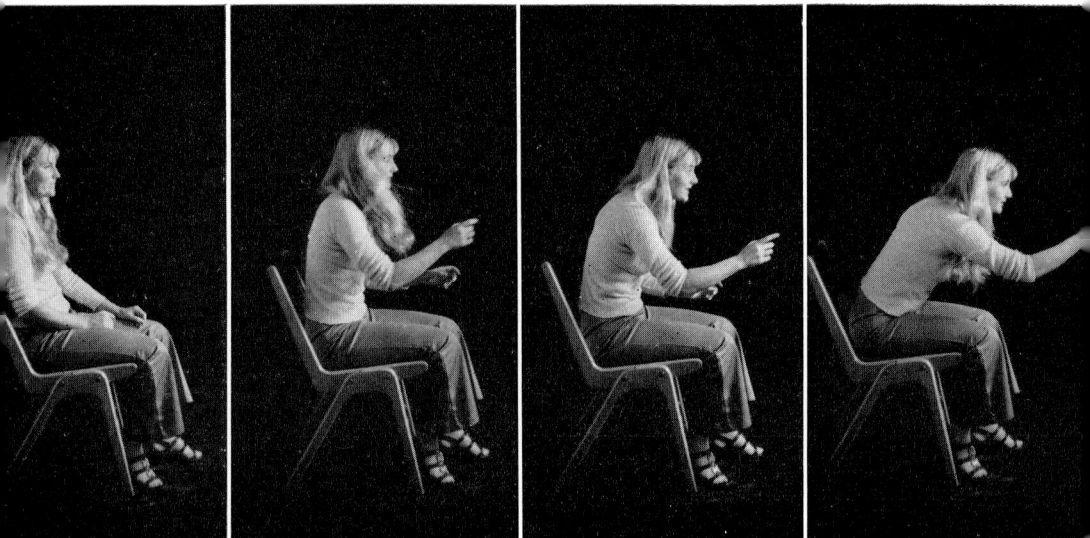

12. P.G.M. Accelerating effort: From a relatively neutral rest position the accelerating hand gesture leads the body into a series of accelerating postural movements, each acceleration being alternated with a slight deceleration. High frequency of decelerating-accelerating in the P.G.M. pattern indicates a strong *deciding* motivation. (see pp. 81, 102, 36)

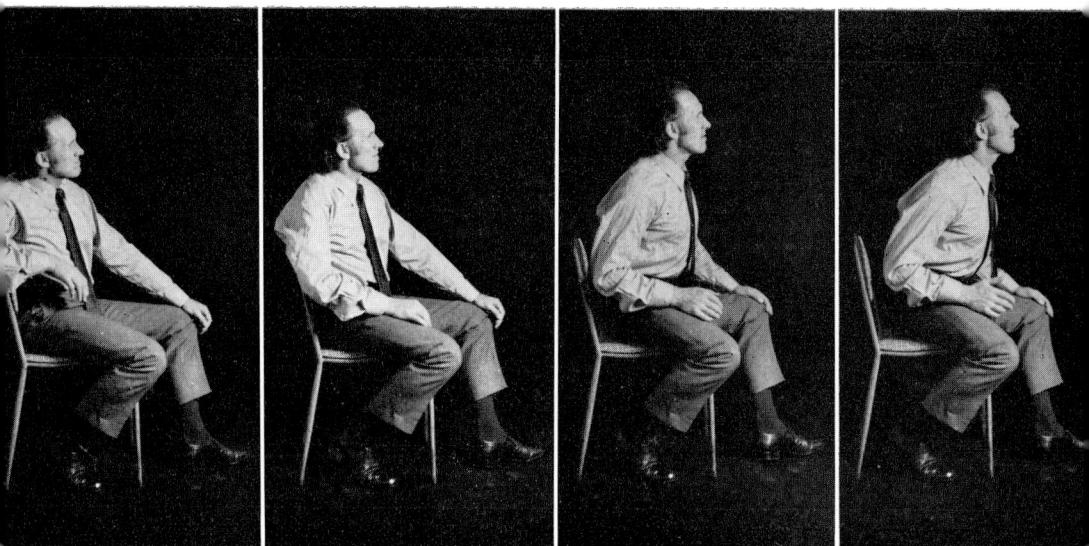

13. P.G.M. Advancing, shaping: Starting from a retreating rest position the advancing hand gesture leads into postural advancing. See the convex curvature of the body (particularly the trunk) in the forward-back dimension: Note that there is little actual locomotion forward. The orientation of the curving of the body is the all important factor. (see pp. 86–7)

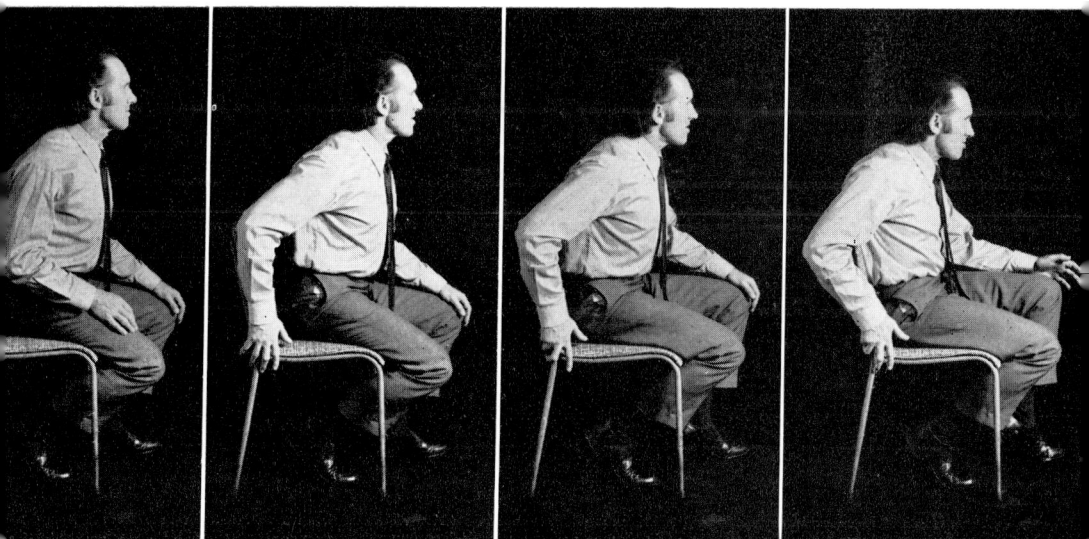

14. P.G.M. Retraining, shaping: From a well advanced rest position the retreating hand gesture again leads but this time into a retreating postural movement. Again note the curve in the forward-back dimensions but this time it is a convex curve. High frequency of advancing-retreating shaping indicates a motivation to *anticipate*. (see pp. 86–7, 102, 36)

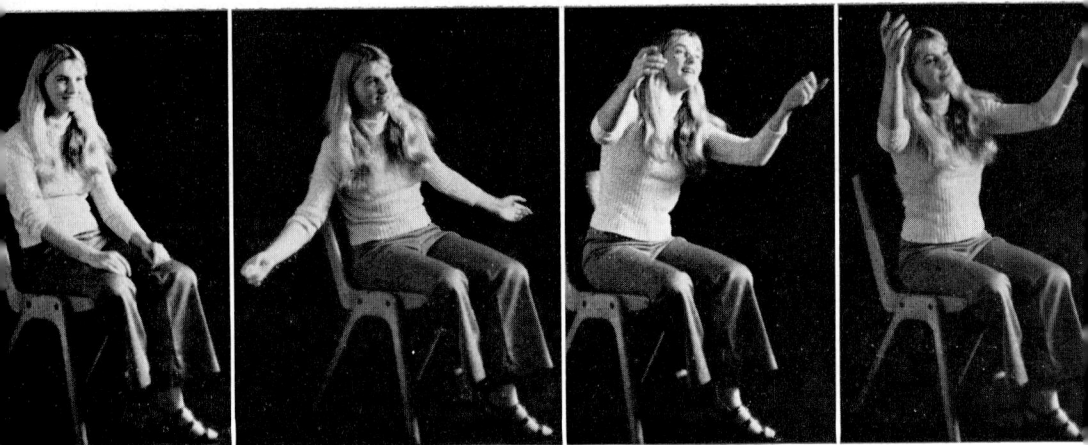

15. P.G.M. Freeing Flow 'effort': From a relatively neutral rest position freely flowing hand gestures lead the body into the activation of postural free flow. Observe the ease and carefree quality of the movement. Although difficult to show in a photograph, each burst of free flow is alternated with very slight bound flow. Activation of free flow like this will often be seen in a person expressing enthusiasm or readiness to join in with a group or project. (see p. 82)

16. P.G.M. Binding Flow 'effort': Highly controlled or bound hand gestures are leading the body into a series of bound flow postural movements. High frequency of both freeing and binding flow in the P.G.M. pattern denotes the readiness to *identify.* (see pp. 82, 109–10, 41)

The significance of P.G.M. movement patterns. *The movement dimensions illustrated are the ingredients which fashion the complex, fluctuating, unceasingly dynamic qualities of our movement. Theoretically the whole range of movement variation is available to every individual and we do in fact use the whole range in our gestures. When it comes to merging our gestures with postures however, in P.G.M. movement, every individual is highly selective in the number and patterning of dimensions of variation he uses. Each person 'selects' a combination or pattern which is highly characteristic and which is repeated time and time again. Such spontaneous selection is indicative of how each individual 'prefers' to deal with his world. This is why it is not really so far fetched to see these preferred P.G.M. movement patterns as reflective of and part of individual, inbuilt and relatively constant motivational states.*

movement are many and various. Directing might be seen in someone making a precise 'pointing' gesture or leaning forward ('pointing' with the head) in order to indicate that he is giving attention to what another person is saying. A cutting movement might be made in the air with the hand in order to draw attention to a point. Indirecting might be shown in a shrug of the shoulders, or a twist of the head in query or interest.

Increasing and Decreasing Pressure

Increasing pressure is the process of exerting force or strength. Decreasing pressure is the process of applying a delicate or light touch. In functional terms increasing pressure is required in quite a small movement; i.e. pressing a licked stamp onto a letter. A greater increase of pressure would be required in jamming a book into an overloaded shelf or grinding ash into the carpet with the foot. Decreasing pressure would be required in positioning a licked stamp before pressing it onto the letter. It would be required in lightly brushing a page off after rubbing out, or manœuvring a delicate piece of equipment.

Expressional and non-functional use of the two dimensions of pressure might occur in the following ways. Increasing pressure is required in thumping the table to emphasize a point (to give the old example). Other less obvious examples would perhaps occur in nodding emphatically or slamming the phone down in exasperation. Decreasing pressure might occur in a nonchalant wave of the hand in the air or in an expression of forbearance.

Accelerating and Decelerating

Accelerating is the process of speeding up, decelerating slowing down. To catch something you suddenly see falling will require you to accelerate. Accelerations can be seen in a crowded bar with people diving to grab an empty space. Deceleration would be required in shaving with a razor or carefully gathering scattered paper clips on a desk and guiding them off the edge into the palm.

Non-functional uses of accelerating might be seen in a person who suddenly gets an idea and positively leaps forward to express it, or in a movement such as a sudden clicking of fingers to indicate irritation at forgetting something. Deceleration might very well be seen in the movements of someone attempting to calm an over excited person, or in an expression of resignation. Whereas accelerating usually has the expressional purpose of speeding things up, decelerating has the purpose of slowing things down. When trying to get others to hurry up, people will instinctively use accelerating movements. To get them to slow down, as with a policeman flagging a car down, they will tend to use decelerating movements.

Binding Flow and Freeing Flow

Increasing control in movement or binding the flow is the process of being withheld, careful, controlled. Freeing the flow or decreasing control is being wild or free in movement. In order to trace carefully round the outline of something you will have to bind the flow of your movement, so too in order to fit something into something else as in sliding a sheet of paper into a plastic cover. In fact most of the complex manual skills we perform require binding of flow or increase of control to varying degrees. To carry a tray full of brimming drinks round a crowded room will certainly require an increase of control, otherwise the results could be disastrous. Free flow or decrease of control is present in adults but often less obviously than in children. A child running helter skelter along a beach will give a perfect example of free flow in movement. Some functions such as shaking a rug or sweeping a huge pile of papers off a desk into a large receptacle will give greater opportunity for free flow. If you have ever seen a film of Picasso drawing you will have seen that he draws with a wonderful free flowing sweep.

In a non-functional sense, if a person looks as if he's being 'careful' then he is probably binding the flow or increasing control. If he makes a 'tight' constricted looking movement then he is probably activating bound flow. If a person on the other hand 'flops' and throws himself about in a free lackadaisical way then he is probably activating free flow. Free flow could probably be seen in a person who throws his hands up in the air in absolute exasperation and bound flow in someone who makes a precisely shaped and carefully executed 'polite' gesture, such as the bow of a Japanese gentleman. The over enthusiastic drunkard who slaps you on the back with great hilarity is expressing himself in free flow whereas the highly formal host who indicates stiffly where you should sit is probably expressing himself in bound flow.

You have probably noticed that whenever an example of expressional use of a movement element has been described it has been qualified with, 'usually', 'probably', etc. This is because no expression is invariably performed with the same movement elements. People express themselves using a great variety of combinations of movement elements. However, there will be a tendency for certain movement elements to occur in certain expressions, but the exact form of any expression will be culturally determined; not invariable or universal.

Shaping

We can vary the process of shaping a movement in the following ways, according to a three dimensional division of space.

The body can shape itself according to the horizontal (side/side), vertical (up/down) or saggital (back/front) plane or according to an overall taking up of space; i.e. the body can literally take up more or less space. The four dimensions of shaping are:

HORIZONTAL PLANE   *Body curves around the:*
Spreading ←——— neutral ———→ Enclosing   Height Axis

VERTICAL PLANE
Rising ←——— neutral ———→ Descending   Depth Axis

SAGGITAL PLANE
Advancing ←——— neutral ———→ Retreating   Width Axis

SHAPE FLOW
Growing ←——— neutral ———→ Shrinking

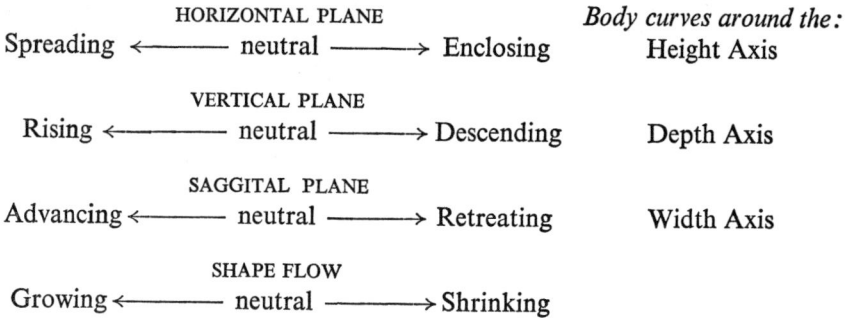

The variation along any of the dimensions, either of effort or shaping, can occur to any degree and in any combination with the other elements.

Perhaps the clearest way of illustrating what is meant by body shaping is to describe some incongruous or inappropriate body shapings. If you asked a person to hammer a nail into a table top you would probably be somewhat surprised if he did the following:

Takes the hammer in his right hand, stands with his right side to the table, whilst spreading himself so that his left hand stretches down toward the floor. As his right hand rises to strike the blow his whole body descends downwards and sideways toward the floor and rises upwards toward the ceiling as the hammer descends onto the nail, rather like a seesaw.

It would be much less surprising if the man took up a relatively enclosed body shape, focused toward the nail, raised his whole body slightly as the hand went up and descended with the descending blow. For the exercise of every type of effort or assertion there is a more suitable bodily shape to match. Of course it is possible to hammer a nail in the way described above. Often one has to hammer in all kinds of peculiar positions but it is most easily and effectively done as described in the second instance.

In looking at the shaping or structure of bodily movement, the prime focus is still on movement quality; i.e. *how* the body takes up its varying shapes, not what shape it ends up in or customarily assumes. What is important is the pathway through which the body moves—never the final position that is taken up. In this sense it is not important that a person folds his arms, but it is important *how* his body shape changes in order to get to the folded arm position.

It has been much more difficult to find words descriptive of body shapes than effort or assertion qualities. Unless sensitized to this aspect of bodily expression we are inclined to look upon bodies as fixed shapes—a matter of physique. A person is either short, thin, fat, etc. Often a habitual but dynamic change of body shape is interpreted as a constant feature of body shape or size.

There are reflections in our usage of language of the fourth shaping dimension phenomenon of bodily growing and shrinking.

Words like deflated, shrank, crushed are all reflective of shrinking changes in body shape.

If you ask a perceptive person to act confident, proud, haughty, you will

Height Axis   *Depth Axis*

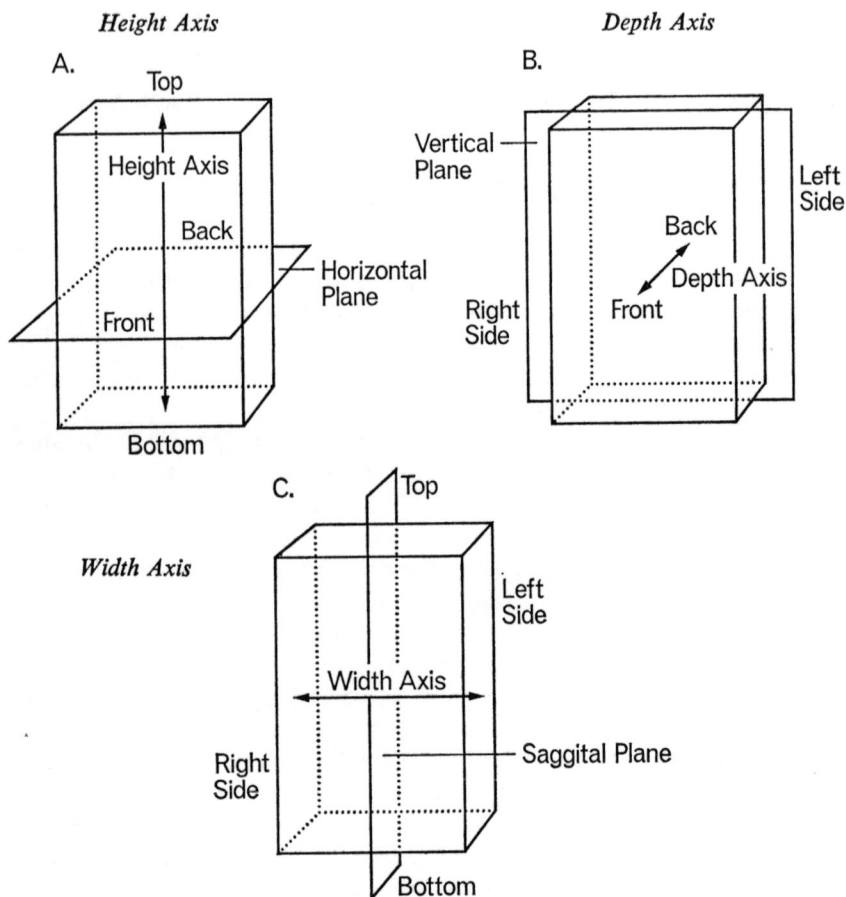

Fig 1   Axes in the body

People have constant preferences for shaping their bodies in various ways. The dimensions of shaping can be visualized by looking at the axes in the body (height, depth, width), around which the body can be curved or 'shaped'. The frequent activation of preferred shaping dimension(s) sets up certain kinds of 'muscular' tensions which indicate and are part of certain kinds of motivational states.

find there is a tendency for the body to 'grow'. Ask them to act crushed, crestfallen, timid, pitiful there will be a tendency for the body to 'shrink', however slightly.

It has been more difficult to find verbal reflections of the other variations in body shaping. So an attempt will be made to describe them by other means.

Shaping is a 'body-centred' process. It does not involve actually moving from one place to another as perhaps the terms advancing and retreating might indicate. If you consider the body as an oblong shaped box with three transversals or axes, shaping is simply a process of curving the body around those transversals. (*See Figure 1.*)

Enclosing and Spreading

Imagine that you are standing immediately in front of a tall thin pole, about 4 inches in diameter. Your task is to mould yourself around the pole. You will probably attempt to *enclose* yourself around the pole. If you consider your body as the oblong shaped box you are curving it forward, the longest transversal (height) acting as the hinge. (*Figure 2.*)

If you were asked to do the same thing with your back to the pole you would have to *spread* your body in order to approximate to the position. Using the box model, it would be the same hinge, but bent back the other way. In both exercises you would find it easier to twist the body slightly in order to mould yourself more closely to the pole. This is due to the limitations of the body structure. We cannot spread and enclose very much. The extreme, of course, would be if you could make the shoulders touch either in front or behind. By twisting so as to put the shoulders on a different level we can enclose or spread more easily.

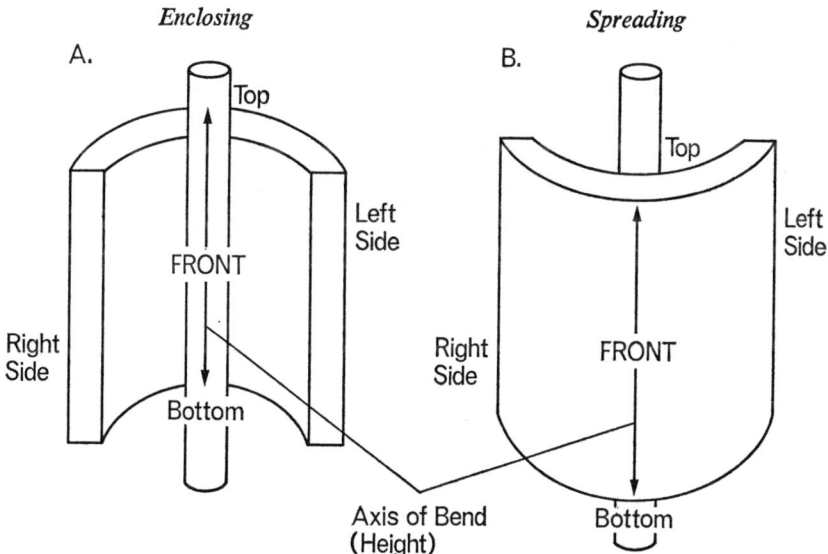

Fig 2   Enclosing and Spreading

Some people have a preference for the enclosing/spreading dimension of shaping. They are constantly (without knowing it of course) curving their bodies backwards and forwards around the height axis.

Descending and Rising

Now imagine that you have a small pipe supported by two rods next to you on the right side. It is a little higher than waist height. You have to mould your right side around it allowing your right foot to stretch right under to the other side of the pipe. This time it is the shortest transversal of the box, the one going through from front to back acting as the hinge. This is the *descending* body shape.

Now you are standing next to the concave half of a large pipe a little taller than yourself. You are asked to stand inside and mould your left side to the wall of the pipe, trying to reach the top. The same transversal acts as a hinge as you adopt the *rising* body shape.

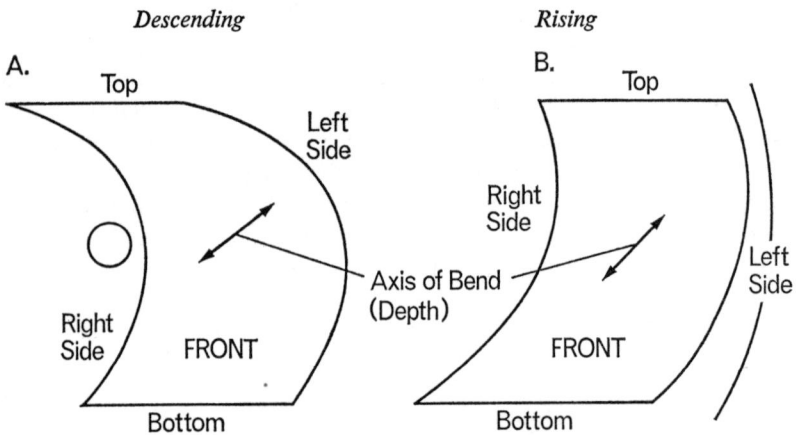

Fig 3   Descending and Rising

Some people feel most comfortable when shaping their bodies according to the descending/rising dimension. They will constantly (again without really knowing it) curve their bodies up and down around the depth (front to back) axis.

Retreating and Advancing

Next, consider you are facing a cylinder on a pole, once again about waist height. You must mould yourself forwards around it. You would instinctively take up a similar body shape if someone punched you in the stomach. This is the *retreating* body shape.

An attempt to mould yourself backwards over the pole will produce the *advancing* body shape. This would naturally occur if someone pushed you hard in the small of the back. The shorter transversal going from left to right across the box is now the hinge.

In the course of adopting various 'held' positions a person will change the shape of his body according to one or a combination of these dimensions of body shapings.

Retreating | Advancing

A. | B.

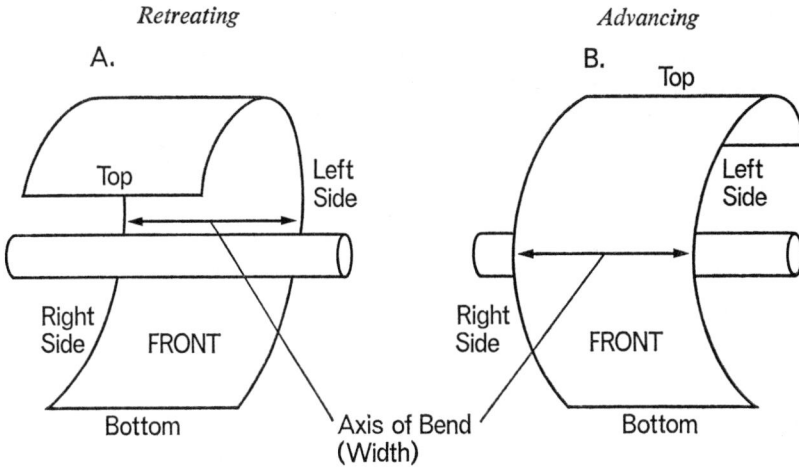

Fig 4 Retreating and Advancing

Some people on the other hand prefer to shape their bodies mostly in the retreating/ advancing dimension. They will habitually (albeit without knowing it) curve their bodies backwards and forwards around the width (side-side) axis.

Sometimes, of course, one may change the position of the body without changing the body shape. If you just fold your arms without moving anything else, then you haven't changed your body shape in the above sense.

You may fold your arms, however, and in the process pass through any of the previously described body shapings. The particular arrangements of the individual limbs has no definite bearing upon the body shape changes that take place.

You are watching a slow-motion film. A man is sitting on a bench with both feet on the ground. He has both a ms spread out each side along the back of the seat. He is going to adjust hisshoe lace. First you observe his left shoulder begins to move and the left arm follows. The left shoulder continues in a diagonally downwards path in the direction of the right shoe. The right shoulder moves straight downward and forward as the trunk moves forward and down, and the right hand moves also to the shoe. The shoulders came closer together as the movement took place. The man has changed his body shape in an *enclosing* way as he has gone to adjust his shoe lace.

Another man is sitting in exactly the same position. The right shoulder begins to move straight downward, so the right side contracts, the left expands. The trunk moves forward and with both shoulders. The right arm and shoulder drop down beside the right leg as the trunk continues to move forward. The right hand touches the shoe. The left shoulder moves slightly across to allow the left hand to also reach the shoe. This man has performed a *descending* shape change in order to reach exactly the same position as the first man.

A third man is seated like the others. The small of the back moves slightly back. Both shoulders move forward simultaneously. The trunk curves forward and down over both knees as both hands go to the shoe. This time there has been a *retreating* shape change in order to get the man into the position to do up his shoe.

Thus it can be seen that just to note the beginning and end 'rest' position could be totally misleading. You could have no idea what shape change took place in order to get the man into the position. Often shape changes take place to a very small degree. Imagine you are facing the thin upright pole again. You just begin to move in order to shape yourself round it and are asked to stop. Already you have made a slight change in your body shape. If you return to normal you have performed an enclosing shape change—even though it was minute.*

Variation of the elements of movement quality occurs in the body practically all the time and in combination with innumerable variations in the positionings and repositionings of the body parts. But in measuring behaviour in order to construct the action profile, the actual positionings of the body are not important. If a man crosses his legs six times, bites his ear twice and stands on his head, it couldn't matter less. What does matter is the frequency with which in doing so he activates the various movement elements and the frequency with which variation is evident along a particular dimension.

THE INDIVIDUAL MOVEMENT PATTERN

For every individual the complex inter-relating of the unceasing flow of effort variation and body shaping variation forms a pattern which is one of the most telling expressions of his individuality that he possesses. His movement pattern is as individual and characteristic as his fingerprints. It has been already pointed out that it is the quality of movement process that is important, not the beginning or end position. It is how the person moves, not what he does that is important. For it is the quality pattern that bears the stamp of individuality, not what positions a person inveigles himself into. This is more likely to be reflective of his race, class or social upbringing, as they are more likely to be reflections of learned habits and skills.

> *There is a difference between the way in which a natural movement quality is performed and the way in which an acquired or learned movement quality is performed.*

There is one more important distinction to be made, because even movement qualities can be learned by people with an aptitude for such learning. Most proficient actors, for instance, are particularly good at it. However,

---

* For a more thorough description of this system of movement analysis see: *A Primer for Movement Description*: Cecily Dell: DNB Inc. 1970—to be obtained from: DNB: (Center for Movement Research and Analysis) 8 East 12th Street, New York 10003.

learned movement qualities which do not appear in the natural pattern can only be performed in a particular way and that is by an isolated part of the body. It cannot be performed as part of a consistent movement which is reflected throughout the whole body.

> *The first is called Gestural movement, the second Posture-Gesture Merging movement.*

This is why any 'big' bodily movement, like a tennis service, golf swing or batting at cricket, will tend to be performed in a highly individual way, even despite the constraints of training. If one tried to perform one such big bodily action using a foreign movement quality (as might occur in trying to imitate someone) then it will happen not as a consistent movement, but as a series of co-ordinated but isolated gestures. Thus the movement will tend to look awkward.

A man playing a series of instruments simultaneously (a literal one-man-band) is performing a gesture system, not a posture-gesture merging. The quality of the movement performed by each limb will be different. The feet may be firmly pounding a drum pedal in a constant rhythm, one hand may be lightly brushing a cymbal with relative slowness or sustainment, while the other hand may be making quick or accelerated dabs at a triangle. If he took his feet off the foot pedals and just concentrated on the brushing, allowing his whole body to participate, you would see a posture-gesture merging take place, and it would be performed according to movement qualities present within his natural movement pattern.

It is because we have the ability to isolate our gestures that we can perform the myriad of practical body functions that we do. Supposing a person were lacking the pressure element

(increasing pressure $\longleftrightarrow$ decreasing pressure)
(strength)   (lightness)

completely in his movement pattern. If he were not able to isolate his gestures there would be an enormous range of functions he could not perform. He could not flick dust off his sleeve, or gently stroke a cat, or stub out a cigarette or use a stapling machine or open a bottle of soda or clean his shoes, or use the accelerator or brake pedal in a car—countless everyday actions would be beyond him.

The distinction between gesture and posture-gesture merging is important because we are concerned to isolate the movement qualities which are part of the natural pattern and not just acquired or learned. Hence it is only posture-gesture merging movement that is used as a basis for analysis and construction of the action profile.

On hearing of the use of movement analysis to measure a certain aspect of personality, people often react with high hilarity, 'Can I not just learn to cross my legs thus and you will assess me as such and such a person?' A natural enough reaction. But in fact experience and experimentation has shown that it is virtually impossible to train a person to change his natural movement pattern. Warren Lamb has tried, giving courses, sometimes spread over years. He has instilled some knowledge of the movement pattern into the student, but change has been marginal or nil! This is, of course, dealing only with the posture-gesture merging movement. People can certainly be trained to perform gestures outside their natural movement qualities, but not posture-gesture merging.

One speculation is that some traumatic shock such as a severe car accident or nervous breakdown might change the pattern, but as yet the possibility has not been researched.

THE BASIS OF INTUITIVE JUDGEMENTS

To return to the question asked earlier; i.e. on what do the good 'judgers' of people base their judgement. The most likely theory is that they are particularly sensitive to the elements of movement quality. They are not so much perceptive to the 'meaning' of any one particular movement but are unconsciously sensitive to the frequency of occurrence of the various movement elements and to the distinction between isolated gestures and full bodily expression (posture-gesture merging), and to the harmony or disharmony between the effort and shaping elements.

An experiment was conducted to find out whether people are in fact sensitive to the distinction between isolated gestures and posture-gesture merging.

It is considered that whenever a communication is accompanied by posture-gesture merging movement expression, then it is that person's sincere and genuine intention that is being expressed. A gesture, however, may be performed without any reflection of the person's true feeling attitude or intention. It may even be used to convey a meaning quite the opposite from the person's true intention. If a person really wants to express amusement, i.e. if he really does feel amused he cannot help but give a good belly laugh (posture-gesture merging). If, however, he just wishes to conform or to please, he will confine it to a polite (gestural) titter activating mouth and throat muscles only. It was considered, too, that people are sensitive to these distinctions when they observe them in other people.

Experiments were designed to help answer the following questions:

1 Is PGM* movement expression in interaction interpreted as a genuine sincere expression of meaning?
2 Is gestural movement expression in interaction seen as an insincere, conventionalized, or somewhat empty apology for a true expression of meaning?

* Posture-Gesture Merging.

To answer these questions five people, 'interactors', were trained to perform simple verbal messages, either with gestural or PGM accompaniment. They then 'performed' these messages individually with a number of 'respondents' (25 altogether) and the respondents were asked to comment in writing about their interpretation of the message conveyed according to whether it was sincere, insincere, convincing, unconvincing, etc.

The results indicated that people do seem to varying degrees to be sensitive to the difference between a verbal communication backed up by PGM movement and one accompanied by gestural movement. There is a tendency for the verbal message accompanied by a total bodily expression or PGM movement to be interpreted as a consistent expression; i.e. where the message is one of welcome, there is a tendency for it to be interpreted in terms such as pleasant as well as sincere and convincing. When, however, the verbal message is accompanied by gestural movement there is a greater tendency for inconsistencies to appear in the interpretations. When the verbal message was clearly one of welcome, the accompanying gestural movement expression caused people to be confused as to the 'real' or intended meaning of the message. The written opinions did indicate that there was a considerable amount of feeling that the message itself was consistent or just plain insincere—or a mockery of a true expression of meaning (for a more detailed account see Appendix I).

As already stated, some people, the 'good' judgers, are probably more sensitive to the frequency of occurrence of the various movement elements and more sensitive to the distinction between PGM movements and gesture movement. If, for instance, one of our 'good' judgers of people is sensitive to the fact that whilst one person displays predominantly time variation in his PGM movement; i.e. changes from acceleration to deceleration, he will perceive him to have certain different personality traits from a person who displays predominantly pressure variation; i.e. changes from increasing pressure (strength) to decreasing pressure (lightness) and so on.

It is probably simply because such a person sees more: i.e. they are prepared to give more 'attention' than others that they are able to differentiate between people on this basis. It makes logical sense to predict that on the action profile assessment the 'good' judgers of people would rate higher on the attention components, *investigating* and *exploring*, than others. This is still only theory, however, as it has not as yet been tested in a controlled way.

The evaluation of the action profile is really only a more disciplined version of the same process. Instead of just being sensitive to the frequency of occurrence of various movement elements, and to the posture-gesture merging (PGM) movement, a detailed record is taken of the occurrence of the various movement elements. This is done using a very simple shorthand notation.* Only movement classified by the observer as true total bodily expression (posture-gesturing merging (PGM)) is notated.

* *See* Warren Lamb, *Posture and Gesture*, Duckworth 1965, page 62.

How long a period of observation is required?

Initially research was done to find out how long it was necessary to spend observing a person in order to gain the full range of movement variation. Each subject was observed until a pattern emerged; i.e. the ratio of the frequency of each movement element to the frequency of the others became manifest. Observation continued until no further change in the pattern appeared. After this had been done with a number of subjects it became evident that $1\frac{1}{2}$–2 hours was adequate to enable an observer to notate a large enough sample to cover a person's whole range of movement variation. It takes longer with some people than others to cover the full range, but two hours is long enough to ensure that even the most broad ranging and complex patterns emerge fully.

Does the movement pattern change?

A study was also carried out in order to determine whether in fact the movement pattern thus established remained constant over time, in different situations throughout different emotional states. A man was observed at intervals in various situations, at a selection interview when presumably he was nervous; at work; relaxed in his garden; and suffering emotional upset after his father had died. The observation periods were spread over a year. In each case the movement pattern which emerged was the same. In addition, reassessments after intervals of between five and eighteen years have indicated only marginal or no change.

Inter Observer Reliability

It is our practice to conduct constant reliability checks. 75 per cent of the assessments are conducted with two observers present and the agreement between the sets of observations is high. It would obviously be better if there were more observers to participate in reliability checks but it has been estimated that there are only about ten fully trained 'effort-shaping' observers in the world. Half of them are in America and half in England and obviously spasmodic collaboration occurs already. There are plans, however, for the more systematic organization of conferences and working sessions to enable greater unification of observation practices.

The construction of the action profile is performed in the following sequence:

At an ordinary two hour interview, detailed observations are taken. An observer cannot possibly notate every phrase of movement. Instead a sample is taken. For each PGM movement the moment elements present are shown. For instance, a man may make a sequence of PGM movement beginning with a light direct head gesture which becomes a light direct movement of the whole body (however slight) followed by a firm sharp cutting movement of the hand which is also backed up by a consistent total bodily movement ended with a similar movement to the first. Such a sequence* might accompany a slight pause for consideration (the light direct movement) ... 'We-ell' ... followed by a reaffirmation of a point of view (the firm sharp cutting movement). '*I still think so ...*' and a return to the previous position to consider the forthcoming answer. It would be recorded that the following movement elements were present in the following sequence.

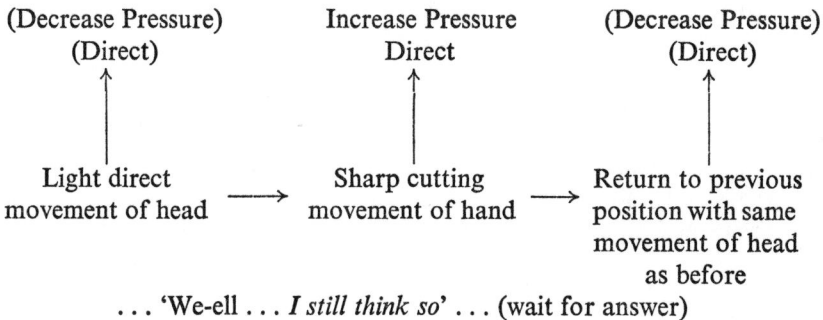

(Decrease Pressure)	Increase Pressure	(Decrease Pressure)
(Direct)	Direct	(Direct)
↑	↑	↑
Light direct movement of head →	Sharp cutting movement of hand →	Return to previous position with same movement of head as before

... 'We-ell ... *I still think so*' ... (wait for answer)

This would simply be represented by a set of symbols which can be easily counted.†

Movement Pattern

Effort		Total	Shaping		Total
FOCUS			HORIZONTAL		
←——————→			←——————→		
Indirecting	Directing		Spreading	Enclosing	
30‡	20	50	20	15	35
PRESSURE			VERTICAL		
←——————→			←——————→		
Decreasing Pressure	Increasing Pressure		Rising	Descending	
25	0	25	20	5	25
TIME			SAGGITAL		
←——————→			←——————→		
Decelerating	Accelerating		Advancing	Retreating	
14	4	18	5	10	15

Table 2

* NB: Not necessarily. No particular movement rhythm ever invariably matches a particular sequence of words.

† *See* Warren Lamb, *Posture and Gesture*, page 62.

‡ The numbers indicate the frequency with which each movement element was seen to be activated.

Similar recordings are made of the changes in body shaping. Any movement element which occurs in gesture alone is not counted and usually not even notated.

At the end the frequency of occurrence of each movement element is summed and a pattern emerges; e.g. a pattern like that in Table 2 might emerge.

This amount of information gives a measure on the first nine action motivations. The degree of strength on the first six action motivations is directly indicated by the total frequency of variation on each of the above six movement dimensions. Strengths on the three interaction categories are derived from a particular kind of relationship between each effort and shaping pair.

It may seem incredible that a link can be seen so clearly between the presence of movement qualities and the presence of action motivations. Much of the evidence for such a link is simply empirical. It is possible to observe, time and time again, that the use of a certain movement dimension invariably accompanies the expression or activation of a certain action motivation. Part III of the book, describing how practical use is made of the action profile, gives a great deal of illustration as to how these links actually show in behaviour.

Meanwhile, there are some theoretical considerations which may cast more light upon the link between movement behaviour and action motivations. These theoretical considerations are discussed in the next chapter.

CHAPTER 6

The Relationship Between the Movement Pattern and the Action Profile

● It has been observed that the utilization of a movement element in a PGM movement is an indication of the presence within that person of a readiness to activate himself in a particular way.

● The ability to activate a particular movement quality in PGM movement is not only an indication that a certain type of motivation is present, *but a necessary and integral part of the ability to act in that way.* In other words being able to do something with your body is just as important as being able to do something with your intellect when it comes to taking certain kinds of action; i.e. according to the twelve action motivation classification in Chapter 2.

Remember it is not simply instrumental or functional use of the body that is being talked about. It is not a matter of being able to physically move your body in a certain direction, or wave your arms and legs in a certain way. It is more the expressional use of the body that is involved.

To repeat the example used earlier: if you thump the table in order to squash a fly—that is an instrumental use of the body. If you thump the table to emphasize a point about which you feel strongly, that is an expressional use of the body. It is in this sphere that the PGM (Posture-Gesture Merging) type of movement is particularly relevant. If in thumping the table to express conviction, you are able to activate the movement quality of increasing pressure, or firmness, in a PGM movement (or total bodily expression) then the movement expression is part of your psychological state of conviction, and not separate from it. You don't just 'know', you are convinced in a cold intellectual way you 'feel' convinced and the movement expression is part of that 'feeling'.

The body-mind distinction is a very old topic of controversy. Modern developments in the various branches of medicine, psychiatry and psychology have shown pretty conclusively that it is an unnecessary distinction. A psychosomatic illness is both a bodily sign of a mental illness, and an integral part of the condition. Similarly the activation of a certain movement quality in PGM movement is a sign of a psychological state of motivation and an integral part of it. The two cannot be separated. One does not cause the other, neither can one occur without the other. They are equally part of a single process.

The connection between the activation of certain movement qualities in the body and the presence of certain psychological states can further be illustrated by pointing to known instances where the inculcation of certain physical, bodily states has caused a corresponding emotional state. It is known, for instance, that simulation of a part of the physical or movement manifestation of fear, namely fast, shallow breathing, if continued for long enough can induce in the subject a feeling of anxiety or fear even though there is nothing to be afraid of and the subject knows this. The tensions set up in the body due to the fast shallow breathing movement are so closely associated with the bodily mechanism to do with the experience of fear that one can induce the other. In some forms of therapy, certain exercises are used which involve the continuous activation of certain movement qualities. This has the result of inducing an intense emotional state in the patient, which is then used by the therapist for releasing repressed emotions and experiences.

TENSION STATES

Another way of looking at the connection between bodily and psychological states is to consider the mechanism of human movement itself. How does it work? How can we perform such a variety of functions with our bodily movement? How can we express ourselves in such a variety of subtle ways? We are so used to thinking of our movement simply in functional terms, sitting down, getting up, walking, carrying, lifting. Even those relatively straight-forward movements require an enormously complex array of co-ordinations, and subtle variation in control. How does it happen?

Movement is produced in the body by the action of the muscles, the inter-play of agonist and antagonist muscle groups. They act solely to create various kinds of tensions in the body in various sequences and rhythms.

Every movement you make indicates some kind of change in muscular tension in your body. All the movement qualities previously described are simply kinds of muscular tension. It is the activation and release of these various tensions that make movement of various qualities. If any one kind of tension is increased to an exceptional degree, it becomes a state of cramp and movement is no longer possible. If for instance you press hard on the table (increase pressure) and go on pressing till you can't press any harder you will get yourself into a state of cramp. If a person is habitually in such a state then 'tension' as it is used in common parlance will be seen. If a person is 'tense' then it will be because one or a combination of the tension states is retained in the body to an exaggerated degree.

Thus in observing the movement qualities present in a person's PGM movement, we are really observing various states of tension. The tensions are present even when a person is still, but they cannot be observed then, which is why they have to be observed during the process of movement. It is conceivable that in the future there will be mechanical means by which the different kinds of varying tension states in the body can be measured. This would be a great advance, for the human eye however well trained and practised is still a relatively inaccurate instrument. Many of the movements observed are minute and the variation in movement qualities might be in tiny proportions.

As mentioned before, each movement quality can be considered a continuum. The pressure dimension for instance is a continuum with extreme decrease of pressure at one end and extreme increase of pressure or firmness at the other end and a neutral state in between. Between the two extremes, variation can occur to any degree. (See Table 3, page 98)

The crosses on the chart indicate points of reversal, i.e. where the direction of the variation is reversed.

⦿ It has been observed that a reversal in the direction of variation is the indication of the ability to use that state of tension actively and to express it in coping behaviour. It can be transformed into the taking of a particular kind of action and can be used to cope with life situations.

If, as the last line shows, a person is observed to retain a particular state of tension unvaryingly; if as in this case for instance a person is seen to possess a constantly 'held' state of increased pressure or firmness in the body, then this is not considered an indication of a workable motivational state. Just as in the physical state it is a kind of paralysis or immobility, so too in the psychological state. It is present but, to all intents and purposes, inactive.

To give an analogy in behavioural terms. Consider for example a person who is 'in a hurry'. Now being 'in a hurry' is coping with a situation by promoting a sense of urgency. (In movement terms by the use of repeated accelerating movements.) If a person sees a need to get things moving more quickly then he can, by expressing an attitude of urgency or hurry at the right moment, actually inject urgency into the situation (probably by causing other people to act faster) and so he can cope with the situation by achieving a speeding up of events. However, this way of acting, so as to promote urgency will only be effective if increased and decreased at strategic and appropriate points. If on the other hand there is no real need for urgency then this activity will be inappropriate, hence ineffective.

Thus the ability to cope with a situation by expressing urgency only comes about through the ability to vary that expression, to turn it on and off, or increase and decrease it. Hence to return to the movement, if it is seen that a person can vary and reverse the intensity of a state of tension along a parti-

D

Types of Variation Along the Pressure Dimension

| Extreme decrease in pressure 'flop' | Decrease Pressure Normal Lightness | NEUTRAL | Increase Pressure Normal Firmness | Extreme increase of pressure 'cramp' |

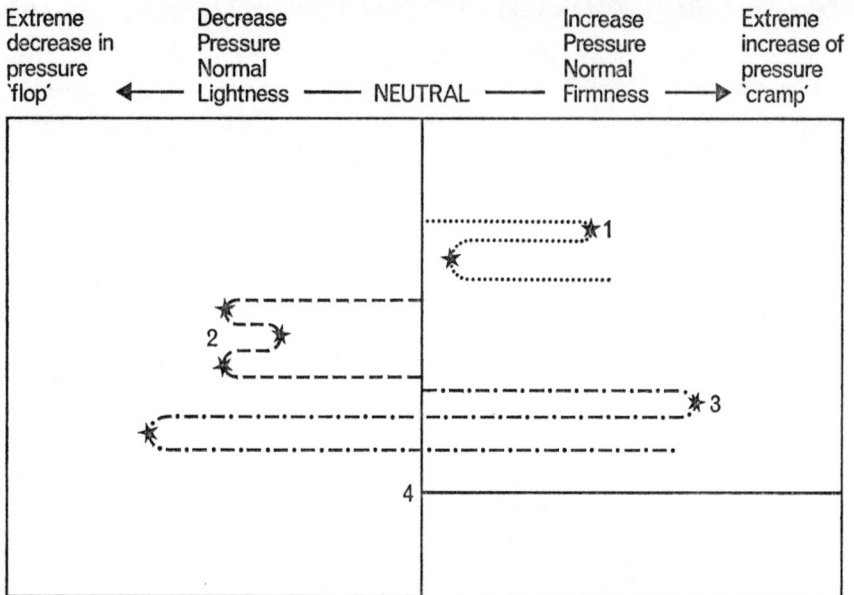

★ Indicates where the direction of variation is reversed

The lines chart the progress of degrees of variation along the pressure dimension

1. (. . . . .)

The first shows a state of tension which varies from neutral to normal firmness, back to neutral and back to normal firmness. These variations need not happen in consecutive movements. It might take some time for this amount of variation along the pressure dimension to occur, or it might happen within a couple of seconds. Such a variation might be seen in a manager seated, one leg across the other knee, grasping the top knee with both hands, pulling on it (increase to normal firmness), releasing (return to neutral), then pulling again.

2. (— — —)

The second line shows a decrease of pressure to normal lightness, then slight variations around that point. Such slight variations are pretty well invisible to the human eye. Such a variation would probably be recorded as 'held' lightness until it reverted back to neutral.

This might be seen in a manager running his hand lightly back and forth across a desk surface.

3. (.—.—.—)

The third line shows a wide variation from increase of pressure to normal firmness, back through neutral to decreased pressure or normal lightness. Such a big variation is easily observable.

This could be plainly evident in a manager who stubbed a cigarette out firmly then lightly brushed a stray piece of ash off the table.

4. (————)

The fourth line shows an increase of pressure to an exaggerated degree and held at that level.

This might be seen in a manager who was terribly angry. Imagine him clenching fists, grinding teeth, increasing the tension till he is in a state of quivering fury, to the extent of being paralysed by it.

Table 3

cular dimension, be it pressure or whatever, then this is an indication that the corresponding psychological state or motivation is active and effective and will enable the person to cope flexibly and efficiently whenever that particular behaviour is required.

To continue the analogy, consider a person who seems perpetually 'in a hurry'. He seems constantly to have an attitude of urgency. However, because it is always there, unvarying and applied indiscriminately it appears simply as fussiness or hastiness and is ineffective in dealing with a situation which really does require an injection of urgency. It is a bit like the boy who cried wolf. He gave so many false alarms, that when he was really in danger no-one took any notice.

If you look back at the chart, line four indicates a perpetual or 'held' state of increased pressure, or firmness in the body. Because it is unvarying it would be considered not to indicate the presence of an effective motivational potential in a person but rather a compensation for a lacking one.

MOVEMENT COMPONENTS IN THE INTERACTION PROCESS

The consideration of the process of human interaction, how people do or do not achieve contact with one another and what are the results of that contact, is beginning to play a larger part in our work. Its importance is obvious but it is a vast subject and there is a great deal more to be learnt. The approach to understanding the process of interaction as described in this book, has so far only been touched upon in the description of the three interaction categories, *communicating, presenting* and *operating*. It has like the rest of the system, been derived primarily from the nature of the behaviour being studied. The fact that it has been primarily the non-verbal aspects of interaction that have been studied has led to the particular approach and theory about how the mechanics of interaction work, described below.

It is becoming pretty well indisputable that an enormous part is played in interaction by the myriad of non-verbal signals given out by the participants. It is beginning to be understood that practically everything a person does, the slightest lift of an eyebrow, shiver of a muscle, shrug of shoulders, the posture he assumes, the focus and duration of eye contact, the distance he sits at, etc., as well as the words he says and tone of voice, all convey a message of some kind and which will certainly be interpreted, either correctly or incorrectly. The process of interaction is best seen in terms of a multimedia network, with all channels working and interacting simultaneously, forming an enormously complex and rich array of data. It makes one wonder how we ever establish contact at all. Certainly it isn't surprising that so many problems in relating occur.

One way of looking at the interaction process is from the point of view of discovering how moment by moment feelings, emotions, reactions to others are displayed. This links with the anthropological study of how the complex interaction systems within various cultures and sub-cultures are set up, here treating the study of a non-verbal interaction system rather like the study of a verbal language. For instance, a certain constellation of bodily movements which in one culture is interpreted one way, may in another culture be interpreted quite differently. Here it is the similarities and patterns within various cultures that are being studied.

Our primary objective has been rather to study individual differences in the non-verbal aspects of interaction. Our interest is to find out what is constant within a person's pattern of interaction behaviour. The study of the qualities in people's movement as displayed in how they energize and shape their bodies has led to the discovery that there are in fact constant individual patterns of interaction. It seems that where the energizing or effort and shaping movement elements are in harmony then the process invites inter-action or like contribution from other people. If, for instance, the movement elements which designate *investigating* (effort) and *exploring* (shaping) are in harmony, then the person will be able to establish a *communicating* type of interaction, i.e. the type of interaction which activates the giving of attention, both in the sense of the participants giving attention to each other and to other things, i.e. *investigating* and *exploring* each other and with each other.

To theorize as to how such a pattern is developed it would seem that if a person does display the effort and shaping components in harmony then this is felt by others to be consistent and therefore invites response. The response the person gets from other people will feed back to him as satisfying and this will gradually establish *communicating* as part of his interactive behaviour pattern. If the effort and shaping components are not in harmony this probably indicates some kind of conflict within the person's attitude which is felt (unconsciously) by others as an attitude which does not invite response.

We do not know as yet how such conflicts are originated or even precisely what is the nature of the conflict in attitude. All we know is that we can observe the phenomenon and its effects upon other people and the process of interaction. Of course, it is a very subtle mechanism and not obviously recognizable in the physical sense, although it is certainly there, and can be seen by a trained observer.

An over exaggerated example might give a clearer picture. Supposing a person approaches you 'looking friendly' (you would probably infer this from the way he shapes his body perhaps with arms outstretched or whatever indicating welcome), then out of the blue he shouts at you loudly and rudely. This would certainly seem to you a conflict in attitude and therefore would cause distress, or certainly surprise. You would not know quite how to react. Such an approach certainly would not encourage a clear interaction process. The shouting man has shaped his body to indicate one attitude and asserted an effort which indicates another. In an infinitely less obvious way when a conflict occurs within the effort and shaping components of movement, a smooth flowing interaction pattern is disrupted. Such a conflict may occur to a greater or lesser degree in three, two, one or none of the effort and shaping pairs. When such conflicts do occur they have been found to be a constant feature in that person's pattern of interaction, unless the conflict is marginal where there is some evidence that it can either decrease or increase. How or why is not yet really known.

CHAPTER 7

The Construction of the Action Profile

THE BASIC ACTION PROFILE

Suppose then you can observe a person for two hours and make a reasonably accurate recording of the frequency of occurrence of the various movement qualities (tension states) and you arrive at a pattern such as the one on page 93. What does it tell you about the person? Obviously, it gives you the action profile, but how exactly is this derived?

Correspondence of First Six Action Motivations to Movement Dimensions

THREE STAGE SEQUENCE OF ACTION

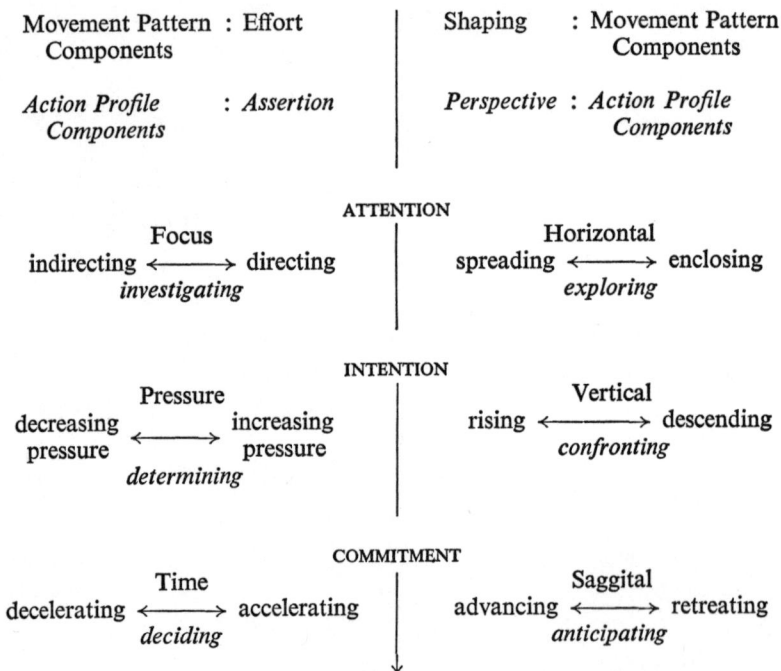

Movement Pattern : Effort
  Components
	Shaping : Movement Pattern
	  Components

Action Profile : *Assertion*
  Components
	Perspective : *Action Profile*
	  Components

ATTENTION

Focus indirecting ⟷ directing *investigating*	Horizontal spreading ⟷ enclosing *exploring*

INTENTION

Pressure decreasing ⟷ increasing pressure pressure *determining*	Vertical rising ⟷ descending *confronting*

COMMITMENT

Time decelerating ⟷ accelerating *deciding*	Saggital advancing ⟷ retreating *anticipating*

Table 4

● The activation of a movement quality (tension state) in the body is an integral part of the activation of a corresponding internal motivational state.*

● The first six action categories are internal motivations.
They correspond to the movement qualities as in Table 4.

Now let us follow the development of an actual movement pattern into an Action Profile. This is a development of the movement pattern shown in Table 2 (page 93). The frequency of occurrence of variation along each dimension is expressed as a percentage of the total amount of variation.

Percentage of Total Frequency of Variation along each Movement Dimension

Effort	Total and (% of grand total)	Shaping	Total (and % of grand total)
Indirecting ⟷ Directing 30　　　　20	50 (30%)	Spreading ⟷ Enclosing 20　　　　15	35 (21%)
Decreasing ⟷ Increasing Pressure　　　Pressure 25　　　　0	25 (15%)	Rising ⟷ Descending 20　　　　5	25 (15%)
Decelerating ⟷ Accelerating 14　　　　4	18 (10%)	Advancing ⟷ Retreating 5　　　　10	15 (9%)
	93	Grand Total: 168	75
	(55%)		(45%)

Table 5

Expressed in percentages we have the action profile so far (on page 104). This is a profile similar to the prototype example on page 44. The great weighting in the attention stage will make this person a naturally attentive, 'research oriented' person. The emphasis on *investigating*, rather than

* As previously defined (page 68) internal motivation is that which impels a person to act according to a certain pattern when there are no external motivating forces, i.e. when you are working for the sake of it, or 'doing your thing' for no ulterior purpose, internal motivation is what makes you take action in your particularly individual way.

	Action	% of total activity
ATTENTION	Investigating	30%
	Exploring	21%
INTENTION	Determining	15%
	Confronting	15%
COMMITMENT	Deciding	10%
	Anticipating	9%

Action Profile 5   ACTION PROFILE DERIVED FROM MOVEMENT PATTERN

exploring, will mean that his appreciation of new ideas will always be rooted in a detailed, probing dissection of the existing situation.

More of his characteristics could be described based on this amount of information, but this is just half the profile still.

The interaction components

The three interaction factors can be derived from the movement information that has already been presented on page 103. Each of the movement elements, you will remember, is a continuum with two extremes or polarities. There is an affinity between the effort and shaping continuums in terms of their polarities. As presented opposite, Spreading is seen to have an affinity with or to 'go with' Indirecting whereas Enclosing has an affinity with Directing. This is considered to be due to the physiological and anatomical structure of the human body. There are similar affinities in polarity for the other movement elements as shown on the table page 102. For easy reference they are: (for each foursome, elements on the same side are in affinity.)

EFFORT-SHAPING AFFINITIES

Indirecting	Directing
Spreading ←——→	Enclosing
Decreasing Pressure	Increasing Pressure
Rising ←——→	Descending
Decelerating	Accelerating
Advancing ←———	→Retreating

Freeing Flow	Binding Flow
Growing ←———	→Shrinking

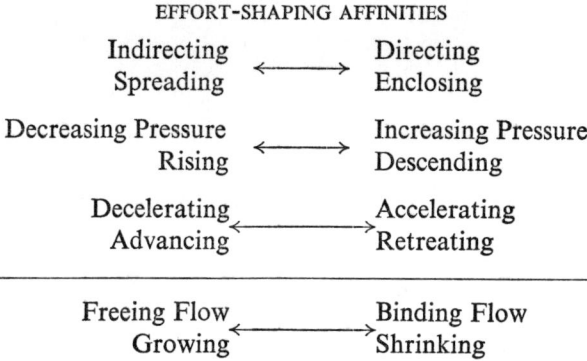

So far as we know to date, only the first six dimensions are relevant for the three interaction factors. Consider the pattern as shown on page 103 from a different angle. Consider first just the attention stage.

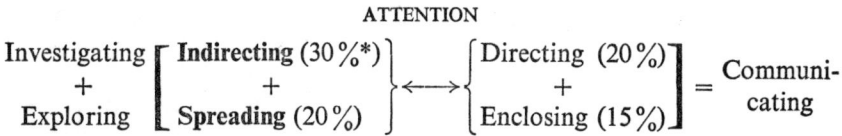

ATTENTION

$$\begin{matrix} \text{Investigating} \\ + \\ \text{Exploring} \end{matrix} \begin{bmatrix} \textbf{Indirecting } (30\%^*) \\ + \\ \textbf{Spreading } (20\%) \end{bmatrix} \longleftrightarrow \begin{Bmatrix} \text{Directing } (20\%) \\ + \\ \text{Enclosing } (15\%) \end{Bmatrix} = \begin{matrix} \text{Communi-} \\ \text{cating} \end{matrix}$$

If the weighting on each continuum is toward polarities in affinity, then the interaction capacity is considered to exist. In this case the weightings are toward Indirecting and Spreading (30 per cent and 20 per cent). These are polarities in affinity therefore the interaction capacity, namely *communicating*, is judged to be active. In contrast consider the following pattern:

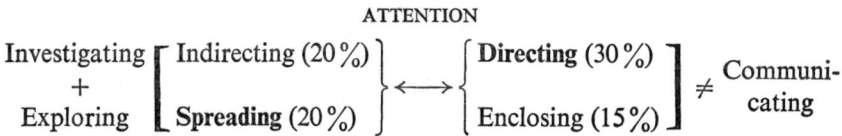

ATTENTION

$$\begin{matrix} \text{Investigating} \\ + \\ \text{Exploring} \end{matrix} \begin{bmatrix} \text{Indirecting } (20\%) \\ + \\ \textbf{Spreading } (20\%) \end{bmatrix} \longleftrightarrow \begin{Bmatrix} \textbf{Directing } (30\%) \\ + \\ \text{Enclosing } (15\%) \end{Bmatrix} \neq \begin{matrix} \text{Communi-} \\ \text{cating} \end{matrix}$$

Here the weightings are toward Directing and Spreading (30 per cent and 20 per cent). They are not polarities in affinity, therefore the interaction factor *communicating* is not considered active.

The illustration on page 106 shows the movement pattern as on page 103 (Table 5) with its corresponding action profile, covering the first nine components.

Communicating is considered slightly less active than *presenting* because the weightings are not so obviously toward polarities in affinity and the weight-

* Numbers indicate frequency of occurrence of that movement element, expressed as a percentage of total movement range.

Movement Pattern / Action Profile

	Movement Dimensions	Frequency of activation	% of total activation		Action	% of total activity	Inter-action
EFFORT	1 Indirecting—Directing 30 + 20	= 50	30%	ASSERTION	1. Investigating	30%	Communicating
SHAPING	2 Spreading—Enclosing 20 + 15	= 35	21%	PERSPECTIVE	2. Exploring	21%	
				ATTENTION			
EFFORT	3 Decreasing Pressure—Increasing Pressure 25 + 0	= 25	15%	ASSERTION	3. Determining	15%	Presenting
SHAPING	4 Rising—Descending 20 + 5	= 25	15%	PERSPECTIVE	4. Confronting	15%	
				INTENTION			
EFFORT	5 Decelerating—Accelerating 14 + 4	= 18	10%	ASSERTION	5. Deciding	10%	Operating
SHAPING	6 Advancing—Retreating 5 + 10	= 15	9%	PERSPECTIVE	6. Anticipating	9%	
				COMMITMENT			
	Total	168	100%				

The extent of the interaction capacity is shown by the shading

Action Profile 6 ACTION PROFILE DERIVED FROM MOVEMENT PATTERN

ings on the third dimension, from which the *operating* factor is derived are not toward polarities in affinity at all. The last two are shown below:

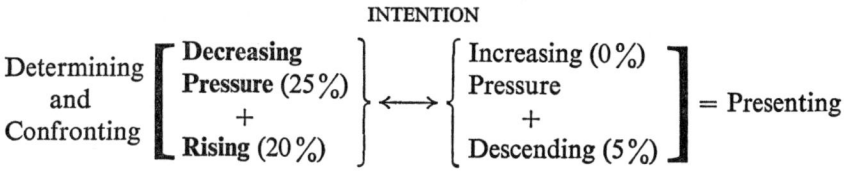

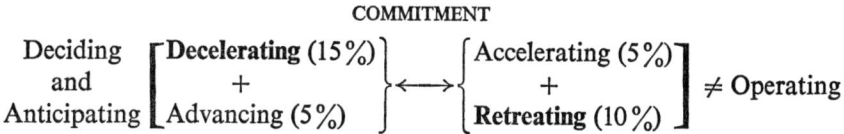

INTENTION

$$
\begin{array}{c}
\text{Determining} \\
\text{and} \\
\text{Confronting}
\end{array}
\left[
\begin{array}{c}
\textbf{Decreasing} \\
\textbf{Pressure (25\%)} \\
+ \\
\textbf{Rising (20\%)}
\end{array}
\right]
\longleftrightarrow
\left\{
\begin{array}{c}
\text{Increasing (0\%)} \\
\text{Pressure} \\
+ \\
\text{Descending (5\%)}
\end{array}
\right]
= \text{Presenting}
$$

COMMITMENT

$$
\begin{array}{c}
\text{Deciding} \\
\text{and} \\
\text{Anticipating}
\end{array}
\left[
\begin{array}{c}
\textbf{Decelerating (15\%)} \\
+ \\
\text{Advancing (5\%)}
\end{array}
\right]
\longleftrightarrow
\left\{
\begin{array}{c}
\text{Accelerating (5\%)} \\
+ \\
\textbf{Retreating (10\%)}
\end{array}
\right]
\neq \text{Operating}
$$

So far the method by which measures of only the first nine action requirements are derived from the movement pattern has been described in detail.

Dynamism, Adaptability and Identification

Dynamism as previously defined is the overall measure of the intensity of application. It is derived from a measure of the intensity of the movement expression.

The detailed recordings taken during an observation session enable a calculation to be made of the ratio of variation of single movement elements, to combinations of two elements and combinations of three. The effort variations are considered separately from the shaping variations. The more combinations of three in relation to combinations of two or one, the greater will be the strength on *dynamism*.

Adaptability

The adaptability measure takes account of the sequential aspect of the components of the action profile. Consider the following profile:

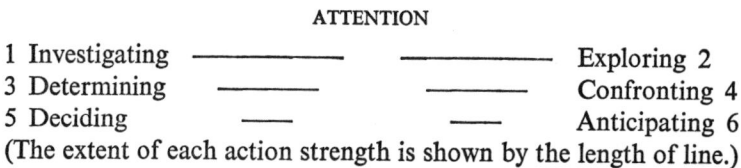

ATTENTION

1 Investigating ————————	————————	Exploring 2
3 Determining ————	————	Confronting 4
5 Deciding ——	——	Anticipating 6

(The extent of each action strength is shown by the length of line.)

Upon entering a new situation a person with this distribution of activity cannot help but give full attention to whatever is novel to him, before he has any thought of taking any sort of action, or even before making up his mind about anything. Because he cannot help but give an enormous amount of attention to anything new he cannot help but take action upon the basis of a full appreciation. Hence he will act in an *adaptable* way. He will act only according to the dictates of the new situation, never simply upon the basis of preconceived ideas or past experience. Therefore on the *adaptability* measure he would score the maximum.

Consider in contrast this profile:

ATTENTION

1 Investigating   ——   ——   2 Exploring

INTENTION

3 Determining   ———   ———   4 Confronting

COMMITMENT

5 Deciding   —————   —————   6 Anticipating

This man, upon entering a new situation is primarily motivated to take action as soon as possible. He feels it incumbent upon him first and foremost to get something moving no matter what. It would seem almost a neglect of duty to him, to pause and review, to just take stock perhaps for months if necessary (like the last man). He has to take decisions in line with projected targets. Because he hasn't given sufficient attention to the new situation, how-ever, to really know what it's about, he can only act, either on the basis of former experience or on preconceived ideas. Hence he cannot act in a truly adaptable fashion. Thus on the measure of *adaptability*, he would score the minimum.

This is not to say that either man will be necessarily the most effective in any particular situation. If the latter, the *unadaptable* man, moved in to a new situation and rapidly applied old methods and they happened to work (probably because the new situation happened to be similar to past experienced ones), then he would appear very successful and so he would be. One suspects that the management 'whizzkids' who can move into a run-down company and turn it round within a year, must work like this. However, there are per-plexing situations where the men of commitment will fail as with the case of Mr. Myer (Chapter 3). Before he took on Kale and Co. Ltd. the run-down Northern English company, he had been highly successful all over the world in getting new factories going. However, this situation was highly complex and entirely different from past situations. Myer couldn't help but try im-mediately to apply old methods—hence he failed. So before you can tell whether a new situation requires a highly *adaptable* manager or not, you need to know if it is really new and different or not. However, one thing is certain, in order to find out how different a new situation really is, you do need an *adaptable* manager to research it for you.

So far, examples of the two extremes of *adaptability* and non-*adaptability* have been given. In between there are many different sequential patterns. For instance:

ASSERTION			PERSPECTIVE
1 Investigating	——	ATTENTION ————————	2 Exploring
3 Determining	————	INTENTION ————	4 Confronting
5 Deciding	————————	COMMITMENT ——	6 Anticipating

Here is a conflict: a manager who is highly *adaptable* in gaining a perspective of a new situation, but highly *unadaptable* in what he actually does about it. He is *adaptable* in attitude but will tend to act in the same old ways. However, gradually the awareness of new perspectives, possibilities, issues, etc., will impinge upon his manner of asserting himself and he will change his way of doing things as well. Thus he would be given a moderate score on *adaptability*.

Consider this pattern:

1 Investigating	ATTENTION	2 Exploring
3 Determining	INTENTION	4 Confronting
5 Deciding	COMMITMENT	6 Anticipating

This pattern indicates a readiness to give full attention to a new situation, but with a strong need to come as soon as possible to the commitment or implementation process. If such a person were under pressure, either to give more time to researching (attention) or to show results (commitment) then the other stage would go by the board (due to the lack of intention). If not under pressure of any kind, such a person would *adapt*. Because of the vulnerability to outside pressures, however (and it is a rare situation where none are present), only a moderate score on *adaptability* would be given.

Obviously this measure of *adaptability* is very qualitative in nature and very dependent upon the nature of the circumstances except for the most or least *adaptable* measures. Thus in reporting upon a manager, where *adaptability* is a particular issue, care is taken to spell out the nature of the manager's *adapting* ability, as above.

Identification

This measure is derived solely from the frequency of variation along the effort flow, freeing ←→ binding and the shape flow, growing ←→ shrinking dimensions. An average of the two measures is calculated and if the frequency of variation is high the measure on *identification* is high and if the frequency of variation is low, so is the measure on *identification*.

The effort and shape flow dimensions are the ones that particularly characterize the movement of infants. In infants the proportion of variation along these dimensions in comparison to the other dimensions is very high and lessens gradually as the child grows. Dr. Kestenberg[17] and her group of psychiatrists who have concentrated upon child studies have found it necessary to concentrate wholly upon the flow dimensions, subdividing them even further into various categories such as evenness or fluctuation of levels, high or low intensity, abrupt or gradual change of flow.

Because the flow dimensions particularly characterize the movement of children, the retention of these dimensions in adult movement are considered to indicate the presence of the 'childlike' qualities of spontaneity, readiness to participate, become involved and enthusiastic, all of which constitute the quality we call *identification*.

CHAPTER 8

Research into the Action Profile as a Valid Description of Behaviour

How do we know that the existence of the various movement qualities within a person's movement pattern does, in fact, indicate the existence of the action characteristics that we say they do? How do we know that if we see a lot of directing ⟷ indirecting in a person's movement pattern that he will therefore display a lot of the behaviour called *investigating* and so on?

First Observations

It all began with the theory concerning the three stage sequence of action: Attention ⟶ Intention ⟶ Commitment.

1 A man named Rudolf Laban[18] (see Bibliography and notes) noticed that action seemed to follow a logical three stage sequence. He also observed in the course of his study of the mechanics of human movement that there were three essential elements which went to make up the effort quality, namely focus, pressure and time. He saw a connection between these three elements and the three stages of action. He observed too that the expression of attention seemed to be facilitated by the use of directing ⟷ indirecting qualities in movement, intention by increasing ⟷ decreasing of pressure and commitment by the accelerating ⟷ decelerating qualities of movement. He observed that the natural emphasis in a person's movement pattern seemed to relate to the emphasis in their behavioural pattern, i.e. those who showed more evidence of directing ⟷ indirecting, were more ready to give attention in various ways, those who showed more evidence of increasing ⟷ decreasing pressure seemed more concerned with expressing intention and those with greater emphasis on the time dimension accelerating ⟷ decelerating did seem more ready to commit themselves. It seemed too logical to be just coincidence.

2 Warren Lamb developed the concepts concerning the shaping qualities and the corresponding 'perspective' action characteristics. This arose from the observation that certain body shapings seemed to facilitate the activation of the effort qualities. It was also observed that these body shapings

could occur either in conjunction with the matching effort qualities, or in isolation. This seemed to indicate that they had a separate functional value and hence were an indication of independent action motivations but of a different order from the 'effort' or 'assertion' characteristics. Thus arose the concept of 'perspective'.

In addition Warren Lamb observed the effects of harmony and disharmony of effort and shaping elements upon interaction and so developed the concept of interaction style.

3 The above concepts were not, of course, developed overnight. Laban spent his life formulating his 'effort' concepts and the 'shaping' concepts only emerged after ten years of concentrated study and constant observation on the part of Warren Lamb. In recent years there has been collaborative evidence from several sources.

4 The detailed study of infant development by Dr. Judith Kestenberg[19] and a group of psychiatrists has revealed that the same movement concepts are applicable to the study of infant development. The developmental sequence follows the logical attention ⟶ intention ⟶ commitment sequence. The directing ⟷ indirecting movement qualities appear first, then increasing ⟷ decreasing pressure and lastly accelerating ⟷ decelerating or time quality. The development of the shaping qualities follow the same course.

There is evidence, too, that the seeds of the adult movement pattern are in existence from birth.[20] So much of a child's early experience in the first most formative years of its life is concerned with learning via the body. The child learns to cope with its environment as much with its body as with its mind and, of course, it is all part and parcel of a single learning process. In infancy the bodily and movement participation is more obvious than in adulthood. In adulthood, however, the minute variations in muscular tension states, as expressed in the individual movement pattern, are like scaled down versions of the big bodily participation that occurs in infancy, but it is probably in infancy that the basic movement pattern is laid down.

A Videotape pilot study

It is only relatively recently that we have begun working with videotape recordings. Minute analysis has been carried out in terms of the behaviour correlates attached to the various movement categories.

In an experiment using this method three managers were gathered together who according to the action profile assessment (on the basis of the movement analysis alone) had three very different action profiles (see the opposite page).

As can be seen, Paisley's activity is strongly weighted toward the attention stage. As much as 35 per cent of his application will be concentrated

Key	Paisley		Child		Travers	
	% of activity	*Inter-action*	*% of activity*	*Inter-action*	*% of activity*	*Inter-action*
ATTENTION			15		10	
Investigating	25				10	
Communicating			6			
Exploring					12	
INTENTION	30		31		10	
Determining						
Presenting						
Confronting	12				28	
			24			
COMMITMENT	15					
Deciding			9			
Operating	8				30	
Anticipating	10		15			
Dynamism	2·0		3·0		3·9	
Adaptability	3·9		2·0		0·0	
Identification	3·0		1·0		2·5	

Action Profile 7 VIDEOTAPE PILOT STUDY

in this way. Of Child's activity, 56 per cent is concentrated particularly in the intention phase of the sequence whereas Travers' activity to complete the picture is primarily located 58 per cent in the commitment stage. They all show a fairly even weighting between the assertion and perspective factors particularly in their strongest area.

The aims of the study were:

1 To find out if the action motivation definitions could be used to analyse the contributions made by individual managers in carrying out a group task.

2 To find out whether these categories were useful and meaningful to a group of observers relatively untrained in these concepts in order to describe the progress of the group interaction.

3 To ascertain whether the assessments made by the observers of the managers in the action requirement terms corresponded at all with assessments made on the basis of movement patterns.

Results

Questions 1 and 2 were certainly answered in the affirmative. The action motivation definitions were certainly found possible as tools for the analysis of contributions made to a group task. In addition the half hour trained observers were able to use the categories in describing the progress of the group interaction with fair facility, although some misunderstanding of the definitions did occur.

The assessments made by the observers correspond to some extent with the assessment made on the basis of movement patterns.

(i) In terms of the first six action requirements. A high correspondence was obtained between observer assessment and action profile assessment in the case of Child (less than 1 per cent probability that the same results could occur by chance). The correlation for Paisley was very much less significant (a 15 per cent probability that the same results could occur by chance) and for Travers not at all.

(ii) In terms of the interaction components, the correlation of observers and action profile assessments was very high for Paisley (all observers rated him predominantly a *communicator*), high for Child (all observers rated him predominantly a *presenter* and two of the four considered some *operating* was present). The correlation for Travers was not so high. (Three observers considered him predominantly a *presenter* and one saw some *communicating*. Only one of the observers considered him predominantly an *operator*.

Brief Conclusion

As this was more in the nature of a pilot study than anything else the results are promising. In this study there were unfortunately many uncontrolled variables such as the subjects' level of *dynamism* and their managerial experience. No doubt a more thorough training of the observers in the action motivation definitions would result in greater accuracy in classification of behaviour. In addition it would be better to vary the nature of the tasks so that there was a sample of *attention, intention* and *commitment* orientations.

All the above amendments came about naturally in the process of a group training course.

Training Course using Videotape

A recent development of the 'Top Team Planning' assignment has been to run training courses on the action motivations for management. The primary aim of such a course is to acquaint managers more thoroughly with the action profile concepts and to give them practical experience with their own action profile in action; i.e. to put their own activity under the microscope using again videotape equipment. During a course it is possible to simulate *attention, intention* and *commitment* oriented situations so that behaviour in all three categories will have a chance to emerge.

The following sequence is followed: Group task (attention, intention or commitment oriented)—play back and detailed moment by moment analysis of the video recording, with managers present and inviting contributions from them. This is followed by discussion on the pattern of behaviour shown by each manager and its applicability to that particular situation. At the end of the five days the managers themselves observe a group interaction and are able to analyse it using the action profile classifications pretty accurately. In every instance the action profile of each manager as drawn on the basis of the movement pattern was accepted, by the manager himself and by his colleagues. Managers are able on the basis of very concrete evidence, not only to accept the accuracy of the action profile but also to see its usefulness. (See p. 161 for fuller explanation.)

PART III

Using the Action Profile

CHAPTER 9

Using the Action Profile to Enhance the Effectiveness of a Top Team

For managers, concerned more with using an approach to managerial be-haviour than with the refinement of theoretical systems, it might be argued that it is more important to ensure that the action profile way of describing behaviour is usable and workable in practical management, than to concern ourselves with sophistications of theory and technique. Suppose the action profiles of a management group can be evaluated and they are 98 per cent accurate, can managers actually use this information? The answer is yes, and increasingly so.

Initially the assessment based upon a movement pattern was used for selection purposes only and was written in terms of a particular job des-cription—hence was only applicable when the man was in that job. There was then no underlying framework that could be used to describe a pattern of behaviour which was constant, whatever the job or situation. That only came six years ago, with the distillation of the twelve action motivations. Now managers can be educated in a set of principles which they themselves can then apply in determining how a manager will behave in different situa-tions. It is really this development which has enabled the application of the action profile method of assessment to the study of management teams. It enables one to consider a manager not only in relation to one particular job, but in relation to different situations and different people and groups of people.

But how does one approach the study of an existing management team, even with the aid of the action profile assessment, and what ultimately are the aims in doing so? It is probably fairly evident by now that the action profile assessment can be a very useful tool for use in filling management vacancies. But how can this kind of study be used within already established management teams?

Why such a study is required:

To begin with, the unpleasant assumption has to be made that within companies managerial ability is often handled in such a way that much of it is unrecognized or misused and hence lost. This occurs in various ways.

1 Managers may find themselves fulfilling roles for which they are not really suited.
2 They may not undergo appropriate development (and 'appropriate' is the operative word here).
3 A team style or joint action profile may develop which precludes contribution from managers of foreign or 'balancing' styles.
4 Unsatisfactory patterns of interaction may develop which prevent full expression of managers' abilities.

The aim in studying an existing management team, using the action profile assessment, is to rectify the above sources of misused managerial ability, to the extent that it is necessary and feasible within any one company.

It would obviously be naive and false to say that sweeping and revolutionary changes can be made within a company on the basis of the action profile information alone, even if it were desirable and that might be debatable. It is obviously a little idealistic blithely to tell a man of 57 who has been an accountant for 30 years that he would have made a marvellous production engineer. It might be unwise also to tell a young man of limited intelligence that on the basis of the action profile he could become a wonderful finance director someday.

All the available information has to be taken into consideration.

The basic data in studying an existing management team is:

1 The action profile of each man.
2 Information gained during interview concerning the views of each manager on such things as:
   (i) The present company situation and his position in it, his prospects, hopes and ambitions.
   (ii) His background, education, training and experience.
   (iii) What he actually does, with whom he meets most often, what he feels to be his areas of greatest strength and greatest difficulty.
3 Company information. Documentation ranging from statements of company policy and objectives to remuneration scales.

In other words as much information as possible about the company and its people is gathered and used in conjunction with the action profile information.

It would also be naive and untrue to say that sweeping and revolutionary changes always occur, as a result of a study using both action profile and other information. The extent of any change will depend entirely upon the need of the company, and the degree to which recommended changes are considered by the management to be possible and desirable.

In any case, as stated at the beginning, this is an account of work in progress. There are many things the action profile information in its present state of research cannot tell you and many things it will never be able to tell you. Having said that, let us consider some of the insights this information can give and some of the ways in which it can be used.

What can be done:

The action profile information in combination with all the other available data can be used to enhance the effectiveness of the Top Team in the following ways:

1 By changing the roles of individuals to fit more closely with their Action Profiles.
2 Bringing new members into the team to supply missing action motivations and weeding out those for whom an effective role cannot be found.
3 Ensuring that appropriate development measures according to the Action Profile are available.
4 Educating managers to an awareness of their own and their colleagues' Action Profiles so they can capitalize on their strengths and recognize complementary action motivations.
5 Instituting formal systems to safeguard the organization in areas in which the team motivation is weakest and ensure that attention is given to functions that might otherwise be neglected.

CHAPTER 10

Fit the Job to the Manager

Experience has shown that a manager performs most effectively and gains most satisfaction when fulfilling a role which demands strengths available to him within the action profile. Conversely, he performs least effectively, and is even subject to pressure and stress, when strengths are required which are not spontaneously available.

It is true that training and experience are essential requirements as well. But they can be acquired. Strengths within the action profile cannot. Therefore it is most essential that a man is suited to his job in terms of his action profile strengths.

However, you cannot just create a tailor-made job for each manager, regardless of the requirements of the organization. In proposing therefore to seek a greater degree of matching between men and jobs within an existing management team, a fairly complex matching process has to go on.

This process can be more clearly indicated by Chart 2.

Out of this process can come some or all of the following possibilities. Within the existing management team there may be:

- Some well suited to their roles
- Some very badly suited to their roles
- Some whose particular strengths can be used to far greater advantage in the existing company situation
- Some whose strengths can be used to greater advantage by some slight change in or addition to present role
- Some whose roles should be contracted

(i) *Some are well suited to their roles*

A good example of this was the buyer in a particular company. His profile was as shown on page 124.

This man has in fact proved to be exceptionally successful as a buyer and has been responsible for saving the company thousands of pounds.

This is the profile of a specialist. Factors contributing to this are:

MATCHING OF EXISTING MANAGERIAL ABILITY AGAINST COMPANY NEEDS

Company needs	*Managerial ability available to fulfil company needs*
Analyse essential functions to be fulfilled in order to achieve company objectives.	Analyse the individual action profile of each man.
1. Are functions presently being carried out by men who according to their action profiles are really suited to them?	1. According to his action profile is he really suited to the function he is presently carrying out?
2. If not, can some changes be made?	2. If not, can his role be changed according to existing definitions of function?
3. Are there gaps which need to be filled?	
4. Are there people within the organization who according to their action profiles could fill those gaps and who could reasonably be moved?	3. Can he fulfil a completely new role?
	4. Is he just over extended or under utilized—requiring extension or contraction of role?
	5. If none of the above does he really have a place in the company?

Chart 2

1 The very heavy weighting in the commitment stage.
2 The outstanding strength in *anticipating*.
3 The total lacks in interaction capacity, except once again in the commitment stage.

He can be summed up as an observant, *determined,* exceedingly farsighted *operator.* He cannot get in touch with people on any terms except straightforward organization of action-programming and setting targets. Hence there are a great many people with whom he cannot interact constructively at all; i.e. all those lacking or weak in *operating.*

Even those who are moderately strong in *operating* but with predominant strengths in *communicating* or *presenting* would find it hard to co-operate with him on many levels. This would immediately exclude him from any general management role.

Example of good matching between job (action
requirements) and manager (action motivations)

		% of total activity	Extent of Interaction activity	
ATTENTION	Investigating	20		Communi-cating
	Exploring	0		
INTENTION	Determining	20		Presenting
	Confronting	0		
COMMITMENT	Deciding	28		Operating
	Anticipating	32		
Dynamism			3·5	
Adaptability			0·0	
Identifying			0·0	

Action Profile 8   BUYER

He is completely *unexploratory*, which may seem at first slightly surprising
for a buyer. However, a clarification on the definition of *exploring* will clear
this. Once the boundary of an area of discovery has been defined, *exploring*
ends and *investigating* begins. *Exploring* is always simply the awareness of
boundaries beyond. Once you define a particular area and start looking into
it you are no longer *exploring*. The market place for a particular product or
set of products is a defined field. Hence *investigation* takes place. This man
is a strong *investigator* so can adequately probe his defined area. The lack in

exploring means in fact that he is never for a moment distracted from his *investigations*. He is totally and persistently concentrated.

The outstanding strength in *anticipating* sets him up to constantly predict and forecast the trends in the market. He is constantly motivated to foresee where things are going and this, due to his concentrated probing, is well backed up by precise information, hence very likely to be a great deal more accurate than predictions made by a great many other people.

His strength in *deciding* enables him to pick just the right moment to buy. He is motivated to commit himself precisely and opportunistly or to bide his time as he sees events are going. Once again his programming is backed up by precise information about his field of operation.

It sounds ideal, and this man has proved himself ideally successful. People have often reported on what appears to be his almost clairvoyant ability to predict the right moment to buy. He has been known to buy the very day before a huge rise in price has taken place in a particular commodity.

(ii) *Some are very badly suited to their roles*

A so-called works manager had the profile overleaf.

This profile is in fact remarkably like the prototype example described in p. 44 as belonging to the truly research minded man. There, it was said that such a man will always be motivated to give full attention to the situation. He will be totally unable to make a decision until he feels he has all the necessary information at his fingertips—and all the necessary information will mean a lot of information for him. This man will never be a *decisive* man of action. He is, however, a good man for going back to first principles and establishing the basis of an operation. He is likely to be a good policy maker and standard setter. He is better as an adviser than as a 'doer'.

The function of works manager requires a large element of *deciding-anticipating* ability. He has to organize, plan, programme, keep the stuff rolling out the door. One might wonder how a man of the above profile could stay in such a position for five minutes, and of course, often such bad positioning automatically gets rectified simply by virtue of the man's obvious inefficiency or unhappiness. However, it happened in this case as can also very often occur, that the man did not really carry out the true function of works manager but found other useful work for himself to do. The outfit of which he was in charge was small in the business as a whole and covered just one small division. The works manager, by name Laver, acquired over time highly specialized knowledge and expertise in this small area and became the only one in the whole concern to have this knowledge at his fingertips. Hence most of his time was spent in advising other people on the basis of his particular area of expertise.

When Laver came for counselling he was highly defensive and refused to accept the action profile, insisting that he was as strong in the commitment

Example of ill-matching between job (action
requirements) and manager (action motivations)

		% of total activity	Extent of interaction activity	
ATTENTION	Investigating	29		Communicating
	Exploring	40		
INTENTION	Determining	10		Presenting
	Confronting	15		
COMMITMENT	Deciding	2		Oper-ating
	Anticipating	4		
Dynamism			2·0	
Adaptability			3·9	
Identifying			2·5	

Action Profile 9   WORKS MANAGER—LAVER

area as in the attention area. He recognized openly that his profile, as we had
it, did not fit him for his present job and had even gone to the trouble of
reading Warren Lamb's book 'Management Behaviour' in order to give
himself a basis for self assessment. So his insecurity was very evident. Most
of the counselling session was spent in trying to convince him that the type
of action profile displayed by a person was not in itself bad, but only in the
context of a particular situation.

The General Works Director confirmed the analysis and has concurred wholeheartedly with the recommendation that he should be given a more advisory role. In detail a recommendation was made as follows:

1 Laver's attributes suggest he is more a 'staff' than a 'line' man but he is not being used in this role.
2 In the production team he should provide an advisory function.
3 As a special project he could head up a very much needed organization and methods review. It is in the company's interests to have its own man active in conducting the survey although consultants might well contribute. Consultants would be briefed to work in conjunction with Laver, who would have continuing responsibility for implementing the recommendations. Such a role is aptly called 'Industrial Engineer' and it needs someone of Laver's practical management expertise as well as aptitude to fill it.

Such a change in role is particularly important for this man. His basic action profile is relatively weak, especially with regard to the overall measure of energy, *dynamism*. As Laver is still young (age 30) the change to a function so much better suited to his particular style could provide an enormous development impetus.

(iii) *There are some whose particular strengths can be used to far greater advantage in the existing company situation.*

If a manager has a strong basic action profile (in the sense of there not being complete absences in any of the action requirements) there are a large number of work situations he can cope with, without actually failing. However, there will be some to which he will be better suited and which will make maximum use of his abilities. One such man's profile is on the next page.

His original position was termed chief engineer and head of a small division. His duties consisted mainly of selling systems to local authorities, electricity boards, etc. It was noted that firstly he was very strong in the attention area, in fact one of the few in the company that was. Secondly, that he was particularly well balanced in the interaction aspects. He was a well qualified engineer, but relatively unrecognized within the company. Nobody had a very clear idea just exactly what he did do and several had a slight suspicion that he was rather a time-wasting wanderer. Those in closer contact with him, however, certainly appreciated his abilities.

In Chapter 14, p. 195, the study of 'team style' within his company will be described in detail. (Just as each individual manager has his own particular style, so too does a management team.) This particular team was found to be strongly biased toward *deciding, anticipating* and *operating* with little motivation towards *investigating, exploring* and *communicating*. *Exploring* was the greatest overall weakness with *investigating* not far behind, i.e. they all

Example of the possibility for changing role to
achieve better matching between job (action
requirements) and manager (action motivations)

		% of total activity	Extent of interaction activity	
ATTENTION	Investigating	17		Communicating
	Exploring	23		
INTENTION	Determining	10		Presenting
	Confronting	10		
COMMITMENT	Deciding	23		Operating
	Anticipating	17		
Dynamism			3·0	
Adaptability			2·0	
Identifying			3·0	

Action Profile 10   ENGINEER—LYLE

wanted to run before they could walk. They were all eager to get to the action
and exploit what they had, without first really questioning and exploring
the basis of their business. Hence many essential questions had never been
asked.

Mr. Lyle had the opposite balancing characteristics. It was considered
beneficial for him to be in close touch with the Managing Director in a strong
position where he could influence policy making. It was recommended that

he should be made marketing planner directly responsible to the Managing Director. This was done and within the very first few months he had discovered how little planning had gone into the vital marketing function. Great efforts had been made to cultivate sales in Asia for instance. The business had grown up in a totally *ad hoc,* opportunist fashion. No-one had even questioned if they could actually make sales profitably in the way they were tackling it. This man is simply motivated to ask such questions and found the ground extremely ripe for his *investigations.* Moreover it is essential to the survival of the company that such *investigations* should be put in hand. The company has reached such a point in its now rapid expansion that concious planning of all resources is of prime importance.

(iv) *There are some whose strengths can be used to greater advantage by some change in, or addition to, present role*

In the same company as the previous example, was a woman executive who held the position of female staff supervisor. Mrs. Tyle was an extremely capable woman but hampered by the prevailing, somewhat prejudiced attitude toward women in the company. With time and training she would have been capable of a senior executive function but it was recognized that in the present climate of opinion she could not be pushed too far too fast. The best way was to increase her responsibility by degrees. Her profile is on page 130.

Notable is her strength in the interaction mode *presenting.* This is a very positive attribute in any training capacity. Where clear demonstration of a fairly cut and dried skill or technique is required, then strong *presenting* capacities are invaluable. The recommendation for Mrs. Tyle then was toward making more use of her *presentational* motivation.

It was considered that she could contribute more than was presently the case by developing her training ability. It was thought worth building on the training experience she already had by getting her to undertake new training programmes.

This could apply even with groups with whom she had had no previous experience, such as sales representatives, and even against opposition. She could rise to a challenge and doing so would help her to develop.

It was considered essential, however, that she was not left in the dark as to any aspect of the subject matter. She was a good trainer in the pragmatic sense rather than a teacher in the sense of true education. It was in *presenting* the subject matter that she absorbed it. So far as possible, therefore, the training manuals to which she worked should be concerned with conducting *investigations* (surveys, research, reviews), forward planning and communications study.

In giving this advice, her considerable limitations in *investigating* and *exploring* were taken into account—hence the proviso that she should not be left in the dark as to any aspect of the subject matter and that if possible the

E

Example of the possibility for slight expansion of role
to allow greater utilization of action motivations

		% of total activity	Extent of interaction activity	
ATTENTION	Investigation	10		Communicating
	Exploring	6		
INTENTION	Determining	20		Presenting
	Confronting	25		
COMMITMENT	Deciding	25		Operating
	Anticipating	14		
Dynamism			1·5	
Adaptability			1·0	
Identifying			2·0	

Action Profile 11   FEMALE STAFF SUPERVISOR—MRS. TYLE

training manuals to which she worked should be concerned with information gathering of various kinds.

(v) *There are some whose roles should be contracted*

Consider the Action Profile 12 opposite.

There is a well nigh equal coverage of the three areas (attention, intention, commitment) and the *dynamism* measure is reasonably high. However, there

Example of the need for contraction of role to
reduce demands on weak action motivations

		% of total activity	Extent of interaction activity	
ATTENTION	Investigating	30		Communicating
	Exploring	4		
INTENTION	Determining	25		Presenting
	Confronting	8		
COMMITMENT	Deciding	3		Operating
	Anticipating	30		
Dynamism			3·0	
Adaptability			2·0	
Identifying			2·0	

Action Profile 12 TECHNICAL DIRECTOR—MR. GALE

is considerable imbalance between the two components in each stage. In the
Attention stage the *investigating* activity is not put into perspective by sufficient
exploration. This means that the information-getting Mr. Gale does of his
own initiative will be narrowly channelled into precisely defined areas. He is
blinkered in the way he looks for information. A similar imbalance occurs
with *determining* and *confronting*. Mr. Gale is *determined* and persistent about
what he wants to get done, but does not face up to the situation straight-

forwardly. He ignores and evades. Because he is *unexploratory* he cannot find a way round a problem he cannot really face up to, so often just ignores it. A similar imbalance also appears in the commitment stage. Here the perspective is present, but the assertion is missing. Mr. Gale is constantly looking ahead, projecting results, aware of the trend of events, but cannot time his decisions or programme his activity accordingly. He will foresee opportunities, but cannot act to seize them.

This kind of imbalance over the three stages of activity is not altogether uncommon but in every case it makes for a very specialized and to some extent limited application.

Mr. Gale was, at the time of the study, Technical Director of the largest division in his company. Not only was he being required to cope with a wide responsibility, as the company was highly technically oriented, but at a time of enormous change. The company had just been taken over by a progressive international group who were rapidly rationalising this old fashioned English concern with its outmoded management methods. This is, in fact, the same company of which Mr. Myer is the Managing Director.

Mr. Gale was valiantly endeavouring to cope with a great deal. However, he was showing signs of stress. He even complained of not being able to cope with the paperwork on his desk every morning.

Recognizing the specialist nature of his abilities, a gradual contraction of role was recommended.

> '. . . without implying any reflection on the man himself, it would seem that he has already been extended to a degree where for his own development, he should first contract before seeking to expand. The aim should be rather to make better use of a smaller range of his attributes than to seek still further adaptation than he has already undergone.
>
> He needs to be protected from getting into a stress situation, from which he would personally suffer, perhaps seriously. Contraction of the scope of his responsibility is the obvious answer. If he can see himself more as a specialist it would then be possible to consider development measures.'

On the basis of this recommendation, Mr. Gale was made Deputy Managing Director. This meant that his role was made smaller, but without obvious demotion. He has a considerable body of detailed technical knowledge and this is still available to the operating divisional managers. Six months after the change, Mr. Gale had become a reasonably competent and useful deputy managing director.

CHAPTER 11

Develop the Manager Appropriately According to the Action Profile

Although as indicated in the previous chapter it is certainly possible to achieve a degree of better matching between men or women and jobs, it isn't possible to obtain ideal matching for every manager. A man who according to his action profile may be relatively unsuited to a particular role may, on the other hand, possess valuable technical expertise or knowledge which the company is loath to lose. The answer, of course, is to prevent this kind of thing from happening in the first place, but this is a long-term process. The most expedient intermediate measure is to ensure that at least such men undergo appropriate development for the role they are fulfilling.

Under the heading of development come the following possibilities:

   (i) Teach the individual to use 'props' . . . techniques and systems, to cover up for those areas where he is lacking in spontaneous motivation.

  (ii) Actually build such 'props' into the system under which the manager functions.

 (iii) Educate the individual as to his 'secondary' strengths, which may be drawn upon more and possibly enhanced a little (personal growth).

 (iv) Provide an environment and selected experiences where the above is made possible.

Points ii and iv, the role of the organization in providing for appropriate development, will be dealt with in this chapter.

PROPS, CONTROLS AND SYSTEMS

Often it has to be recognized that a particular action limitation is undevelopable in the growth sense. The most sensible way of dealing with such limitations is simply to recognize them and to take precautions against their possible harmful effects. This can be done by using various systems and controls. Sometimes these can be built into the man's job, particularly in the case of middle managers. It may be more difficult to implement such a process when it comes to senior managers. It is a question of degree. A top manager must ultimately be able to stand on his own feet without being supported by the system to a high degree. This is not to say that all senior managers must be perfect, or even to suggest that they should do all things equally well. Experience has shown that they certainly do not. However, in the top management team, built in safeguard systems and controls can only function to a certain extent, beyond which the manager must stand on his own.

At senior level the safeguarding against weak areas can be as efficiently executed through the complementing of persons within a particular management team. If the Managing Director is weak on *investigating,* then he must have people in his team or on his board who are strongly *investigatory* and so on. For the moment let us concentrate on the institution of controls and systems as protection against gaps in spontaneous motivation.

The advice to supply a man with some kind of prop against a particular weakness has been found to be most appropriate in the first and last areas of the action sequence.

ATTENTION

Investigating   Exploring

COMMITMENT

Deciding   Anticipating

Various techniques for coping with these areas have already been established and are used by managers in varying degrees. One wonders, however, how often they are used by those most in need of them. Management by objectives, for instance, is obviously well suited to the encouragement of *anticipating*. It can be a highly valuable tool for those lacking in a spontaneous *anticipatory* motivation. Not surprisingly, however, it is those already strong in *anticipating* who often gravitate toward Mbo. They instinctively have a feel and sympathy for such a system. But they, of course, are precisely the people who benefit least, particularly if their present job doesn't happen to require an enormous amount of *anticipation*. This is not to say that such a person wouldn't benefit at all from Mbo, but it is less essential for him than for the man lacking in *anticipation*. It would always be a struggle for the *non-anticipator* to operate an Mbo system but a beneficial one nevertheless. If nothing else he is made aware of his lack of *anticipation* and readiness to look ahead and set objectives. The action profile is invaluable in enabling one to differentiate the managers who really should be directed toward a particular technique.

In Action Profile 13, *Investigating* is obviously the most serious limitation. *Deciding* and *Confronting* are small but developable in the growth sense. *Investigating* is not developable in terms of growth. The advice given was as follows:

The need for techniques and controls to cover a weakness
in *Investigating*

		% of total activity
ATTENTION	Investigating	5
	Exploring	20
INTENTION	Determining	25
	Confronting	10
COMMITMENT	Deciding	15
	Anticipating	25

Action Profile 13 MR. LAYSON

'He needs to be provided with controls to guard against inadequate investigation. Specific intellectual training in *investigating* techniques would be relevant. To protect him from making mistakes due to inadequate *investigation*, efforts should be made to see that information is always readily accessible to him. He must literally be fed with as much detailed information as is practicable.'

Now, consider Mr. Irland's profile overleaf. He seemed to be always becoming entrenched in battle against some particular problem—so much so that he never released himself sufficiently to take a fresh look at the situation and so come up with a new way of approach. The recommendation was that he should use a formal creative problem-solving technique:

'A slight shift of emphasis from the need to get to grips with a situation to a more relaxed attitude of enquiry and appraisal will be beneficial. It needs simply an effort not to get too earnest too soon.

The need for techniques and controls
to cover a limitation in *Exploring*

		% of total activity
ATTENTION	Investigating	10
	Exploring	2
INTENTION	Determining	24
	Confronting	20
	Deciding	10
COMMITMENT	Anticipating	34

Action Profile 14   MR. IRLAND

It is in the nature of a relaxing of assertion rather than an increase.

This will result in a greater readiness to look at old problems with a new eye. Whenever he feels he is becoming entrenched in a situation, it will require an effort to relinquish the resolution to battle on, and rather to take the approach of going back to square one and really considering perhaps radically different methods of approach.

Experience with a structured approach to creative problem solving may help.

Mr. Hurst (see Action Profile 15) has a different need. The *deciding* faculty is practically non existent. Hence this man finds it extremely difficult to programme his activities. He almost has no sense for time at all. When studied he was endeavouring to cope with the job of salesman—admittedly of a highly technical and personalized nature. It wasn't competitive door to door consumer selling. Nevertheless, he was in trouble due to his inability to pro-

The need for techniques and controls
as insurance against lack of *Deciding*

		% of total activity
ATTENTION	Investigating	15
	Exploring	5
INTENTION	Determining	24
	Confronting	24
	Deciding	2
COMMITMENT	Anticipating	30

Action Profile 15   MR. HURST

gramme. The only chance for him was seen to be the imposition of a strait-
jacket-like programme control:

'The policy on his development should be based on two main considerations:

1 He needs to be given (as though being propped up), everything
possible in respect to a system he should operate, the methods he
should use, or the tactics he should employ. There should be no
reticence about organizing him to the full.
2 All the "propping up" as indicated above should be related to objectives which he is invited to declare on his own initiative. It is
important that he should feel he has specified his own personal
objectives without too much prompting. It is in the manner of
attaining them that he needs help.

It will spur his development considerably if he can be made aware of his poor sense of timing and how he can inject more urgency into his working activity. This is a matter for self-awareness and every suitable occasion should be taken to demonstrate the need to him and perhaps challenge him to do something about it.

In general, it should be impressed upon him that time is short, that in business time costs money, and that it is not necessarily a compromise of standards to seek to get more done in the time available.'

Note that it is emphasized that he must contribute his objectives of his own initiative. This is because he is already strong in *anticipating*. He knows what his targets are, but he cannot programme himself to reach them, hence concentration on training him to clarify objectives would be largely a waste of time in that it would not get to the real basis of the problem. The opposite applies to someone who is already strong in *deciding* but weak in *anticipating*. See Action Profile 16.

The almost complete lack of *anticipating* in combination with the predominant strength in *deciding* is a particularly interesting feature in this man's profile. He is highly motivated to take decisions but almost totally without consideration as to their implications. He can programme his day to day activities efficiently, but they are out of context with any systematic pursuit of objectives.

He will take a decision as if for the moment only. He may programme his day by day activities but there will not be an ongoing process or staging of activity toward a realistic target. In combination with the overall action pattern, this lack in *anticipation* was seen to be a considerable problem:

'His big limitation is in failing to exercise an *anticipatory* faculty. This puts him, as it were, in a constant state of apprehension as to whether something might happen for which he is unprepared. He works as though constantly expecting to be surprised by developments.

While hard experience may have pre-disposed him to this state of apprehension he remains basically unable to look ahead or project ahead. It is important that he should have detailed forward plans to work to, otherwise many of his decisions may be shortsighted and opportunist.

A similar problem exists in respect to work relationships. He will deal with people opportunistly, and they are likely to feel it. As a manager he is clear and positive in dealing with subordinates but over emphasizes the "here and now" situation. No-one is likely to get much of a prospect from him of where they are going.

The limitation on *anticipation*, together with his earnestness and *determination*, makes him vulnerable to working himself into an an-

The need for techniques and controls
to cover for lack in *Anticipating*

		% of total activity
ATTENTION	Investigating	15
	Exploring	5
INTENTION	Determining	24
	Confronting	24
COMMITMENT	Deciding	30
	Anticipating	2

Action Profile 16   MR. LIGHT

xiety state. Putting pressure on him through ultimatums, criticism or incentives could impose too great a burden.

In his case provision for realizing the development possibilities is a particularly important need and will help to release him from over-anxiety.'

A 'propping up' procedure as follows was recommended:

'On the basis that he is unlikely to be a complete failure, and that there is a good chance of making him into a success, he can be recommended subject to action with him in the following two areas:

1 Provision of forward planning procedure and regularly working with him to keep them up to date. This could be along the lines of a "management by objectives" procedure.

2 Giving him the opportunity to broaden as a manager. He is one of the few people of whom it can be said that almost anything in the management field, including management courses, which serves to broaden his perspectives or enlarge his scope of appreciation of what business management consists of, will be beneficial.

He is amenable to training and it should be given him in as relaxed a framework as possible. He can gain more from personal counsel—it is important that he should not be made to feel dependent on anyone. As mentioned earlier, he should not be given anything in the nature of an ultimatum. He is over eager to create his own pressures: his main need is to be given broader perspectives.'

The advice in point 2 is to do with the lack in *exploring*. However, this is more in the line of growth development as some real growth could perhaps be possible in this area.

THE HAZARDS AND USEFULNESS OF INTELLECTUAL
TECHNIQUES AND CONTROLS

Although such propping up procedures as described above can to some extent succeed, they can obviously never replace a natural strength in a particular area. A naturally *unanticipatory* manager, no matter how many controls, techniques or sophisticated equipment he tries to use, will never be as competent or useful as a spontaneously motivated *anticipatory* manager in areas where *anticipation* is important. In the first place, where the spontaneous motivation is lacking, the actual process of using a stop-gap tool or technique is pretty unrewarding. A non *exploratory* person just would not find structured problem-solving or brain-storming much fun—at least not for long. In the second place the person using a tool instead of a spontaneous motivation, no matter how earnestly he tries, will tend (a) to use the tool in a somewhat inflexible and inappropriate way, and (b) will, in due course, tend to lose patience with it and neglect its use to some extent or altogether.

So why bother, you might ask? Well there are two ways of approaching the problem. To some extent a manager can be so structured into a situation that he is provided with the necessary control. As with Mr. Layson, for instance, it was suggested that information should always be readily accessible to him, to safeguard against his limitation in *investigating*. 'He must literally be fed with as much detailed information as is practicable.' Now this advice will mean that he is treated in a very different way from someone strong in *investigating* and of whom the following might have been said:

'He can be relied upon to always give full attention to the situation. He will probe, thoroughly and in detail. No matter how complex the situation, he will always seek to find all the facts.'

The second point of view from which the providing of techniques and controls as props can be viewed, is in the self awareness the experience of those controls and the use of those techniques can provide for the manager. The *indecisive* manager struggling to plan his programme flexibly and consistently will become much more aware of his limitation in this area, than if he'd just been told about it. He may also become much more aware of the fact that other managers may be naturally strong in those areas in which he is weakest. Hopefully this could lead to the readiness to draw on other people's strengths. The complementing of people's action motivations is perhaps the most constructive way of dealing with limitations.

Mr. Hurst may struggle to overcome his limitation in *deciding* (2 per cent) and this is necessary for his development as a manager, but he will never be as effective in this as, say, Mr. Light who naturally puts 30 per cent of his energy into *deciding*.

However, Mr. Light may have a limitation in an area where Mr. Hurst is strong. Thus the two if working together could complement each other, each providing different strengths and adding a different type of activity to the joint effort.

THE SAFE ENVIRONMENT FOR GROWTH DEVELOPMENT

Any attempt to provide experiences whereby a manager is required to draw more heavily upon secondary strengths within his action profile (with the objective of enhancing them) is a very delicate procedure. If secondary strengths are in fact enhanced, this virtually amounts to a change in the personality. It is not just 'learning' or 'doing' something new, it is 'being' something new. It can be an exhilarating experience, as any such change though marginal is felt by the person to be immense. However, it is certainly a somewhat hazardous procedure to try and bring it about.

If the experience is, for instance, too severe and the demands upon secondary strengths too rigorous, the manager will simply revert to his old well established strengths, however inappropriate they are. If on the other hand the demand is too slight, nothing will happen. Thus it is a delicate procedure requiring delicate handling. In effect, therefore, it is not sufficient just to provide isolated experiences. It is also necessary to provide an entire climate or environment in the context of which this kind of development can safely take place.

What can the company to do provide a suitable environment for personal growth?

(a) How should the chief executive or superior approach the task of development with a particular manager?

(b) What is a 'safe' environment for growth development?

Environment in General

(i) Mr. Lyle.

His profile and an account of how his role was changed appears on page 128. It was considered that he needed first and foremost to have the environment created where his patient, apparently relaxed approach could achieve results equivalent to that attainable by more urgent, obviously attacking approach. The following factors were considered necessary:

- (a) Recognition of his person style; that he is dynamic as a manager even though not obviously aggressive.
- (b) Giving him opportunity formally to make a presentation of his plans and objectives to colleagues in other divisions. (Recognizing his relatively limited *presenting* capacity.)
- (c) Backing him up with conferred status and authority. (Recognizing his lack of emphasis on *confronting*.)
- (d) Listening to his advice on the timing of activities and not attempting to hurry him up. (Trusting to his own strength in *deciding*.)

He was thought to be someone for whom it was worth creating such an environment because realization of his develoment potential could pay handsome dividends to the company. He was exceptional in the degree to which he could appreciate the full scope of company activities and to be in a position to do so was considered itself to be a great fillip to his development.

Much more than with most people the key to his development was seen to lie in the relationship with his Managing Director. It was particularly vital that there should be recognition of his personal qualities. This alone, if communicated, would have far more constructive effort than attendance at any number of management courses.

This is aimed at establishing an environment of recognition. As mentioned earlier, Mr. Lyle had talents which had hardly been recognized. To realize his potential abilities fully, he needed to be given the opportunity, not simply to 'prove' himself in the results sense, but to be appreciated for what he could do according to his own particular style. It was necessary to positively recommend such recognition for Mr. Lyle precisely because his particular style was considerably different from the team style and hence likely to be misunderstood and underrated.

(ii) Mr. Baker.

His action profile is such that he is limited in giving attention, both in *investigating* and *exploring*. He is strongest in intention, particularly *confronting*, very strong in *deciding* but weak in *anticipating*. Overall he is low on *dynamism*. Here is his profile:

The need for protection against undue requirement
for *Investigating, Exploring* and *Dynamism*

		% of total activity	Extent of interaction activity	
ATTENTION	Investigating	8		Communicating
	Exploring	2		
INTENTION	Determining	24		Presenting
	Confronting	29		
COMMITMENT	Deciding	28		Operating
	Anticipating	9		
Dynamism			1·5	
Adaptability			1·0	
Identifying			3·5	

Action Profile 17   MR. BAKER

The basic action profile is relatively weak, particularly in respect to the interaction capacities, and the total energy measure, *dynamism*. Hence to make any kind of worthwhile contribution, he needs to be carefully placed and supported. He is only a self starter under certain special conditions. It was thought that these conditions could be obtained by establishing an environment where there was no sustained pressure upon him to maintain a consistently maintained level of vigour. On the other hand, it had to be a lively environment where people would respond to his forthright application and where he had the skills to ensure that he did not feel himself to be bashing his head against a brick wall.

It was also considered important that the environment should be fairly well known and that he was not concerned with new and untried matters.

He literally needed one person to be constantly available to him as adviser. It should preferably not be a superior but someone only indirectly involved with the work of his department in whose objectivity he had complete reliance.

The idea here is to establish an environment where he is not required to show too much initiative and hence be made vulnerable because of his lack of *dynamism*. It is designed to protect him against his weaknesses in *investigating* and *exploring*, by providing that he should not be precipitated into new and untried situations and should learn skills of information acquiring. On the positive side his strengths in *determining* and *confronting* will cause him to be most effective in a lively straightforward situation.

A large factor in a manager's environment is the people he works with. Sometimes this factor is of prime importance as in the case of Mr. Lyon. His profile is unusual and is shown opposite.

In this case the *identification* factor is important. Although the spread of action motivations is good, and the coverage of the interaction capacities is well above average, there is an underlying weakness in the profile due to the low measure on *dynamism*. This usually indicates that careful placing is needed as in the previous case of Mr. Baker. There are other important factors. Note that the first of each pair of the three action stages; i.e. *investigating, determining, deciding* are all 20 per cent of the total energy distribution; i.e. the assertion side of activity is evenly spread over the three stages.

Such an even spread may at first sight seem highly desirable. However, experience indicates that it has the strange effect of actually reducing activity due to the very balancing factors. Such a person is always in a state of flux from one stage to another. He can never settle on one. He may, for instance, seem *indecisive,* although strictly speaking strong on *deciding,* because as soon as he has implemented a decision he is almost at the very same time giving attention to new information bearing on it, which very likely may cause him to form a new intention—and so on.

An additional factor stems from the intensity of activity going into the perspective getting vs. assertion areas. Although Mr. Lyon is more evenly spread on the assertion side, his total activity is more intense on the perspective side.

This all adds up to the following characteristics:

> 1 He has a great sense for what is appropriate, both as to where he
>   fits in and in respect to company activities. This is exercised to a

The need for a suitable people environment

		% of total activity	Extent of interaction activity	
ATTENTION	Investigating	20		Communi-cating
	Exploring	3		
INTENTION	Determining	20		Presenting
	Confronting	22		
COMMITMENT	Deciding	20		Operating
	Anticipating	15		
Dynamism		1·5		
Adaptability		2·0		
Identifying		3·0		

Action Profile 18   MR. LYON

great extent as an intuitive feel. He will, for example, have a feel for when he has gone far enough in pushing a demand, or in making a concession, or whether or not a thing is worth doing (perspective emphasis).

2 He is himself highly disciplined in backing up this compensatory balancing way of working. Where he feels that something has to be put right or an adjustment has to be made, he will pursue it with *determination* and persistence. In both these respects his application is spontaneous and of an intuitive nature.

Mr. Lyon, in addition to the above, is strong in interaction capacity and *identifying*. He can relate to most people, and can appreciate their approach. Moreover he is ready to become involved and can easily participate in almost any type of activity.

Because he is so ready to fit in with things and particularly people, it is very important that he works with people who will draw the best from him. At the time, he was working as a buyer under a highly determined, almost obstinate, authoritarian works accountant and also accountable to the equally determined executive chairman. Lyon could fit in with these men perfectly well, but only to the detriment of his own contribution. In line with all this the outline for development was in terms of providing a suitable 'people' environment:

> 'He has an inbuilt compensatory mechanism, an instinctive tendency to even out extremes plus a great sense for appropriateness. This can have a cancelling out effect. It means that in a situation where he is exposed to strong but varying personal influences he will take initiative to placate and keep the balance between those influences rather than strike out on his own and take initiative in those areas where he is strongest. Hence the most beneficial situation for his development would be a working liaison with a complementary person, who would not need placating but would rather encourage the type of initiative Mr. Lyon is best suited to take.'

The best arrangement was outlined, which was that Lyon should be responsible to the head of administration services, an unassuming attentive man already in charge of much of the development programme previously set in motion. It was recommended also that Mr. Lyon should work in close collaboration with the management accountant, once again a relatively unassuming and unassertive, but highly perceptive and farsighted person. The interaction attributes overlap well, so an effective group should emerge, with Mr. Lyon especially able to display much greater initiative than before (and this did indeed happen).

The last two managers, Lyon and Baker, could almost be termed 'delicate' particularly in terms of the basic weakness of their action profiles, so they call for fairly careful treatment. This may well sound like a lot of mollycoddling and some may say that an organization cannot afford to carry too many such delicate cases. However, despite some problems in making full use of such people, they certainly can make a considerable contribution.

There are many, of course, who have a much more robust basic profile. Such a person is Mr. Slessor. (Action Profile opposite.)

He has a high level of *dynamism,* the coverage of interaction capacities is reasonably wide and there are no very bad gaps in the assertion areas; i.e. *investigating, determining, deciding,* which do seem to be particularly important in general management. Mr. Slessor was at the time of assessment acting

The need for a challenging environment

		% of total activity	Extent of interaction activity	
ATTENTION	Investigating	18		Communicating
	Exploring	2		
INTENTION	Determining	29		Presenting
	Confronting	19		
COMMITMENT	Deciding	12		Operating
	Anticipating	20		
Dynamism			3·5	
Adaptability			2·0	
Identifying			3·5	

Action Profile 19   MR. SLESSOR

simply as an engineer installing new machinery in a new factory. He had no management experience as such. However, in view of the basic sturdiness of the action profile it seemed worth utilizing him in this capacity, particularly as most of the work in the new factory had been completed. It was suggested that he should be introduced to the job of production manager. This was, of course, only in the context of other carefully worked out changes in the organization.

In view of this, the development advice was:

'Simply to give him a much bigger challenge would be a way of spurring his development. As he offers a great deal, it could well be worth taking a risk in his case.

In responding to a new challenge, he is likely to reveal a tenacious grip over the job and a sort of "hinder me if you dare" attitude. This can cause him not to co-ordinate his activities as fully as might be possible with those of his colleagues and it is in this area that he needs help.

He will gain much from having his activities scrutinized and rigorously criticized where merited. In this way he can be helped to see himself as others see him. He requires particularly to be challenged on his *deciding* ability. He can be *confronted* with errors in timing, scheduling, programming, organizing wherever they occur. He can improve slightly in this area, in a personal growth sense, and a constant challenging on this score may go a long way toward bringing about improvement.'

The recommendations in this case are all geared toward putting the pressure on and creating a challenging situation, utilizing the strongest middle intention area. He is the kind of person who can respond to a rousing challenging situation and will in fact be motivated to the greatest extent by it.

In each case the aim has been to create a 'safe' environment. By this is meant a situation where a man's strengths are being drawn upon and weaknesses not unduly stretched. If the management situation is predominantly invoking those strengths in which the manager has long established confidence, then he will be a confident man. From this base of confidence he can then feel secure enough to venture into newer areas. This may in turn bring about small changes in the action profile itself. Mr. Slessor for instance (see profile page 147) may begin to channel slightly more of his energy into *deciding* and *investigating*.

The thinking behind this view is in line with the theory about the action profile; i.e. that it is a very fundamental and well established part of the personality and any change occurring in the distribution of the components making up the pattern will be slight and felt to be a major experience.

Opposing the view given above, it may be argued that the way to get a person to develop a less apparent action capacity is to put him in a situation where he cannot use his strongest capacities (i.e. they are inappropriate), and so he has to rely on lesser capacities and by doing so enhance them. However, experience with many managers in many situations indicates the following:

● A manager placed in a situation where his established strengths are inappropriate will feel inadequate, insecure and will begin to show signs of tension.
● In situations of inadequacy, insecurity and stress, people rely more and more on long established behaviour patterns even to the

extent of reinforcing them still further; i.e. they do *not* develop weaker areas or rely more on attributes in which they have less confidence. On the contrary they develop the already well developed strengths still further.

Thus it would seem that development inducing situations which draw upon and emphasize weaker areas, can only be short excursions. If the development is to flower, there must be a 'safe' home ground to which the person can always return, where he spends most of his time and where he can re-establish his confidence in exercising the old comfortable strengths while gradually integrating and establishing new areas of strength. This leads to a consideration of more detailed action which the managing director, immediate superiors, and perhaps development officer (if there is one) can do to provide for suitable excursions in order to encourage development.

How should the chief executive or superior approach the task of growth development with a particular manager?

The action profile of Mr. Lever, the office manager (now head of administration) of Fulham Operations Ltd., is on page 150.

In the personal growth sense the intention stage, *determining* and *confronting* are considered undevelopable. They are just not sufficiently evident to form a basis for development. In the commitment stage, both *deciding* and *anticipating* are potentially developable and to the extent that they can grow, the matching interaction capacity, *operating* can also grow in proportion. The 'safe' environment recommended for him was one which would bolster the weak middle intention area:

> 'In his case he is likely to become more highly motivated by it being made clear to him that he is needed and that there is confidence in his being able to take on more responsibility. He will tend to defer unless given such self assurance and it is a prerequisite for the development measures.'

On the basis of this an 'excursion' into the world of *deciding* and *anticipating* was advised:

> 'The increased demands could be systematised to some degree in the sense that his duties can be specified according to a definite programme and clarification of objectives. He is likely to get through more work more effectively the more that he has to cope with pressure of time. It has to be a positive pressure in the sense of some penalty being conferred in event of failure and not simply putting him under a sense of obligation.'

Mr. Child is an efficient production manager. He has a well balanced action profile (page 151), with a high measure on *dynamism* and a very good coverage of the interaction areas. He has one rather unusual feature: a very low

The need for intention back-up to allow
excursions into *Deciding* and *Anticipating*

		% of total activity	Extent of interaction activity
ATTENTION	Investigating	25	
	Exploring	35	
INTENTION	Determining	1	
	Confronting	8	
COMMITMENT	Deciding	15	
	Anticipating	16	
Dynamism			2·0
Adaptability			2·5
Identifying			3·5

Action Profile 20   MR. LEVER

measure on *identifying*. This means he is highly self contained and detached. His manner is such that he is unable to invite spontaneous interaction from other people. He is aloof, not in the sense of being snooty or unfriendly, but simply self contained. He cannot easily participate spontaneously in the activities of others. This is an interesting factor in combination with his strong abilities in interaction. When he does interact with people albeit on a rather formal basis he is highly effective.

The need for a 'private' environment to
allow a general broadening development

		% of total activity	Extent of interaction activity	
ATTENTION	Investigating	20		Communicating
	Exploring	6		
INTENTION	Determining	26		Presenting
	Confronting	24		
COMMITMENT	Deciding	9		Operating
	Anticipating	15		
Dynamism		3·0		
Adaptability		2·0		
Identifying		0·0		

Action Profile 21   MR. CHILD

Primarily with this quality of aloofness in mind, development advice for
Mr. Child was given as follows to the Managing Director.

'Development in his case should be conducted, as it were, privately, so
that he is never made to feel that others are aware that he is exposing
an area of deficiency. This can best be done by a correspondence course
like form of study in management techniques. A number of brief
courses or seminars which have the effect of sparking him to further
reading and study would be the best means. In addition, there should

be opportunity for him to discuss his experience both in attending courses and in his reading, with a sympathetic colleague. This last point is important. He is a man who can gain a great deal from having counsel available. He does not invite it but he needs it.

He is not a man to make excuses or to delude himself on any of his limitations. It is more than ever important to him that he should not fail or be made to appear at a disadvantage. He should not therefore be caused to bite off more than he can chew and he himself is probably the best judge of when he is ready for a bigger responsibility. It is a big component in measures for his development that he should regularly be consulted on what more he could do.'

As can be seen the development advice itself is primarily in terms of knowledge rather than personal growth or change. Mr. Child was considered undevelopable in this respect. He was at this time in a critical stage of re-adjustment. He had just been appointed production manager under Mr. Myer and was coping with a totally new management approach. It was thought therefore that critical gaps in management expertise were the first priority, and these the Managing Director was most capable of diagnosing. It was considered that advice would be of most benefit couched in terms of how the Managing Director should approach the problem of development with Mr. Child. What his attitude should be rather than what exactly he should see the man was trained in.

A much younger man (Mr. Leonard), in the same company and with a fairly similar profile, was treated in some respects similarly, in others quite differently. His profile is opposite.

His greatest strength, *confronting,* causes him to be strongly and straight-forwardly aware of what is required of him. Because however the *determining* factor is considerably less developed, he may not always act upon this clear recognition. In fact due to the fairly low measure on *dynamism* he does not take enough initiative on anything. Hence the basic development need was seen to be the encouragement of greater initiative. The development programme itself was seen as an area where he could take such initiative.

The guidelines given to the Managing Director were that he should rely primarily on his *confronting* strength (the readiness to face up to demands with complete realism and honesty) but to back him up in the *determining* area, by putting him under some pressure to really get to grips with the needs he recognized. In addition, it was advised that he should be encouraged into excursions into the other likely developable areas, *exploring* and *antici-pating* by:

(a) Discovering the prospects for himself and the company and setting his own realistic objectives (*anticipating*).
(b) *Exploring* the means by which he could develop himself in order to achieve those objectives.

Possibility for development excursions
into *Exploring* and *Anticipating*

		% of total activity	Extent of interaction activity	
ATTENTION	Investigating	18		Communicating
	Exploring	13		
INTENTION	Determining	10		Presenting
	Confronting	30		
COMMITMENT	Deciding	12		Operating
	Anticipating	17		
Dynamism		2·0		
Adaptability		1·5		
Identifying		2·5		

Action Profile 22   MR. LEONARD

He is the management accountant in Mr. Myer's company and as he was still young (age 30) it was considered possible for him to develop considerably and perhaps take on a bigger administrative role as well as the strict financial one.

The aspect of development advice described in this section is in order to guide the chief executive or superior not only on what areas can be developed and by what means, but how he should approach the whole question of development with a particular man. What should his attitude be—should he bolster him up and give him extra confidence as in the case of Mr. Lyle, should he take care not to expose his weaknesses publicly and see that he has close personal help as with Mr. Child, or push him into taking his own decisions and organizing himself as advised for Mr. Leonard. The tenor of this kind of advice will vary enormously sometimes from one extreme like applying all the pressure possible, to the opposite of releasing and diminishing every possible source of pressure. Sometimes the differences are much more subtle, but nevertheless just as important.

CHAPTER 12

Educating Managers as to their Action Profiles

Experience has shown that managers are often mistaken or at least unclear as to what strengths are spontaneously available to them. A similar confusion may occur in recognizing where colleagues are particularly strong.

This matters because it can lead to wasted abilities. Such waste can occur in many ways. Managers may actually seek positions for which they are not suited. They may attempt to imitate the 'style' of a senior manager too much unlike themselves. They may fail to exploit their own strengths to the fullest extent. They may also fail to use props, intellectual controls, systems and techniques in areas where they really need them. Not surprisingly, as already mentioned, people are usually more attracted to the techniques or aids which cover areas in which they are already naturally strong.

Within a team, lack of recognition of each other's strengths may result in failure to use complementary abilities to the best advantage. Instead of relying upon a suitable colleague in an area where he is not naturally strong, a manager may actually compete with his stronger colleague or just attempt to rely upon his own depleted abilities.

It is important that managers are clear as to the distinction between spontaneously available strengths and consciously acquired techniques. It is important because they will always be on safer ground with the first than with the second. It is important too in preventing inappropriate development measures. Sometimes a manager, sensing a lack somewhere in his spontaneous motivation, may endeavour to actually 'change' or 'grow' in that area. If it is indeed a real gap in spontaneous motivation there will be no change and his efforts will be wasted.

A manager was studied who was found to be very limited in *confronting*. Sensing this lack, he tried to actually make himself more of a *confronter* by dint of sheer will power. After repeated failure he had at last albeit grudgingly and in some bewilderment to give up. The situation was remedied when it was pointed out to him that this was a lack in spontaneous motivation that could not be changed. He had to approach this problem, not by attempting to change himself, but by using other people's strengths in this area, or by initiating props of various kinds for himself. With this approach he has had some success.

The education of managers as to their own and colleagues' Action Profiles although important can be a considerable task. It requires quite a comprehensive education.

This education can be approached in various ways. It can be given by the means of one or a combination of the following:

    (i) Individual counselling sessions
    (ii) Individual courses
    (iii) Group courses and meetings
    (iv) Seminars and teach-ins on the Action Profile concepts.

COUNSELLING

The counselling session involves a verbal exposé by the consultant of the manager's action profile and discussion as to the implications thereof in terms of development, career opportunity and present achievements and difficulties.

The first stage in the counselling session is to describe the framework of management activities. It is important that the definitions are made as clear as possible and plenty of practical examples are given, before any reference is made to the person's own pattern. It is necessary to pay particular attention to those areas which are least evident in the manager's profile as not surprisingly most misinterpretation occurs in these areas. Depending upon past experience, background, upbringing and so on, the misinterpretation is basically of two different kinds.

1 The person feels that he is in fact strong in this area because he is very aware of a constant effort to overcome the limitation. This is often the case where the manager has been in a situation where his lacking motivation has been much required, or where in the course of his upbringing it has been required as a socially desirable motivation. *Determining,* particularly in its aspects of self discipline, often falls into this category. This is something which in our society is often particularly desired of children, hence a lack will be early felt. Other motivations such as *anticipating* are rarely a first priority requirement. How often is a child told he must look ahead more; be more farsighted? Hence a lack here is unlikely to be consciously recognized until required by another environment or unless it is pointed out. Then it can be related to experience and will fall into place.

It was mentioned above that a person lacking a required motivation is often conscious of an effort to provide that motivation. In addition he may often consciously provide himself with controls, systems and techniques of one kind and another to act as a kind of stop gap. This, of course, may be confused with a natural strength in the area. A well informed and sophisticated executive, for instance, who is lacking in a spontaneous motivation toward *anticipating* will undoubtedly provide himself with all the techniques of forward planning available to the manager. It is necessary to point out that although this is an essential precaution to take, it is still only making the best of a bad job. Under the pressure of day to day events, despite his brilliant 5-year strategic plan he will still be caught on the hop due to lack of *anticipation*. So it is necessary that this lack in internal motivation is recognized. The best way to remedy it is, of course, to introduce a few strong *anticipators* into his team.

2 A person may have an intuitive awareness or feeling only for those aspects which are strong in his own profile. For a manager strong in *anticipating* but weak in *deciding*, for instance, a description of *anticipation* may immediately strike a chord. He has immediate experience of how it feels to be constantly *anticipatory*. However, the description of *deciding* will be an academic procedure for him and will provoke only an intellectual response. He knows what is meant by 'decision making'. It is very common in management jargon. He knows he has to make decisions and he knows that eventually he does. He is unlikely to appreciate at first, however, the fact that some people have an inbuilt sense for the timing of decisions, that they probably achieve more by their sensitivity to the 'right' moment than by forcing a decision because they know it is their duty.

It often seems to be exceedingly difficult for managers at first to feel a real 'empathy' for or understanding of those motivations which do not occur strongly in their own pattern. Sometimes it is even difficult to gain intellectual acceptance from them of the fact that as good or better results can be achieved by a completely different way of working.

Emotional breakdown as a result of this exercise in self awareness

The method used to present the profile revelation is so designed precisely to eliminate this danger.

1 As mentioned above, the individual profile is only discussed in context with the whole system.
2 The information is presented in the form of an integrated pattern, not just a bald list of good points and bad points.
3 No limitation is picked out in isolation. It is always seen in balance with its complementing strengths.
4 Nothing is seen as ultimately good or bad, only suitable or unsuitable for a particular situation.

5 The profile is always discussed with reference to the man's present job and the demands being made of him, the company situation and future prospects for the man within the company.
6 The emphasis is always constructive. Ways are explored in which existing strengths can be utilized more and for ways in which props can be provided for weaker areas. Advice is given on the kinds of positions which are seen as being suited to the particular manager's action profile and likely areas suggested into which he could profitably move.

Measures against the possibility of emotional upset occurring then are built into the procedure. It can be claimed that they have worked. To our knowledge there just haven't been any instances of emotional breakdown occurring as a result of this kind of personal revelation.

Benefits deriving from the counselling session

Further positive benefits which accrue as a result of the counselling session are:

1 To a certain extent it provides a new frame of reference into which the day to day activities of management can be fitted. Just the first six action requirements; i.e.

Investigating and *Exploring*   = Attention
Disciplining and *Confronting* = Intention
Deciding and *Anticipating*   = Commitment

provide a useful working checklist. If management is to function effectively all six have to be activated. In the general day to day run of getting things done, the left hand three are of prime importance. They must all be carried out however for any one project or course of action, if not all by one person, at least by someone. Only the first step can be achieved in the counselling session, however, toward conveying a full and workable understanding of this frame of reference.
2 The revealed action profile provides a useful framework against which the manager can compare his experience. It can clarify the somewhat dim awareness he already has of the precise nature of his strengths and weaknesses and how they operate. It can provide a rational explanation for puzzling failures, and feelings of discomfort in certain jobs or aspects of a job.
3 It can give confidence in strong areas. Often a person is found to be strong in an area which he hasn't been called upon to exercise fully. This can give him the confidence to seek greater activity in this area.

4 It can rationalize his fear of certain aspects of his work and give him confidence and support in his natural desire to avoid too much concentration in those aspects.
5 It can give him a definite guide as to what types of work he should seek and what types he should avoid.

The last stage of the counselling session is to advise on development. This too is based on the action profile and very precisely moulded toward individual needs.

The nature of development advice given in counselling sessions.

Not all the development advice can be given to the manager during counselling. There is a limit to what the individual can absorb in one session. Normally just two or three key points are given.

The distinction between the two different kinds of development is clarified in terms of the manager's own strengths and limitations.

1 Where and how he can promote his own personal growth.
2 What he can do in terms of controls and techniques to back up areas of weakness.

How is a development area defined?

According to the action profile, an attribute is defined as developable in the growth sense:

1 If the attribute is already sufficiently evident to provide at least a basis for development.
2 If there is room for movement (i.e. it is not too close in extent to the next strongest component).

If personal growth is considered possible, for instance in *deciding,* then this is conveyed to the individual concerned in the counselling session. The whole concept of *deciding* will be explained to him and perhaps a course of action enabling greater utilization of this ability mapped out for him. It is always stressed that the change of necessity must be relatively small, but that a small change can be very significant, and can 'feel' like an enormous difference in the man's approach. An example of this is a man who was considerably lacking in the *confronting* attribute. He now boasts proudly that he positively gets a kick out of *confronting*. He loves to face up to people and situations. However, by anyone's standards he still can hardly be rated as a *confronter,* particularly compared to people predominant in this area: but he feels the difference to be enormous. It is certainly significant in that he doesn't carry his lack of *confrontation* or evasiveness to the extreme of cancelling appointments, and not turning up at difficult meetings, as he used to do.

Secondly, in the counselling sessions, those areas where growth development looks difficult are pointed out. The approach here is to discuss with the man ways and means of establishing controls to cope with these weaker areas. A man who is very weak and undevelopable in *investigating* for instance will be asked to think up ways of providing himself with information, systems, ways of seeing that he is always fed with sufficient information. He may be encouraged to utilize another person's strengths in this area if this is possible.

In every case the development advice given is tied very closely to the particular needs of any one individual. Sometimes a straightforward gap in a particular area of expertise or knowledge is noted and advice given to rectify it. For the most part, however, the development is geared toward enhancement of the motivational strengths already evident and protection against incorrigible limitations.

Perhaps the impression has been given, until now, that full acceptance of the action profile is always obtained. The number of times some disagreement occurs would be in the region of 1 in 100. In some cases insecurity is evident to a high degree. One such case was the Company Secretary of a company. He admitted that his 'face did not fit' with the Managing Director and we had already received the same information from the Managing Director. Another case has already been mentioned (page 126). Mr. Laver was a works manager —a job more associated with the commitment, *deciding-anticipating* end of the action process. Laver had the opposite profile, being strongly motivated at the attention end of the sequence. If you remember, he insisted that he was just as strong in *deciding* and *anticipating* and remarked openly that he had read Warren Lamb's book[21] and had assessed himself as adequate in the commitment area for his job. The contrary action profile findings gained wholehearted concurrence from the Works Director who agreed that this man should be moved into a far more suitable 'advisory' type of role.

In such cases great pains are taken to present the positive side of this approach. However, where the fear and insecurity is already so entrenched it can be difficult to alleviate it completely.

In other cases, disagreement may arise due to a mistake in observation. The counselling session gives an opportunity for checking observation, so differences of opinion can be ironed out in consultation.

INDIVIDUAL COURSES

An individual course is usually considered most relevant for a manager who has particular problems. Such a course will essentially be an extension of the counselling session. A much more thorough and intensified education will be given in the action profile concepts and concerning the manager's own action profile. Specific problems will be dealt with in these terms and specific development procedures mapped out in detail.

An individual course of a slightly different nature might be given to the personnel manager, or someone suitable (according to the action profile of course) to enable them to incorporate the action profile material into their current appraisal, development or manpower planning schemes.

A development only now being explored is to train such a man to interpret the bare action profiles himself, thus enabling a more first hand knowledge of company factors to be applied to the interpretation.

This is done via group meetings and courses. The aim here is to educate a group of managers, by various means, up to a point where there can be open discussion of each other's action profiles. The purpose of this is to achieve a more comprehensive co-operation between members of the team based on:

1 Knowledge of each other's way of working or 'action profile'.
2 Recognition of each other's individual strengths and how they complement one another.
3 Recognition of team strengths and weaknesses.
4 Recognition of patterns of interaction.

To date, this is the most sophisticated application of the action profile material. Several small group discussions have taken place (of two or three senior managers) but as yet only three where a whole senior management team (ten managers in one instance) was concerned. Both were conducted very successfully and usefully. A five-day group training course has as yet only been attempted once, and two-day courses twice, but with considerable achievement which gives promise for this type of application.

THE GROUP COURSE

Here is an account of a group course from the point of view of its educational function in creating awareness under the first three headings, viz: knowledge of others' way of working or action profile, recognition of others' strengths and how they can complement each other, and recognition of team strengths and weaknesses. The objectives of the course were as follows:

1 To give each manager practical experience of how his action profile affects his behaviour, individually and in group interaction.
2 To give managers experience of how personal styles interact. To show that each different style has its particular contribution.
3 To show that the optimum combination of personal styles may vary according to the object of the task, meeting or assignment. For example, if the task is primarily one of investigation it would be best to have people strong in *investigating* working on it.
4 Practice in evaluating tasks in terms of the 12 action requirement

F

categories. For example, is the task primarily one of *exploring, determining, anticipating . . .?*

5 On the basis of 1 and 2, to enable each manager to formulate his own development programme.

The method of achieving these aims was:

1 To enable each executive to discover for himself the effects of his action style both from the point of view of getting a certain task done and in terms of his own particular contribution within the group and that of his colleagues.

2 To give each executive evidence of his behaviour during each session in such a concrete form that he can use this as a basis for planning a more constructive use of his own strengths and in particular greater and more appropriate exploitation of his colleagues' strengths.

The concrete evidence of behaviour was given in the form of a replay of a videotaped recording of the previous session, and a detailed analysis thereof. By the end of the first few days, the managers were able to make a realistic attempt at the analysis of their own contribution and that of other people in terms of the action profile categories. Warren Lamb, the author and an associate performed a group task for them and they analysed it with a fair degree of accuracy (a bit too accurate!).

Sessions or tasks were designed according to the three stage sequence of action.

1. *The Giving of Attention*

An exercise was used to draw upon the *investigatory* and *exploratory* capacities within the group. It is known as the 'safe saw' problem.* The group is asked to pretend that it has been employed by a manufacturer of circular saw blades. Their task is to make the blade safe enough for a ten year old child to use, within a cost increase limit of 25 per cent. This problem requires primarily an *exploratory* approach, backed up by *investigation*. Precipitate intrusion of the other activities, especially *deciding* and *anticipating*, is likely to result in rejection of ideas which otherwise could be built on in order to gain a workable solution.

The action profiles of the group are shown opposite.

As can be seen, Tearney is the strongest in *exploring* (25 per cent), Docker (20 per cent) is also strong. Next is Lawson (with 10 per cent). In *investigation* Bailey (21 per cent) is the strongest, Shelley next strongest (15 per cent) and Lawson and Tearney both have 10 per cent.

It was predicted before the exercise was carried out that it would be

---

* Permission to use this exercise has kindly been granted by the copyright owners: Synectics Inc. of Cambridge, Massachusetts.

Key	Docker % of total activity	Docker Inter-action	Bailey % of total activity	Bailey Inter-action	Lawson % of total activity	Lawson Inter-action	Tearney % of total activity	Tearney Inter-action	Shelley % of total activity	Shelley Inter-action
ATTENTION										
1 Investigating	5		21		10		10		15	
2 Exploring	20		8		10		25		5	
7 Communicating										
INTENTION										
3 Determining	25		22		10		25		30	
8 Presenting										
4 Confronting	10		5		25		5		25	
COMMITMENT										
5 Deciding	15		23		25		15		10	
9 Operating										
6 Anticipating	25		21		20		20		15	
10 Dynamism	3·5		3·5		3·5		3·5		3·0	
11 Adaptability	2·0		0·5		0·5		2·0		1·0	
12 Identification	3·5		3·0		3·5		3·9		0·0	

Action Profile 23 GROUP COURSE TEAM

Tearney who would lead the way to the solution. But it was thought that in such a commitment orientated group he would have considerable difficulty in keeping the group to pure exploration of ideas.

It was considered that the most opposition might come from Docker, Bailey or Lawson due to their strong *deciding* and *anticipating* motivations.

The first prediction was in fact borne out. Tearney did come up with the seed of an idea which eventually led toward a solution. It was fortunate, too, that he is also highly *determined* (25 per cent) because he had to bring the group back to basic *exploration* time after time—ten times in fact in the space of three quarters of an hour.

The problem clearly states that it is a blade modification that is required, which calls for *exploration* into the basic design of a circular saw blade, and questioning of such fundamental assumptions as that: If a blade cuts wood it must cut flesh. In order to cut wood a blade has to be metal, round and with teeth.

The 'commitment' weighted managers were not prepared to question these assumptions and so were inclined to ignore the possibility of modifying the blade and go for various alterations to the whole saw (which they saw as more immediately practicable)—guards and safety switches of one kind and another. Tearney constantly pointed out that this wasn't the problem and drew them back to the questioning of fundamental assumptions again.

A detailed analysis of the contribution of each manager according to the first six action requirements is on pages 166 and 167.

As the total contribution of each manager varied quite considerably, the analysis was made from two points of view:

1 For each individual what percentage of his total contribution was contained in each of the six action requirements. (Table 6)
2 For the group, what percentage of the total activity under each action category was contributed by each manager. (Table 7)

From a theoretical point of view the first question one has in mind in performing an analysis like this is:

● Do people contribute to a task (over a relatively short period of time in this instance ¾ hour) in the exact proportion, as indicated by the 'action profile'?

The analysis (Table 6) says no. Bailey, for instance, who according to the 'action profile' puts 25 per cent of his application into the *deciding* category, during this exercise applied 0 per cent of his energy in this way. Shelley, who according to the action profile concentrates 30 per cent and 25 per cent into *determining* and *confronting,* showed signs in this exercise of only 11 per cent and 23 per cent respectively.

Docker on the other hand has shown a distribution fairly similar to the action profile distribution. And surprisingly, although he is the second strongest in *exploring*, it was he who gave Tearney most opposition in his search for the solution, due to his even stronger motivation toward *deciding* and *anticipating*.

The second question to be considered is:

- Can people, for a limited period, restrain their contribution in situations where they recognize that their own spontaneous strengths are not really appropriate?

As Table 6 shows, the answer is yes. Shelley is a case in point. Because it was an *investigatory-exploratory* oriented task, Shelley restricted his own contribution primarily to *investigation* (33 per cent) and *exploration* (33 per cent) (with a little *confronting* (23 per cent) and *determining* (11 per cent), his strongest areas normally, creeping in). As a percentage of the total group activity in these areas, however (Table 7), his contribution is fairly small, *investigating* only (10 per cent) and *exploring* only (15 per cent). He has therefore been most successful in restraining himself from making an inappropriate contribution even to the extent of limiting his total contribution. Perhaps it is significant that he is by far the eldest and most experienced manager in the group.

Docker on the other hand, the youngest and least experienced manager, has been least successful in restraining himself from making inappropriate contributions. Of the total group activity in *determining, deciding* and *anticipating* (in all of which Docker is strong) he supplied respectively 50 per cent, 50 per cent and 45 per cent. He contributed no *confronting* but then he is very low on *confronting*.

The next question to ask is:

- What did the managers gain in terms of learning to recognize their own and their colleagues' strengths according to the action profiles?

After playback and analysis of the video recording, they were able to recognize the predominant emphasis in type of contribution made by themselves and their colleagues.

Docker: Was recognized to contribute considerable *exploring* (20 per cent of group activity) but to have almost destroyed his own ideas by a precipitate swing to the later stages of activity, in particular *deciding* (50 per cent) and *anticipating* (25 per cent). He was all too ready to *anticipate* how even his own wilder *explorations,* and those of Tearney, would not work.

Bailey: Was seen to contribute (for him) an enormous amount of *investigating* (70 per cent of his own contribution and 25 per cent of the group contribution). This was considered unusual for him and attributed to the general weakness of the group in *investigating*.

Analysis of Contribution to Safe Saw Problem

	Docker		Bailey		Lawson		Tearney		Shelley	
	No. of contributions	% of Individual contribution	No. of contributions	% of Individual contribution	No. of contributions	% of Individual contribution	No. of contributions	% of Individual contribution	No. of contributions	% of Individual contribution
Investigating	7	22%	9	69%	9	25%	7	29%	3	33%
Exploring	4	13%	1	8%	4	11%	8	33%	3	33%
Determining	7	22%	0	0%	0	0%	6	25%	1	11%
Confronting	0	0%	1	7%	13	33%	1	4%	2	23%
Deciding	5	16%	0	0%	5	14%	0	0%	0	0%
Anticipating	8	27%	2	16%	6	17%	2	9%	0	0%
Total individual contribution	31	100%	13	100%	36	100%	24	100%	9	100%

Table 6. % of total individual contribution contained in each of the six categories

Analysis of Contribution to Safe Saw Problem

	Docker		Bailey		Lawson		Tearney		Shelley		Total group contributions	
	No. of contri-butions	% of group contri-bution	No. of contri-butions	% of group contri-bution	No. of contri-butions	% of group contri-bution	No. of contri-butions	% of group contri-bution	No. of contri-butions	% of group contri-bution		
Investigating	7	20%	9	25%	9	25%	7	20%	3	10%	35	100%
Exploring	4	20%	1	5%	4	20%	8	40%	3	15%	20	100%
Determining	7	50%	0	0%	0	0%	6	43%	1	7%	14	100%
Confronting	0	0%	1	6%	12	75%	1	6%	2	13%	16	100%
Deciding	5	50%	0	0%	5	50%	0	0%	0	0%	10	100%
Anticipating	8	45%	2	11%	6	33%	2	11%	0	0%	18	100%

Table 7. % of total group contribution in each category, contributed by each manager

Lawson: Was seen to contribute a great deal of *confronting, deciding* and *anticipating* (75 per cent, 50 per cent and 33 per cent of group activities) but in a way that was not obstructive to Tearney's *explorations*. Although he tended to 'jump the gun' and was very ready to start organizing the manufacture of guards, etc.—he responded sensitively to Tearney's insistence on further *exploration*. When Tearney finally got his *exploration* to an almost workable stage (a suggestion for a particular type of blade design) Lawson seized on it and helped to work it through to a workable solution.

Tearney: Was seen to be the 'star' of this exercise. His broad *exploratory* appreciation and *determination* to keep at it stood out remarkably.

Shelley: Recognized for his attempts at constructive co-operation in terms of his readiness to contribute predominantly in terms of *investigating* and *exploring* even though this meant that in total his contribution was small.

The next exercise was simulated in order to require behaviour predominantly of an Intention, *determining* and *confronting* nature. Each manager was required to 'persuade' a colleague into something which he knew would draw opposition from the colleague.

The third exercise was simulated in order to require mostly Commitment, *deciding* and *anticipating* behaviour. They were told that in two hours the group Managing Director was to sign their company over to a disliked competitor. They had 20 minutes in which to make their plan of action.

In each case the video recording was played back and an analysis made as for the safe saw problem. The total distribution of contribution after the three exercises is shown on pages 170 and 171.

● What the managers learnt:

1 That over a series of exercises, covering attention, intention and commitment oriented activities, although each exercise was short (no more than ¾ hour; often less) that the action profile pattern became fairly well evident in the behaviour of each manager.

   In particular it was interesting to note that in relation to the total group activity within a particular area, those areas where an individual manager was predominant in contribution corresponded very closely to predominances in the action profiles (see page 163).

   (i) Shelley and Bailey are the strongest in *investigating* (15 per cent and 21 per cent versus 5 per cent, 10 per cent and 10 per cent) and they contributed the most *investigating* during the exercises (22 per cent and 22 per cent versus 20 per cent, 20 per cent, 6 per cent).

   (ii) Tearney is by far the most *exploratory* (25 per cent versus 20 per cent, 8 per cent, 10 per cent and 5 per cent) and he contributed 56 per cent versus 12 per cent, 4 per cent, 16 per cent and 12 per cent of the total *exploration*.

(iii) Tearney, Shelley and Docker are strongest in *determining* (25 per cent, 30 per cent, 25 per cent versus 22 per cent and 10 per cent) and they contributed most of the group *determining* (35 per cent, 29 per cent and 25 per cent versus 9 per cent and 2 per cent).

(iv) Lawson and Shelley are the strongest *confronters* (25 per cent and 25 per cent versus 10 per cent, 5 per cent and 5 per cent) and they contributed by far the most *confronting* during the exercises (52 per cent and 39 per cent versus 6 per cent, 3 per cent and 0 per cent).

(v) Docker, Bailey, Lawson and Tearney are all strong in *deciding*. Docker and Lawson contributed strongly to the group in *deciding* (34 per cent and 37 per cent) but Bailey and Tearney not so strongly (17 per cent and 8 per cent).

This could have been because all the exercises were of relatively short duration (no more than 35 minutes). Bailey and Tearney may have been overshadowed in each situation in *deciding* motivation whilst sensitive to the need for compensating activity in other areas.

(vi) Docker is the strongest in *anticipating* (25 per cent versus 21 per cent, 20 per cent, 20 per cent and 15 per cent) by a small margin and he contributed by far the most in this area (52 per cent versus 11 per cent, 33 per cent, 4 per cent and 0 per cent).

2 The managers came to recognize clearly how their colleagues contributed to various situations.

3 They learnt that each kind of contribution was more or less applicable to a certain type of situation or task, e.g.:

(i) Tearney was clearly the star of the *exploratory-communicating* creative problem solving task. Without him the group would not have arrived at an acceptable solution. He performed adequately during the *determining-confronting* exercise and played a subsidiary but useful role in the *deciding-anticipating* exercise.

(ii) Shelley was obviously more suited to the *determining-confronting* situation.

His 'aloofness' was recognized (score on *identification* of 0·0) and this recognition enabled the other managers to cope better with the impression of detachment that he conveyed.

(iii) Lawson was seen to be highly effective in the *deciding-anticipating* situation. His strong *confronting* was recognized as having a beneficial clarifying effect in certain situations.

Analysis of contribution to three exercises: Attention, Intention and Commitment oriented

	Docker		Bailey		Lawson		Tearney		Shelley	
	No. of contri-butions	% of Individual contri-bution	No. of contri-butions	% of Individual contri-bution	No. of contri-butions	% of Individual contri-bution	No. of contri-butions	% of Individual contri-bution	No. of contri-butions	% of Individual contri-bution
Investigating	13	13%	14	32%	13	15%	11	14%	14	20%
Exploring	6	6%	2	4%	7	9%	27	35%	6	8%
Determining	21	21%	8	17%	1	2%	29	38%	24	36%
Confronting	2	2%	1	2%	20	22%	0	0%	15	32%
Deciding	28	29%	14	32%	30	33%	7	9%	2	4%
Anticipating	28	29%	6	13%	17	19%	2	4%	0	0%
Total individual contribution	98	100%	45	100%	88	100%	76	100%	61	100%

Table 8. % of total individual contribution contained in each of the six categories

Analysis of Contribution to three exercises: Attention, Intention and Commitment oriented

	Docker		Bailey		Lawson		Tearney		Shelley		Total group contribution	
	No. of contributions	% of group contribution	No. of contributions	% of group contribution	No. of contributions	% of group contribution	No. of contributions	% of group contribution	No. of contributions	% of group contribution		
Investigating	13	20%	14	22%	13	20%	11	16%	14	22%	65	100%
Exploring	6	12%	2	4%	7	16%	27	56%	6	12%	48	100%
Determining	21	25%	8	9%	1	2%	29	35%	24	29%	83	100%
Confronting	2	6%	1	3%	20	52%	0	0%	15	39%	38	100%
Deciding	28	34%	14	17%	30	37%	7	8%	2	4%	81	100%
Anticipating	28	52%	6	11%	17	33%	2	4%	0	0%	53	100%

Table 9. % of total group contribution in each category, contributed by each manager

(iv) Docker—was seen to be a little confused. It became obvious where his strengths lay but he seemed not to have the capacity of applying them appropriately.

(v) Bailey—was recognized as supplying mainly the missing *investigatory* motivation. The 'intensity' of his assertion motivation (*investigating* 21 per cent *determining* 22 per cent, *deciding* 23 per cent) was recognized and its effects discussed. He was finally able to accept almost a complete lack in *confronting*.

4 At the end of the course the managers were able to state:

(i) Where they themselves were spontaneously strongest and weakest.

(ii) Where their colleagues were strongest and weakest.

(iii) Where they could develop in the growth sense.

(iv) Where they needed to use props (and what props) or the complementary strengths of colleagues (and what colleagues).

EXERCISES IN GROUP COMPOSITION

The next exercises concerned groupings according to similarities in style.

1 'Commitment' group:
Bailey (total 45 per cent in commitment area)
Lawson (total 45 per cent in commitment area)
Docker (total 40 per cent in commitment area)
2 'Attention-Intention' group:
Shelley (total 20 per cent of attention, 55 per cent intention)
Tearney (total 35 per cent of attention, 30 per cent intention)

They were each given the same topic to discuss:– To define marketing and suggest ways in which marketing management in their own company could be improved.

What the managers learnt

That a predominant weighting in a group toward a particular area of motivation is very powerful. The emphasized motivation will be expressed regardless of the nature of the task.

The above topic fairly obviously required predominant attention, and perhaps a little intention activity, stemming from the second half of the question.

It was interesting to see that the groups even *defined* the nature of the task after performing it, according to their predominant group motivation.

1 The 'commitment' group saw the task as requiring:
Most attention ⟶ through intention ⟶ to commitment.

2 The 'attention-intention' group saw it as requiring:
Most attention and some intention.

The actual performance when analysed bore out these interpretations. The 'commitment' group arrived at a precise definition (via Bailey the *investigator*) very rapidly and then moved on to work out ways and means of actually implementing workable improvements, using the definition as an anchor point.

The 'attention-intention' group spent about three quarters of the time in discussing the definition of marketing, and *exploring* the implications of same. A general idea was arrived at, as to how the marketing management could be improved. It was an idea much better founded in principle than the first group's ideas. Contrary to the first group they made no attempt to work out any details of implementation.

What the managers learnt

That groups can be arranged according to action profile information, so that the predominant motivation suits the task.

Exercises in analysis of situation, problems, tasks, etc., according to action requirements

This was done specifically via studies, and incidentally throughout the other exercises. It became obvious that managers have to bear in mind their own pattern as an influence even upon original analysis of the requirements of a situation.

CHAPTER 13

Educating Managers on
Patterns of Interaction

This too was a product of the group course, but it is a more complex subject and requires additional introduction.

UNSTRUCTURED VERSUS STRUCTURED INTERACTION SITUATIONS

An unstructured interaction situation is defined as: A situation where the process of interaction is free from any kind of formalization, in the way of accepted rules or procedure.

A structured interaction is defined as: A situation where the process of interaction is governed by accepted rules or procedure.

A chance meeting of colleagues in the corridor, which turns into a discussion will be an unstructured interaction, whereas a debate is a highly structured interaction. In the unstructured situation, the participants are free to create their own interaction 'climate' be it predominantly *communicating, presenting* or *operating,* or a mixture of both, according to their own pattern. In the structured situation, however, the interaction 'climate' has already been created. A debate, for instance, presupposes a *presentational* mode of interaction and the rules are there to keep it so. A consultation between patient and doctor in his professional capacity presupposes a *communicational* climate, though this is less rigidly structured than a debate situation.

It is fairly obvious and has been found to be the case, that the spontaneous interaction abilities are expressed most clearly in unstructured situations. In fact the natural ability is often hampered by the imposition of the 'rules' of the corresponding structured situation, but this is not necessarily so.

A structured situation will provide the appropriate interaction climate for a person who is weak in a particular mode of interaction and a lack in natural interaction ability can be substantially overcome if there is opportunity for the situation to be appropriately structured.

The revelation of individual interaction styles and group patterns of interaction was designed with the following objectives in mind:

1 To show the function and importance of interaction modes.
2 To show what can be done to provide against a gap in interaction ability.
3 To show that the effectiveness of an interaction mode varies according to the requirements of the situation.

The three exercises previously mentioned as attention, intention and commitment oriented were also (unavoidably as they were group exercises) *communicating, presenting* and *operating* oriented. There were in addition three more exercises of a different nature, but also respectively *communicating, presenting* and *operating* oriented.

The three exercises already described were primarily of an 'unstructured' nature whereas the additional ones were primarily 'structured'. The exercises were defined as follows:

Analysis of each manager's contribution during the unstructured situations is shown below:

Exercises in Interaction for Group Course

	Structured	Unstructured
Communicating	Synectics* session: A structured procedure for promoting creative problem solving. Rules are designed to prevent loss or destruction of ideas no matter how wild, and to allow constructive building on likely ideas.	'Safe-saw' problem. Questioning of basic assumptions and building upon and preservation of ideas no matter how wild and unlikely required.
Presenting	Debate with two teams, each presenting a case.	'Persuading' exercise. Strong presentation of a clear issue required.
Operating	Mbo procedure; necessitating one manager to extract objectives, programme, control, etc., from colleagues.	'Take over' situation—a plan of action required.

Table 10

* Synectics Inc. the founder organization of this technique is situated in Cambridge, Massachusetts. The English counterpart is ABRAXAS, New Malden, London.

Table 11 shows that over the three situations, the distribution of actual behaviour bore a close resemblance to the distribution shown in the action profiles (page 163).

Analysis of contribution to three unstructured situations in terms of the three interaction modes

	Docker		Bailey		Lawson		Tearney		Shelley	
	No. of contributions	% of Individual contribution	No. of contributions	% of Individual contribution	No. of contributions	% of Individual contribution	No. of contributions	% of Individual contribution	No. of contributions	% of Individual contribution
Communicating	22	62%	10	58%	2	10%	32	60%	20	36%
Presenting	3	8%	0	0%	0	0%	21	40%	21	38%
Operating	11	30%	7	42%	19	90%	0	0%	15	26%
Total individual contribution	36	100%	17	100%	21	100%	53	100%	56	100%

Table 11. % of individual contribution contained in each of the three interaction categories

Analysis of contribution to three structured situations in terms of the three interaction modes

	Docker		Bailey		Lawson		Tearney		Shelley		Total group contribution	
	No. of contributions	% of group contributions	No. of contributions	% of group contributions	No. of contributions	% of group contributions	No. of contributions	% of group contributions	No. of contributions	% of group contributions		
Communicating	22	25%	10	12%	2	3%	32	37%	20	23%	86	100%
Presenting	3	8%	0	0%	0	0%	21	46%	21	46%	45	100%
Operating	11	21%	7	13%	19	36%	0	0%	15	30%	52	100%

Table 12. % of group activity contributed by each individual in each of the three interaction categories

What the managers learnt

1 From the analysis they learnt more about the nature of the interactive modes, and came to recognize more clearly the effects of their own interaction pattern. Lawson, for instance, who was at first puzzled by being told that he was not a *communicator*, had this made patently obvious to him. It happened time and time again that after a statement of his, there would ensue for a few moments dead silence from everyone else. He pronounced his opinions or suggestions so positively and with such an air of commitment that he simply did not invite *communicative* participation from others. It was very clearly just as if he was 'reporting' the results of his own private *investigation* and *exploration*.

2 From experience with the structured situation, they learnt how they could use this method as an aid in areas where the spontaneous interaction ability was weak. It was seen for instance that whilst the weak *presenters* performed rather inefficiently during the unstructured 'persuading' exercise they were able to make clear concise *presentations* during the structured debate exercise.

   Lawson has already reported using the 'Synectics' technique where he saw the need for a *communicational* climate. He was able to gain (for him) a previously unheard of level of participation and co-operation from a group of women workers, by using the Synectics technique to involve them in solving problems within their own department.

3 The managers were able to see that a particular interaction mode was more or less appropriate according to the nature of the situation. In the 'safe-saw' problem, for instance, it became very apparent that it was Tearney's ability to promote a *communicative* climate which enabled the solution to emerge.

The 'safe-saw' problem described earlier (page 162) has provided the basis for the study of group interaction within hundreds of groups. It has been used to show how difficult it is for a random mixed group of people, without direction or control to find the solution to a problem involving original creative thinking. In 90 per cent of cases the solution is lost, not because the ideas aren't there but because they are rejected or destroyed in the normal processes of group interaction. In most cases the seed of the solution is suggested at least by someone. By this is meant that someone suggests a half formed idea which if worked on constructively could lead the group to the solution. In one out of ten groups, however, such embryo ideas are ignored, laughed out of court or crushed in some other way.

To tie this in with the three stage division of interaction modes the interactive process required for this type of exercise is *communicating*. If a group is made up solely by *communicators*, a climate is set up whereby every idea is fostered, built on and stored if found unsatisfactory. It is only when the later stages of intention and commitment, in the form of *presenting* and *operating* intervene, that ideas are rejected, ignored and lost.

A *presenter*, for instance, in such a group, is motivated primarily to express intention. He wants to get to grips with something and feel that something concrete is happening. Hence he will reject ideas which at first sight appear inappropriate, and seize upon the first one that looks immediately possible. He will then declare his preference and proceed to fight for it. This will obviously cause conflict of one kind or another and severely disrupt the creative process.

An *operator* on the other hand will be constantly looking for something to implement. He will seize on other people's ideas if they look good but predominantly with a view to *anticipating* the result. Any really new idea is therefore likely to be rejected as the *operator* can only *anticipate* on the basis of present experience and he is thus more likely to bring up difficulties than advantages. Again this is a distraction from the basic creative process. The beginning of a new idea is always pretty unlikely and any precipitate *anticipation* of results will invariably invalidate it in its infant form.

This is an oversimplified analysis for as stated before, you cannot divide people into just three categories. A person's interaction pattern is always some mixtures of the three styles, with varying weightings in the components.

In speaking of the intrusion of *presenters* and *operators*, is meant the intrusion of these tendencies within individuals and their predominance over the other interaction modes.

To go back to the five managers, the action profile chart (page 163) shows that there is a considerable readiness to establish a *communicational* climate, a little intrusion of the *presentational* mode, but a heavy weighting on the *operational* mode. Significantly the strongest *communicator*, Tearney, is completely lacking in *operating*. Thus he was able to maintain consistently a *communicational* mode of interaction within the group, even throughout many attempts to move onto a more *operational* orientation.

Some extracts from a typescript of the interaction will show this more clearly.

1 A discussion of various mechanical devices, guards, safety switches, etc., has been going on for a period and Tearney attempts to bring them back to the problem as it was given:

Tearney: The only thing we've been paid to do as a group from the blade manufacturer, is to make that blade and that's it.
    (He is bringing the group back to give more attention to the original task.)

Lawson: The thing is that we've gone beyond that. We've assumed that we can't make a blade.

Shelley: O.K. You've bought us back Ted (Tearney) and that's good. Is it feasible to manufacture a blade?

Docker: Let's consider it straight and square. If it cuts wood it cuts flesh (said with determined finality).

(He is expressing disbelief that re-attention to the original question will do any good as well as the desire to get onto a more immediately practicable solution.)

Tearney: O.K. That's a statement you made but is that so? Is it not possible to have a different kind of blade? (Said in a conciliatory way.)

(He is insisting that re-attention should be given but with care not to reject Docker's contribution too roughly.)

Docker: Objecting (words unclear).

2 Tearney went on to explore aloud an idea for altering the structure of the saw blade.

Tearney: Alright. It was to be driven by the same machine that cannot change. It's in motion so it has . . . the other thing I suppose is if we had a blade . . .

Docker: (Interrupting.) We're cutting through this table now—as we agreed the blade is guarded top and bottom, sorry top, the only place it's not guarded is the bottom. We need a device where the blade automatically only goes down to the thickness of the wood, so that the guard springs back.

Tearney: (Resuming, not to be put off.) O.K. here's an idea. (Warding Docker off with his hand.) If you could develop (to Docker: you will pick flaws in this because it's not absolutely mechanically sound . . . you have a good point). If there were some kind of sensing device at the end of each tooth or in the shank here so that when it's running free, centrifugal force will just make it round and not a sharp edge.

(He has *communicated* his idea, both preventing Docker from rejecting it out of hand . . . 'you will pick flaws in this . . .' and at the same time ensuring that Docker doesn't feel rejected '. . . you have a good point . . .')

Bailey: But let's not forget point D (the cost restriction).

(He is *anticipating* details of implementation already!)

Lawson: (Continuing on Tearney's point.) Yes, until you exert pressure on something that's really hard, tougher than flesh, will it actually start operating (directed at Tearney).

(He is seizing upon Tearney's idea and seeing if it can be worked through.)

(Confused mumble from everybody.)

Docker: Yes. But according to point D, it mustn't come up to 25 per cent more of the retail cost.

(He is taking up Bailey's obstructive *anticipatory* behaviour.)

Tearney: (Laughing to soften his insistence.) That's a mathematical problem to do with manufacturing. First we've got to come up with a couple of solutions—then let someone else sort that out (directed at Docker).

(Again he is bringing them back to the initial *exploring* activity and he is still concerned to keep everyone with him.)

This kind of process went on many times during the discussion. Every time the others leapt ahead to consideration of adaptations of the existing machine, Tearney insisted that they return to consideration of the basic blade design. Throughout the entire process, however, he was able to keep the peace. He acted as a harmonizer and an 'includer'. He never allowed even what he saw to be the most inappropriate suggestion to be rejected out of hand. In his behaviour during this exercise, Tearney showed clearly the constructive function of *communicating*; i.e. to allow free consideration, review, questioning, *investigation* and *exploration* of even the wildest idea, in a climate where everyone has his say, different points of view are tolerated, and ideas are jointly built upon until eventually a solution is reached.

Unstructured Exercise in Presenting

In the *presenting*, persuasion exercise, Shelley showed clearly his stronger *presenting* motivation. He was the only one of the whole five to be unanimously recognized as having actually persuaded his colleague. The colleague too was the only one who admitted to being persuaded completely. He chose a very clear and simple issue and stuck to it doggedly throughout the interaction. His 'victim', Docker, produced a mass of evasory argument, but Shelley was never put off the basic issue. He was not, however, seen to be aggressive or bullying in any way. He simply was able to share his own clarity of intention and firmness of purpose with Docker.

The others were all less successful to varying degrees for different reasons. Tearney made a good *presentation* but was too long winded at the beginning. It is as if he has to go through a *communicational* ritual before he can get to the *presentation* stage. He gets there in the end though, and when he does is effective. Docker instead of *presenting* a clear issue, was more concerned to get Shelley to agree to a particular plan of action based upon their previous discussion (i.e.: Shelley's *presentation*). Lawson in his turn attempted to *operate* Bailey into an idea which he worked into a whole plan of action, even giving indications as to the most expedient programming of events. Bailey remained unresponsive and totally unconvinced. He commented later that he felt he was being virtually 'taken over' by Lawson and organized into action before he was even convinced it was the right action. Bailey himself couldn't even think up an issue, or get anywhere near one. Instead he chose to discuss with Lawson a problem which he knew Lawson already recognized and was prepared to do something about. (This incidentally drove it home to Bailey that it was unrealistic for him to expect to ever 'become' more of a *confronter*. He just doesn't see the world in terms of issues; black and white things to be faced up to, and he never will.)

Unstructured Exercise in Operating

Lawson was clearly outstanding in the *operational* (take over in two hours) situation. In this situation, Tearney began talking first with his *communicational* ritual. The others said later that this gave them time to think but that none of them actually listened to what he said. After about ten minutes Lawson came forth with a concise plan of action. Objections were raised and opinions sought in order from each one. From then on the group was with Lawson, with Tearney backing him up (in clear *presentational* mode by this stage). The plan of action, sequence of events, programme, objective, were all worked out rapidly, precisely and exactly within the time limit set.

At the beginning of this section three points were mentioned categorizing what the managers learnt from these interaction exercises. There is a fourth, however, which became evident as the course progressed.

4 A further aspect brought out by these experiences was the pattern aspect of a person's interaction behaviour. By this is meant that it became evident that a person will try always to lead with his strongest attribute. If he is strong on all aspects of interaction, but *presenting* is strongest, he will endeavour first to initiate a *presentational* climate. If this doesn't work, or the situation obviously demands another mode, only then will he employ his secondary strengths. Tearney, for instance, always tried initially to establish a *communicational* climate. He did this even in the *operational* situation, until pressure from the group forced him to adopt more of a *presenting* mode.

CHAPTER 14

Team Style and the Business Climate it Creates

Every senior manager who has had experience with working in more than one senior management team, would probably agree that any established team has its own distinctive character or 'style' just as an individual has. It is very often remarked, for instance, how important it is that a new member should fit in with the 'style' of a team. But how can team 'style' be pinned down, analysed and defined so that a proper attempt can be made at fitting a new member into it? The action profile concept provides a way of doing this, by enabling extrapolation from characteristics of the individual styles to the team style.

The action profile concept adds definition and clarity to the obvious fact that no two individual managers possess the same style of management. Therefore it enables the otherwise rather vague concept of style, both individual and team, to be pinned down precisely in terms of spontaneously available motivations, and conversely limitations or gaps in spontaneous motivation. As managers differ according to the areas in which they are strong or weak, and none is strong in all, their combination in a team will result in a certain mixture of strengths and weaknesses, which will result in a distinctive team style, which in turn will create a particular business climate.

In the absence of a tool for defining the components of individual style, the combination of individual styles into a team style becomes a somewhat accidental affair. There is a tendency as a result for the team style to become to varying degrees lopsided. Evidence suggests that if a team becomes severely unbalanced, there will be a decrease in effectiveness.

It is not surprising that lopsidedness occurs. There is a very human tendency for people to gravitate towards others who are reasonably like themselves. Managing Directors are no less subject to this tendency than anyone else. In one extreme case, a Managing Director was found to have established a team, with a joint style and profile which was an exact replica of his own.

Indeed, to some extent an overlap of approach is desirable and necessary.

Otherwise there is no joint basis or common ground, on the foundation of which differences can be expressed. In this respect the interaction components are particularly important. In discussing action profiles with a colleague, a manager once remarked 'No wonder I've never been able to get on with you, we have no common network of interaction.' He was strong in *communicating* and *operating* with a complete absence of *presenting* whilst his colleague was strong in *presenting* and nothing else. However, although an overlap is necessary this can be achieved without necessitating complete similarity in approach.

Given the action profile information, an effective team can be constructed by combining men of complementary profiles. The aim will be to achieve a reasonable balance across the action requirements, particularly the first nine —the basic six action requirements and the three interaction modes. There is evidence that for a senior management team the *dynamism* level has to be uniformly high, except in management capacities where a high level of trained intellectual ability (e.g. finance) is required. *Adaptability* is a quality needed mainly in fairly specific situations (i.e. where the company is venturing into previously unencountered areas). It seems that in general the spread of *identification* needs to be high.

Using the action profiles of an existing management team, the joint profile or team style can be analysed in a number of ways, to serve a number of different purposes.

> 1 The team can be treated most simply as a collection of individuals required to cover certain essential functions and in doing so create a reasonably well balanced business climate. If the twelve action requirements are not covered to a certain level the business climate created by the team will be in danger of becoming dangerously over-emphasized in some directions and under-emphasized in others.

To deal with the first six action requirements first: if no-one *investigates* there will be lack of definition, lack of detailed information, lack of penetrating analysis of the situation. No-one will question: What is it? What are we? What type of company do we want to be? If no-one *explores* no-one will be looking for all the possibilities and alternatives available at any one time. No-one will question whether there are other markets which the company could enter, or other products which it might produce. No-one will question: What else is there? Do we have to do it like this?

If no-one *determines* there will be a lack of purpose, resolution, persistence against obstacles. There will be a lack of conviction that what the company is doing is right, hence inability to stick with anything. No-one will assert: Yes this is what we *should* be doing. If we keep pushing we'll win in the end. If no-one *confronts* there will be confusion about the most important immediate needs. There will be evasion of obvious demands, lack of readiness to face up to the facts of a situation realistically. No-one will assert: The central issue is this. You can't escape the facts, what is obviously needed now is such and such.

If no-one *decides*, nothing will actually get implemented. The moment by moment sequencing of events will be confused. No-one will be looking for opportunities to be seized. There will be no sense of urgency or preparedness to wait for precisely the right moment. No-one will say: Right, let's do it now. No, let us wait a little until the time is more propitious and get the moment right. If no-one *anticipates* no-one will be watching the trends. There will be no appreciation of a time objective for anything. No-one will foresee the results and implications of present activities or forecast changes in the situation. No-one will say: If we do such and such then this will happen. Our product will have died in ten years' time, so we need an alternative.

2 In addition the team can be treated more realistically as a complex interaction unit.

For this the analysis needs to take account of the spread of interaction abilities and the *identification* factor.

Within the above distinctions, the depth of analysis can vary according to the purpose of the analysis:

(i) Spread of predominant strength (scores of 3·0* or more) across the twelve action requirements.

This is applicable to a healthy, well balanced team and will indicate in what direction the strongest joint motivation is pushing. It can be useful for highlighting differences between groups within a team.

(ii) Spread of adequate strengths (score of 2·0 or more).

This for any team will give an indication of the degree to which essential functions are being carried out. This is the most commonly used form of analysis.

(iii) Spread of limitations (score of 1·0 or less).

For a considerably unbalanced team this will give an indication of real 'danger' areas.

For an organization in difficulty, an analysis according to (ii) and (iii) above can prove a valuable diagnostic tool in establishing the real source of difficulties within the organization. If the team is found to be severely unbalanced, the following remedies can be applied:

(a) Addition of members with appropriate balancing characteristics.

---

* For analysis of team style across the whole twelve action motivations, it is necessary to express degree of strength on all action motivations according to a rating on the four point scale. Absence of an action motivation would be represented by a score of 0·0, greatest strength by a score of 3·9.

(b) Allowing greater influence to be executed by an existing member with appropriate balancing characteristics.

(c) Weeding out members with superflous strengths (i.e. already well covered by the other members).

(d) Instituting formal systems to safeguard against weakest areas.

IMBALANCE IN TEAM STYLE

In the team of which Mr. Myer was the Managing Director, there was found to be a serious bias. To remind you of the situation: this was a traditional English company taken over by an American international Group. The Americans were, of course, concerned to make the firm profitable as soon as possible.

They rapidly set about introducing all the regular systems and methods. The company, however, seemed (at least to the Americans) to take an inordinately long time to respond. This was due firstly to the neglect on the Americans' part to really study this new situation at the very beginning, and their application of old methods willy nilly, imposing them on a management team completely uneducated in these methods. The slow recovery was also due, however, to the particular team style evidenced by the English group.

A table showing the spread of strengths across the first six action requirements is shown opposite.

Reference to the chart shows that the top team have in common two characteristics to a remarkable degree of unanimity. They are:

1 Investigating (21 per cent team activity)
6 Anticipating (23 per cent team activity)

The predominance of these two factors, with no-one failing to show activity in these areas, is exceptional. The company can be said to have a top team of *investigator/anticipators*.

This means that everyone is observant, keen to find out the facts, ready to pay attention, keen to define standards, responsive to opportunities for providing definition, predisposed to establishing matters of principle and pursuing established procedure. All this is, or can be, positive. There is then a jump from observation to *anticipation* of the likely consequences. On the basis of what he sees, everyone tries to look into the crystal ball. There is a prevailing manner of observant farsightedness. Everyone is concerned to make predictions on the way things are going to set his objectives, to speculate on the outcome of events and, inevitably, to speculate on how he personally will make out. Much of this is good. It has to be viewed, however, as to how well qualified and experienced are the executives to derive useful information and how well versed they are in projecting, and so likely to make sound

Imbalance in Team Style

	Myer—M.D.	Gale—Tech. Dir. Div. 1	Trevor—Div. Dir. Div. 2	Salter—Export Mgr.	Tyler—R & D Div. 2	Tison—Prod. Controller Div. 2	Long—Sales Mgr. Div. 2	Laurie—Head of Design	Child—Prod. Mgr. Div. 1	Slessor—Construction Engineer	Leonard—Finance	White—Personnel	Total	% of Total
1 Investigating	10	30	10	25	23	20	20	17	20	18	18	23	234	21%
2 Exploring	12	4	25	25	18	10	5	10	6	2	13	36	166	*14%
3 Determining	20	25	10	5	2	10	20	10	23	29	10	8	172	14%
4 Confronting	8	8	30	20	18	5	5	23	22	15	30	2	186	15%
5 Deciding	25	3	5	5	21	15	25	20	9	12	12	8	160	13%
6 Anticipating	25	30	20	20	18	40	25	20	20	24	17	23	282	23%
Total	100%	100%	100%	100%	100%	100%	100%	100%	100%	100%	100%	100%	1200	100%

Table 13. Spread of strengths over the first six action motivations (% of total activity)—Kale & Co. Ltd.

*Areas of low emphasis are boxed.

forecasts. The evidence is not encouraging. Seven of the executives are lacking in breadth of experience and their knowledge relates to specialized craft areas. Their actual performance in terms of results achieved contributes to this assessment.

The implications are more serious when it is realized that not only are they severely limited as indicated above, but that they are predisposed spontaneously to 'jump' from observation to speculation without much effort to the intervening stage of resolving of purpose and facing up to the realities of the situation. (*Determining* and *Confronting* constitute only 14 per cent and 15 per cent of the team's total activity.) It is true to say that among the top team there is actual indiscipline (absence of authority, or of readiness to persist) and refusal to *confront* (evasion of the real issues and self-delusion). This is a generalized statement, but a fair statement of prevailing tendencies.

When people combine in their behaviour both of the *determining* and *confronting* activities, it indicates concentration on facing up to the reality of the situation and finding the effort to cope. Only Trevor, Laurie, Child, Slessor and Leonard (five out of twelve) are without handicap in this respect, and only Child and Slessor are positively strong. There is thus a big pull away from discipline and reality which these two men alone cannot be expected to counterbalance. As already reported, the Managing Director himself, although highly self-*determined*, does not so *present* or demonstrate the situation to his executives as to encourage discipline in the sense of firmness, persistence, tenacity, refusal to allow any unwitting evasion of pressing immediate demands.

There is evidence that lack of purpose exists to a higher degree than it should. Although executives, in the main, work long hours, they do not allocate their time precisely and they flit from one thing to another. Time spent in discussions is prolonged and three or more people may be involved, often unnecessarily. Mistakes are often laughed away as 'one of those things' and are liable to be repeated.

No controlled studies with a view to seeking proof of such lack of purpose have been made but there is sufficient indication to substantiate the finding that executives are disposed to behave in this way. Individual performances over the past two years, so far as it is possible to assess them in the light of the dislocation caused by the merger, support the charge of lack of resolve and realistic appreciation of needs—not in preparedness to spend time but in their way of using the working time available (*deciding* only 13 per cent) and their readiness to be accountable for results achieved—or not achieved. Men with the experience and seniority that Gale (Technical Director) and Salter (Export Manager) enjoy, for example, should have been able to achieve more, if only in the respect of their colleagues and subordinates. The prevailing group style of *investigating/anticipating*, with absence of *determining*, is characteristic of lack of readiness to be accountable for performance, and of self-delusion about what is being done.

It may seem a harsh accusation when it can be shown that in some respects executives have responded loyally and staunchly to the demands placed upon them. The move to the new factory is a case in point. Even so, the points made above still apply. There is great devotion to duty and yet indiscipline in personal management behaviour.

Mr. Trevor's (Divisional Director) style of leadership could possibly be applied so as to face people up to this situation and make them aware of the needs they must discipline themselves to meet. He could probably make a greater contribution than is the case at present but his own *determining* limitations make it important to find exactly the right role for him (he is strong in *confronting* (30 per cent) but weak in *determining* (10 per cent)).

The pull of the predominant group style is such that relative newcomers, particularly Laurie (Head of Design) and Leonard (Finance), are in danger of being influenced by it and there is some evidence that it is responsible for Laurie's relapses into arrogance and Leonard's almost isolationist self containment. Certainly both men would now be performing differently if they were members of a stronger group.

As a group the executives most need the sort of influence which Child or Slessor (both strongest in *determining* and *confronting*) could assert. Neither is suited to the role which Mr. Myer has carried out and clearly neither has the skill, intellectual brilliance, or industrial experience to have achieved all that Mr. Myer has done over the past two years. It is worth considering, however, whether their leadership potential can be developed and applied.

As can be seen, there is not only the revelation of the considerable bias in action motivation here, but some suggestion as to how the balance could begin to be rectified. Firstly, just the recognition that there is a bias and a very fundamental reason for it is a step forward. Secondly, revelation of the people most suited to counteract the tendency can help. However, in this kind of process one is always confined by the realities of individual experience, training and expertise. If a man who has the needed balancing characteristics just does not have wide or relevant management experience then it isn't practicable to suggest he take a different or more leading role.

In this case suggestions were made to push one of the men with the greatest strengths in the balancing characteristics (primarily *determining* and *confronting*) e.g., Slessor, toward achieving a more influential position. The other, Child, was already exerting some influence as Production Manager. Slessor was, however, the construction engineer, without real managerial responsibility. It was recommended that he should be developed toward taking a senior management responsibility as quickly as possible, and to appoint him production manager of the smaller division within the company. The Managing Director agreed that he showed considerable potential and was prepared to make the appointment.

Ironically, just at this time, it was discovered that he had been involved in illegalities and had to be dismissed. Thus was lost this possibility of redressing, to some extent, the behavioural balance in the team.

Another man suggested as having one of the needed balancing characteristics was Trevor, 'director' of the smaller division. As an example of the difficulties encountered in trying to deploy people's strengths due to complications of experience and training, Mr. Trevor is an interesting case. He is an American, moved in primarily because of his great experience of the products of the particular division. The division had been making a serious loss. Under Mr. Trevor's leadership it improved slightly, but despite his experience, recovered much more slowly than the other major divisions and is even now barely satisfactory despite the intervention of the Group Managing Director himself and numerous American experts. For a line manager Mr. Trevor has an unusual action profile (opposite).

There is a much greater concentration of energy in the second of each pair, the 'perspective' areas, *exploring, confronting* and *anticipating*, than in the 'assertion' areas of *investigating, determining* and *deciding*. The perspective attributes make up 75 per cent of the total expediture of energy in fact and this is an unusually high proportion for someone acting as line manager.

Weighting in favour of the 'perspective' areas result in a readiness to prepare the conditions for action but not such a preparedness to actually take action in a directly assertive manner. If the weighting in favour of the perspective side is somewhere in the ratio of 2 : 1 then this results in only a slight preference for setting up the conditions for action which may be expressed as an outstanding skill in delegating. If, however, the weighting is more in the line of 3 : 1 in favour of the perspective side, as with Mr. Trevor, then there will be little preparedness to directly take action at all, which of course, is a great handicap in a direct operational role.

The action profile showed Mr. Trevor to be not only a great delegator but also a great co-ordinator as he is in addition strong in the human relations areas. The concentration on the perspective areas means that he has an outstanding feel for how various aspects of the organization relate:

'In his approach to management action, his attitude is rather akin to that of a designer or architect. He acts to structure the environment; to get the conditions right. He is outstanding in his sense of perspective and proportion. He is intensely aware of how various aspects of a situation are related and balanced. He is not afraid, however, of upsetting the balance or disturbing existing relationships. In fact it is by doing that very thing that he gets things done. He cannot stand by and let an unsatisfactory situation continue. He must act to stir it up. In one sense he is almost a professional "stirrer".

'By "stirrer" it is not meant that he is an indiscriminate meddler. He does not blunder into a situation rashly precipitating activity. He is sensitively aware of where movement and possibly disruption will be beneficial. This catalytic ability; the ability to promote constructive change, stems partly from his outstanding ability to face up to a situation (*confronting* 30 per cent).

A strange Action Profile for a line manager

		% of total activity	Extent of interaction activity	
ATTENTION	Investigating	10		Communicating
	Exploring	25		
INTENTION	Determining	5		Presenting
	Confronting	30		
COMMITMENT	Deciding	5		Operating
	Anticipating	20		
Dynamism			3·0	
Adaptability			2·5	
Identifying			3·5	

Action Profile 24 MR. TREVOR

He must take a stand, make clear his position, recognize immediate needs, and declare what has to be done. This gives him a provocative, challenging aspect—not "aggressive" in the brute force sense—but in a quietly realistic way. He is good at facing other people up to the needs of the present, at making the situation clear to them. It is by doing this that he initiates change and constructive activity. He will not necessarily be pushing in taking the initiative to right matters by his own immediate effort.

'He is particularly strong when it comes to interaction. Although bad at organizing people (low on *operating*) he establishes very positive relationships of a friendly yet challenging nature. In addition, he is understanding, ready to listen and spontaneously interested in others (strong in *communicating*). His leadership is not of the rousing, "follow me to the death" type, however. He is certainly dynamic, but he has a quiet detachment with it. People will be challenged, stimulated, made to face up to their responsibilities, counselled or advised. They will not feel organized or programmed or swept up in a wave of participatory zeal. He leads and initiates action not by applying more effort, but by re-arranging the area of application.'

Because Mr. Trevor displayed this unusual style, in combination with the needed *confronting* attribute, one suggestion was that he should be given a function termed 'Director of Services'. It would have been a function created around Trevor's style of management, rather than the other way round. As such, both his challenging *confronting* ability and his outstanding co-ordinating abilities could be used to the full. Unfortunately, no other man in the group had his experience and knowledge of the products of the division. Thus he could not be released and is still struggling with production and sales problems.

About nine months after the report had been written, close contact was had with his two immediate subordinates at a training course. Both reported intense frustration due to what seemed to them to be entirely irrational behaviour on the part of Trevor. He was making decisions seemingly just to please the Managing Director. They were just 'fake' decisions which he rarely followed up and which were anyway totally out of touch with the realities of the situation. He displayed a rigidity and lack of flexibility which often indicates an over-compensation for lacking motivations, in his case weakness on all the assertion factors particularly *determining* 5 per cent and *deciding* 5 per cent. If the action profile analysis is right, Trevor was being forced to act under pressure, completely against his natural action pattern. This can result in an emotional upheaval for certain people. In Trevor's case, with his enormous sense for perspective and basic adaptability he was able to live with compromise—but what a waste of a man's abilities!

Since that report was written, a second survey was made of the next level of managers. Several younger men were identified, both strong in overall management potential and possessing strengths in the weaker areas, hence contributing toward a more even spread of motivation across the team. A great many changes had taken place since the first reports were submitted and some of the findings in the first report had to be reviewed in light of the second study.

The team as it is now constituted shows the spread of activity indicated in Table 14 (opposite).

The team has obviously been streamlined to some extent and the organization structure made more compact. The promising young managers identified by the study and, of course, already recognized to some extent, were fairly rapidly moved into positions of greater responsibility, namely Laurie (from design to technical manager then technical and production manager of the

Correction of Imbalance in Team Style

| | Leonard—Financial | White—Personnel | Myer—M.D. | Gale—Deputy M.D. | Div. 1 | | Div. 2 (smallest and least profitable at time of studies) | | | | Total | % of total after changes (present team) | % of total before changes (previous team) |
					Laurie—Tech. & Prod.	Dorel—Sales	Trevor—Div. Director	Child—Prod.	Layson—Tech. & R. & D.	Locke—Sales			
1 Investigating	18	23	10	30	17	20	10	20	5	10	163	16·3%	21%
2 Exploring	13	36	12	4	10	5	25	6	20	25	156	15·6%	14%
3 Determining	10	8	20	25	10	25	10	26	25	25	184	18·4%	14%
4 Confronting	30	2	8	8	23	5	30	24	10	5	145	14·5%	15%
5 Deciding	12	8	25	3	20	30	5	9	15	15	142	14·2%	13%
6 Anticipating	17	23	25	30	20	15	20	15	25	20	210	21·0%	23%
Total	100%	100%	100%	100%	100%	100%	100%	100%	100%	100%	1000	100%	100%

(column group header: Staff covers Leonard—Financial, White—Personnel, Myer—M.D., Gale—Deputy M.D.)

Table 14. Showing spread of strengths across the first six action requirements for management—present team of Kale & Co. Ltd.
Total weighting of strengths is compared with that of previous team (see page 187).

G

larger division). Dorel moved in as sales manager of the larger division, Layson as technical and R & D manager of the smaller division and Locke as sales manager of the smaller division. Most importantly the spread of action motivation became much more even. There is still a weighting in favour of *anticipating*, but *determining* now has as much emphasis as *investigating*. *Deciding* also has a stronger spread.

In analysing a team in the way just described, as stated before, it is really simply from the point of view of seeing that there is sufficient action motivation spread about the members of the team to ensure that most of the vital management functions are performed. It is treating the team just as a collection of individuals, and of course, this is a highly useful and fundamental exercise. If the relevant motivations are not present, the company will be managed ineffectively. It can be a great help to a managing director to know precisely, in this straightforward way, where his team's strengths and weaknesses lie.

TEAM DYNAMICS

However, a team, if it is acting as a team and not just a collection of individuals, is a much more complex unit. The areas of action covered by the team members acting singly may be different from the kind of action produced as a function of team interaction. To analyse the style of a team in this sense, therefore, we need to look particularly at the intermix of interaction motivations and how this intermix relates to the spread of straight action motivations and to the *identification* factor.

If, for instance, there is a weighting in favour of say two of the straight action motivations of the same stage of action; e.g. the Attention stage—*investigating*, *exploring* and the spread of interaction motivation is similarly weighted toward the Attention stage; i.e. *communicating*, then this would result in a very homogeneous and complete style of team interaction. Singly the team members would tend to promote the activities of *investigating* and *exploring* and collectively there would be a joint sparking off of these activities. It would be a uniformly research minded team in fact. The predominant 'manner' of relating would be one of mutually inviting ideas, suggestions, alternatives, considerations, etc.—and the spontaneous motivation of each individual would enable him to respond fully and appropriately.

Such a high degree of uniformity in team interaction would, of course, be unusual. In any event it will only be a matter of weighting, there will usually be some odd men out. It would be too much to expect to find everyone conforming exactly to the team style. However, the weighting of attributes and the joint style it produces is important. It is a determining factor in the initiating of action to the extent of affecting what does and does not happen as a result of the activity of a particular management team.

The spread of the *identifying* factor across a team is relevant in that it will govern the degree of unity or cohesiveness within the team. With a strong spread of *identifying*, there will be an involving, 'all in this together' atmosphere. Many things will be sparked off spontaneously, and there will be an easy, casual interchange amongst the members of the team. A team with a thin spread of *identifying* may nevertheless produce plenty of constructive action (if the spread over the interaction areas is strong) but there will be a more formal atmosphere. Less will occur spontaneously and hence perhaps less altogether.

The following accounts and comparison of the team styles of two different groups within the same company will reveal more vividly the above factors.

The company is the one of which Mr. Irving described (page 55) is now the production and technical director.

As mentioned in the account of Mr. Irving, the company, Fellows Acre Ltd., is a medium sized engineering firm, separated geographically, with divisions in Bristol, Manchester and Nottingham. The Bristol section deals with the internal administration and sales side of the largest divisions, the Manchester section with production for all divisions and Nottingham with administration and sales of the smallest division, involving only two acting executives, including the executive chairman. The Manchester group as a team and the Bristol group as a team are compared. Broadly, therefore, it is a sales oriented group in comparison to a production oriented group.

Below is a comparison of the two groups in terms of spread of strengths over the whole twelve action motivations. To enable a comparison to be made over the entire twelve action motivations, however, it has been necessary to change the numerical interpretation of the individual profiles. Whilst the first six action motivations can be presented in percentage terms it is more difficult to treat the others in this way. Thus all have been converted to ratings on a four point scale which is the manner of presentation used normally for some clients. In Table 15, the total sum of ratings on each action motivation is shown for each team to enable an easier comparison.

Reference to the chart reveals considerable similarity in the weighting of strengths. Both show predominant strengths in *anticipating* (85 per cent and 81 per cent respectively of each group showing adequate strength) and *operating* (78 per cent and 90 per cent) with a fairly high average on *dynamism* (90 per cent and 100 per cent). Both are most seriously limited in *exploring* (50 per cent and 36 per cent) and adaptability (35 per cent and 40 per cent).

The most evident differences are that whereas the Bristol team has a very strong weighting in favour of *deciding* (78 per cent) the Manchester team has a strong weighting in favour of *determining* (81 per cent). The Manchester team in addition has the *identifying* factor very much more in evidence (90 per cent).

These characteristic styles of the two teams were described as follows. (In the first account the Bristol team is treated in isolation as the Manchester team had not as yet been studied. In the report on the Manchester team, the two groups are related and contrasted and comments made on possible implications of the differences in style.)

Team Comparison

	Bristol Team sales oriented N=14		Manchester Team production oriented N=11		Difference
	No. of Strengths* (2·0 or greater)	% of Group	No. of Strengths (2·0 or greater)	% of Group	
1 Investigating	10	71%	7	63%	8
2 Exploring	7	50%	4	36%	14
3 Determining	8	57%	9	81%	㉔
4 Confronting	8	57%	5	45%	12
5 Deciding	11	78%	6	54%	㉔
6 Anticipating	12	85%	9	81%	4
7 Communicating	6	42%	6	54%	12
8 Presenting	8	57%	6	54%	3
9 Operating	11	78%	10	90%	12
10 Dynamism	12	85%	11	100%	10
11 Adaptability	5	35%	5	45%	10
12 Identifying	9	64%	10	90%	㉖

Table 15. Showing spread of strengths over the twelve action motivations—Fellows Acre Ltd.

Comparison of Bristol (sales oriented) team and Manchester (production oriented) team.

* Strength is defined as score of 2·0 or greater as measured on 4 point scale. This was previously defined (p. 185) as 'adequate' strength = i.e. sufficient to ensure that the activity is adequately covered. Areas of greatest difference are circled.

Team Style of Bristol Team (Sales Oriented—Fellows Acre Ltd.)

The outstanding general strengths, looking at the sum of motivations, are in the readiness to act in three ways.

    1 *Deciding*—having sense of timing; starting off a process of implementation at the appropriate moment; decisiveness in order of

time priorities; seizing opportunities; flexible on the spot programming. (78 per cent of group showing adequate strength.)

2 *Anticipating*—looking ahead, farsightedness, foreseeing consequences of action; evaluating practicalities; constant anticipation of future developments; systematic future programming. (85 per cent of group showing adequate strength.)

3 *Operating*—on the spot organising of people; creating sense of urgency or slowing down of pace, spurring people on or delaying activity with awareness of objectives; controlling the action; sharing own process of deciding and anticipating. (78 per cent of group showing adequate strength.)

The three are all related, forming a well integrated and somewhat complete manner of approach to business. This particular combination results in the smooth running of an established system. It is the turning of the handle of a well phased, well oiled machine. The spontaneous behaviour is so well balanced in this direction that the company would run somehow in the face of even the most unsuitable systems of organization and this is positive. In a favourable environment, it would take a lot to stop the running of this machine. However, there are implications of this approach in which inherent dangers are exposed:

1 Competitiveness—this is a feature associated with the *operational* approach. It can be positive if combined with a sense of corporate purpose, identification with a unified company image. It then becomes directed outside. Otherwise it remains internal and causes fragmentation and lack of co-operation. There is, however, a reasonable pull toward the *confronting, determining* activities in management. This would enable the development of a strong sense of purpose and the establishment of a real company image. There is not, however, a great response in the Managing Director's style of leadership to this possibility, especially in the establishment of a company image. Emphasis along the lines of propagating a sense of common purpose could usefully be encouraged.

2 Lack of *adaptability*—this is also associated with the *operational* combination in management behaviour. It is a very definite limitation in the company (only 35 per cent showing strengths). This does not imply an inability to seize opportunities but rather a lack of the ability to really change attitudes toward management and company responsibility. It implies a rigidity and lack of readiness for real change within the organization in relation to changes in the environment.

The possibility of competitive fragmentation mentioned above, is rendered a more potent danger by a general weakness in the area of participatory readiness; the ability to include one another in activities, to achieve a feeling of unity and working together. People who have this quality are good team welders. The balance in this team is against it (only 64 per cent of group strong on Action Requirement 12—*Identification*). The Managing Director has this quality but is heavily outnumbered. Thus achieving common purpose and image could provide a more fruitful line of development.

A great weakness in the team lies in the lack of readiness to apply an *exploratory* approach. Only 50 per cent of the group show adequate strengths. Those positively strong (score of 3·0 or more), i.e. able to promote a stronger emphasis on this activity, are the Managing Director, Lyle (chief engineer of small division), Sand (works manager) and Drew (office manager). This overall weakness implies a general lack of readiness to adopt a creative attitude, to be ready to look outside the running of the existing system in search perhaps of completely new and as yet unheard of ways of looking at the company. There could be a lack of innovative ideas in a general sense, a comparative lack of emphasis on the need for development of new products, new markets—in short, everything to do with broadening the outlook, the habit of always looking for new and different possibilities and alternatives. Lyle, Drew, Sand and the Managing Director, all exercise the readiness to take this view but there are reasons beyond their sheer paucity in number why they are not a more potent influence in this particular way.

The overriding facility in the company is, as already mentioned in *operating* —turning the handle of a running machine. All the *explorers* are as strong as everyone else in this respect, so there may be some tendency for them to concentrate on this and so just swim with the tide.

In addition, both Mr. Etheridge (Managing Director), Mr. Drew and Mr. Sand have difficulty in *communicating* effectively in a way to really put the *exploratory* outlook over. Sand is further restricted as an influence by his propensity to look at his area of responsibility too much in isolation and distinct from the company as a corporate whole. Lyle can *communicate* this attitude and ideas arising from it, effectively, yet perhaps not always backed by sufficient conviction (weak *determining*, *confronting* and *presenting*) to overcome the overriding pull against such an approach.

The Managing Director has an outstanding readiness to be continuously coming up with new ideas and suggestions. This is combined with a tendency to give an impression, either of being already committed to one of the alternatives, or of not *presenting* a full and straightforward picture. It could, when seen in relation to the opposite dominant tendency in the team, create some insecurity and unease as to quite what his intentions are. People lacking in the *exploratory* capacity are very inclined to see what was meant as merely a tenuous, *exploratory* suggestion, as either some definite statement of purpose—or a commitment of some description. If such expectations are often not realized, this could be experienced as unrewarding and disturbing.

The limitation in *adaptability* mentioned above, stems from the tendency not to go back to first principles; to give attention to the original basis of the now formalized and established system. This means that although there is a system which does whatever it does relatively smoothly, there is a lack of definition and attention to what it *should* be doing, as opposed to what it *is* doing. This can lead to the strange contradiction of the efficient running of what may in fact, to some extent, be a basically inefficient set up. This comes about through a lack of awareness at the primary stages. If one is simply not aware of the basic principles on which an organization is built, it is difficult to change them. The ability to do this comes from the spontaneous readiness to act in an *investigatory-exploratory* way. There is certainly some pull toward an *investigatory* readiness (71 per cent of group strong) but this, without a matching *exploratory* readiness, leaves appreciation of first principles too narrowly confined. There is no broadening of awareness to allow a balanced perspective. Often these abilities can best be developed through personal interaction. A way to develop the *investigatory-exploratory* attitudes would be to encourage more of a *communicating* atmosphere (there is great possibility for such development—on Action Requirement 7 there are six development possibility ratings with five positive strength ratings). This means that the fostering of an *exploratory*, discussion type interchange within the team, with less emphasis on straight organization, will be beneficial.

Team Style of Manchester Team (Production Oriented)—Fellows Acre Ltd.

The managers at Manchester taken as a group, show evidence of a team character different, but not entirely opposite, from the group at Bristol. However, the differences can explain some of the difficulties that have been occurring between the two groups. As a whole the Manchester team is outstanding in the extent to which it possesses the characteristics of:

1 *Determining*—having firmness of purpose; determination, persistence against difficult odds; resistance to pressure, strong conviction. (81 per cent of group showing adequate strengths.)
2 *Anticipating*—looking ahead, farsightedness, foreseeing consequences of action; evaluating practicalities; constant anticipation of future developments; systematic future programming. (81 per cent of group showing adequate strengths.)
3 *Operating*—on the spot organising of people; creating sense of urgency or slowing down of pace, spurring people on or delaying activity with awareness of objectives; controlling the action; sharing own process of deciding and anticipating. (90 per cent of group showing adequate strengths.)

It is interesting to note that these are precisely the characteristics most predominant in the general manager, Mr. Irving's own motivational pattern. This is not to imply that this is necessarily wrong. However, it is as well to recognize the fact.

As a joint style of management, this means that there is great motivation toward really getting to grips with the demands of production. There is an environment of *determination* and persistence, a great willingness to really stick at the job.

This is a strong management style, particularly as it is backed up adequately though not strongly by motivation toward *investigating, confronting* and *deciding*. It means that on the whole decisions are well phased, not taken blindly without due attention being given to the facts and the important issues are to some extent delineated and faced up to.

The weakest area is the motivation toward the *exploring* activities (only 36 per cent of group shows adequate strength). This magnifies the tendency to stick at a problem and tolerate frustration, rather than to find a way round the obstruction. *Exploring* includes the readiness to look for alternative methods, to instinctively consider how many different ways a problem can be tackled. This is not to say that a predominance of an *exploratory* attitude is a valuable objective, for a strongly *exploratory* approach is more suited to a creative environment applicable to the initial planning stages in management, a function of staff rather than line personnel. In the Manchester situation it will suffice that this gap is recognized. It will help if those strong in the *exploratory* approach; i.e. Tiller (Development Engineer) and Laver (Works Manager) are recognized as being capable of contributing usefully in this special sense.

As mentioned above, the readiness to apply *investigation* is not strong (63 per cent of group strong). This means that while there is in fact some readiness to give attention to method, it seems that this is one area that needs serious attention. This is primarily because the motivation toward simply preparing the ground in terms of establishing method, is so subordinated to the desire to want to get to grips with what is seen as the real work in the light of the final objective; i.e. to get the stuff out of the door. Enough emphasis is given to the preparatory stage to prevent disaster, but not enough for it to result in increased efficiency in the overall running of the business. (Later a recommendation was made concerning the need for an organization and methods review, employing outside consultants if necessary.)

There is a further strong feature in the Manchester team which should be mentioned. This is the high degree of participatory involvement or *identification* (90 per cent of group strong). This results in a highly unified team and a strong group identity.

This is one of the features which distinguishes the Manchester team from the Bristol one. In the Stage 1 report the relative lack of unification at Bristol was pointed out as a factor in the possible development of rivalries between managers within the team. It was mentioned that the inherent competitiveness could be dangerous unless unified and turned outward. The Manchester team is unified, however, and this probably results in less interpersonal rivalry. However, there is a very strong and unified 'team' rivalry and at present this seems to be directed largely at the Bristol people particularly in their role as sales versus production. Apart from this, the two groups are fairly similar except that the Bristol group is strongest in *deciding* (78 per cent) whilst the Manchester group is strongest in *determining* (81 per cent). This makes for a difference in emphasis but certainly not so as to necessarily impair the co-operation of the two groups.

It will aid co-operation, however, if the nature of this difference is recognized. The Bristol people must be instinctively aware of the weight of *determination* and resolve emanating from Manchester. This may be interpreted as obstinacy and heavy-handedness in some instances. On the other hand, the Manchester group may feel a slight suspicion at the lightweight more tactically *operational* approach at the Bristol end. In reality the two styles combine very well to provide a strong overall managerial approach.

A point made about the Bristol team was that predominant stress on the 'commitment' stage of management activity as evidenced in strengths in *deciding, anticipating* and *operating* leads to a certain *unadaptability*. This is reinforced by the similar weighting within the Manchester group. It is because there is little spontaneous readiness to go back to first principles and question the very basis of the business. Hence there is still a real need for the 'advisor' type role so that people of a predominant *investigatory, exploratory* tendency can provide this questioning function. Obviously the production end needs to have an *operational*-action based orientation. But this emphasizes the necessity to ensure that a complete imbalance in the company as a whole in this direction is not allowed to crystallize.

The precise way in which findings such as the above are used, varies according to the situation. In this case the main findings were embodied in specific recommendations.

1 The need for slight rebalancing toward greater readiness, to *explore*; i.e. the need to find out if they are making the right thing and selling it in the right place.

This was achieved by specific recommendations concerning people displaying strengths in *exploration*. In the Bristol team, Mr. Lyle (already described page 127) was seen to be a saving grace. As mentioned before, at the time of the study he was chief electrical engineer concerned mainly with selling systems to local authorities. The recommendation was that he should be appointed marketing planner, so that his strength in *exploring* could be influential in policy making.

At Manchester two men stood out in this respect, Mr. Tiller, then the Chief Development Engineer, and Mr. Laver, manager of the tiniest works. Mr. Laver has also been spoken of before (page 126). It was mentioned that he had the typical research minded action profile with fairly low dynamism—making him much more suited to an advisory, rather than line, operational role. Mr. Tiller, an *explorer* of great *determination* and *dynamism,* was being somewhat wasted at the routine testing end of the R & D function: not that he ever really kept to the routine. He spent much of his time in fact diverting himself 'testing' rather wilder ideas than those coming from the R & D manager. The man who was at the more creative end of R & D was a highly qualified, academic, aloof, precise, unimaginative technician. The company had employed him because they appreciated his unyielding application of 'controls'. His budgets were impeccable and his programming admirably inflexible.

A comparison of their action profiles—showing the first six action requirements and the dynamism measure—is on the opposite page.

The most obvious difference between the two men is that whereas Stirling concentrates 50 per cent of his energy into the *Intention* stage, Tiller concentrates 50 per cent of his energy into the *Attention* stage. Whereas Stirling is low on *dynamism*, hence limited in the amount of activity he generates, Tiller is high on *dynamism*. This means that the approach of the two men is very different.

The Chief Development Engineer

Tiller combines ideas with 'guts' and with 'go'. Almost everything about him comes under one or some combination of these features. Each needs to be explained in more detail.

He shows a restlessly questing outlook, constantly on the lookout for new possibilities which offer new interests or new excitement (30 per cent exploring activity). This leads to his having a ready fund of new ideas, more in a broad ranging sense rather than tied to his technical expertise. He is an ideas man, motivated to want to create. He is a natural creative designer but his restlessness is such that he may be led too early into diversionist channels. He cannot help but be under the constant temptation of distraction. His type of ideas aptitude would be appropriate in an unstructured free ranging environment such as is often associated with artistic enterprise.

Closely linked with his propensity for *exploratory* ideas is the readiness to work strenuously and tenaciously so as to give a good account of himself (25 per cent *determining* activity). He is also motivated by recognition of the need to justify his existence. He is highly disciplined in how he organizes himself at work. It is important to him to have a cause which he believes in and to which he can dedicate himself. It is in this respect that he shows guts— he will not allow himself to be put off anything which he believes it right to do. He is a *determined explorer* in the sense of venturing into a world of ideas in a determined pioneering manner.

The third main feature, his 'go', arises mainly from his *dynamism*. In other people this might be related to *decisiveness*; in his case it is more closely related to the questing restlessness referred to earlier. He will go out to quest

Comparing Suitability for R & D function

		Tiller Chief Development Engineer	Stirling R & D Manager
		% of total activity	% of total activity
ATTENTION	1 Investigating	20	20
			5
INTENTION	2 Exploring	30	
	3 Determining		25
	4 Confronting	25	25
	5 Deciding		
COMMITMENT		10	10
		10	15
	6 Anticipating	5	
Dynamism		3·9	2·0
Adaptability		3·0	2·0
Identification		3·9	1·0

Action Profile 25 MR. TILLER AND MR. STIRLING
||||| Area of greatest emphasis is shaded

for ideas, and he will put himself out so as to force a thing through. He is not a person who will be slow to go out and get what he needs or wants or the job requires him to have.

The R & D Manager

In contrast to this, Mr. Stirling takes up an exceedingly clear, convinced stand on any issue. He has great *determination*, persistence and forthrightness in the way he faces up to the demands of the job, although he does not make this obvious. He has great self conviction and a sense of his own purpose (25 per cent of activity in both *determining* and *confronting*).

He is sparing in the amount of sheer energy he expends. He has a very clear picture of what needs to be done, but will do it with the maximum economy of effort, in terms of straight action.

He is naturally systematic in organizing his own work and he has a similar influence on others. He is a good organizer of people—will give clear directives especially in terms of programming and setting objectives (strong *operator**). He has a strong *anticipatory* faculty, which means he is very ready to set objectives and predict trends on the basis of his clear *confrontation* of present needs. His timing, however, in terms of setting priorities and ability to decide at precisely the right moment is not as well developed as it could be.

His straightforward appraisal of a situation is based on a thorough probing and *investigation* of relevant facts. He is less able, however, to adopt an *exploratory* attitude and hence introduce different alternatives in method or mode of approach. He is not creative in his attitude to management, and is unlikely to come up with many novel ideas, but he is valuable in his application of thoroughness, straightforwardness and system.

Tiller looks a much more obvious candidate for the creative side of R & D. He has limitations though which also had to be taken into consideration.

Although highly *exploratory*, he is limited in *anticipation*. He tends to be so interested in what is going on around him that he does not apply much energy toward projecting ahead. He does not naturally establish objectives, and he will plan ahead only if compelled to do so. He works as though he has great conviction that whatever ideas arise of whatever job he comes to grips with, then the future will be assured. (Greater motivation toward *exploring* 30 per cent than *investigating* 20 per cent with low *confronting* 10 per cent.)

Complementation of strengths is often the answer.

It was seen that by combining him with another design engineer, Gussman, renowned for his design flair and precision of application, the two could make a highly complementary R & D team. The design engineer is strong in *investi-*

* Not shown on action profile.

gating, anticipating and *deciding*. His *investigations* would ensure that Tiller's wild ideas were kept within the bounds of reason and thoroughly tested for viability. His *anticipation* would ensure that the ideas were in line with projected trends in the industry and in line with company objectives and his *decisiveness* would ensure that projects were programmed adequately, and flexibly in tune with an ever changing environment.

In the light of this recommendation, naturally the R & D manager's position had to be taken into account.

> Stirling has rightly earned great respect for his engineering skills and intellectual powers. His management attributes, however, have caused him to regularize the procedures of development engineering in a way which is more appropriate to a big company or a research institute rather than a moderately sized company such as Fellows Acre Ltd. dependent on a quick and flexible response to market opportunities. His contribution is better channelled into detailed work on specific projects. He can be given a number of important projects to work on and should be looked upon as a 'star' engineer (analogous to a 'star' salesman) who might well earn a high salary but should never become an overall manager; like the successful 'star' salesman who is ineffective as sales manager. It is conceivable that Stirling may leave under these conditions. It has to be seriously considered whether the benefits to be gained from the Tiller, Gussman team is worth the loss of Stirling.

The executive directors did think the Tiller-Gussman team was worth the loss of Stirling and so the change went ahead.

The second bias in the preparedness to take action in the Fellows Acre Ltd. teams as brought to light by the team analysis was dealt with as follows:

> 2 The need for controls against over concentration on the 'commitment' stage of management action (. . . you may be great at operating systems, but what are the systems like that you are operating?)

The weighting in both teams toward the commitment stage and away from the attention stage had a particularly obvious manifestation in extreme untidiness in the general organization and methods area. Efficient methods and systems were just not being laid down. What systems there were had been allowed to grow up in an *ad hoc*, haphazard manner but, of course, they were being worked in a highly co-ordinated way. The effectiveness of the operation, however, was being negated by the illogicality of the systems. Hence the following recommendation:

> 'The company is already considering a proposal to employ consultants on organization and methods and it is strongly recommended

that this be followed through as comprehensively as possible. The study of methods obviously has to be co-ordinated with the proposed plans for integrating and possibly relocating the Works. There would appear, also, a need to review the stock control system. A reorganized production control and planning department is already under preparation. It is highly desirable that all these matters—organization and methods, stock control, production planning—should be studied as part of a co-ordinated view of production facilities as a whole.

The problem of organizing such a survey, whether by outside consultants or carried out internally, obviously needs careful examination relative to the need to keep production going in a (currently) difficult business situation. Mr. Irving is clearly well able to decide the priorities but it will help him to be provided with as much information as possible. Laver has the aptitude to provide this and in such a close knit team such as exists at Bristol there is a definite advantage in having someone from within to head up the procedure.

Indeed, consultants attempting a survey along the lines indicated above are likely to have problems in getting their recommendations implemented because of the weight of motivation away from *investigating and exploring*. It is in the company's interests to have its own man active in conducting the survey although consultants might well contribute, and Laver is recommended as suitable for the role. Consultants would be briefed to work in conjunction with Laver, who would have continuing responsibility for implementing the recommendations. Such a role is aptly termed "Industrial Engineer" and it needs someone of Laver's practical management experience as well as aptitude to fill it.'

As can be seen this recommendation, in addition to the main concern, pointed to a concrete opportunity for exploiting Laver's 'attention-giving' strengths.

It is a fairly run of the mill recommendation to make, but it happened to be highly appropriate for this particular company. Many of the other companies studied would gain no benefit at all from an O & M survey.

TEAM STYLE ANALYSIS AS A DIAGNOSTIC TOOL

As discussed at the beginning of this section, the analysis of team style, through revealing gaps in spontaneous motivation, can often throw light upon the source of difficulties within an organization, which otherwise could be wrongly interpreted and hence wrongly treated.

Kale and Co. Ltd., for instance, considering the team as it was constituted at the time of the first study, would not have benefited in the least from an o & M review; yet from an outside analysis, antiquated systems may well have been diagnosed as a major problem. The result of an o & M reorganization with such a team, predominant as it was in the willingness to *investigate* (hence to establish system) with far less motivation toward *decisive* action or implementation of those systems, would have had nil benefit. The beautiful new systems would have been resented and just not used successfully. In fact this had actually been happening before the study was done.

With Fellows Acre Ltd., however, there could be no such danger. They would be only too pleased to work a system, any system so long as it was laid down for them and they were not expected to fiddle around with it.

In Fellows Acre Ltd. there is little sign of formalized forward planning techniques. Without knowledge of the behavioural weightings in the company this could be seized upon as a fundamental need. The institution of formalized forward planning would, however, be superfluous, as the managers are already spontaneously motivated to plan ahead. Not that an Mbo exercise or such like would do the company any positive harm but it wouldn't be focusing on a fundamental need.

A similar mis-diagnosis could have been made in the case of Kale & Co. Ltd. They certainly weren't pursuing any objectives very obviously. But it wasn't the actual objective setting they needed, but an injection of a bit of realistic determination to get moving in pursuit of the objectives.

MATCHING COMPANY BUSINESS CLIMATE TO THE BROADER
INDUSTRIAL-COMMERCIAL CLIMATE

So far in the discussion of team style, the emphasis has been upon achieving a reasonably even spread of motivation across the twelve action requirements in order to prevent areas of weakness arising due to gaps in spontaneous motivation. But there is another side to it. One cannot help feeling that a completely balanced team, with a totally even spread across the twelve activities of management, must be a rather undynamic, mediocre affair. Surely it must be beneficial to have a degree of bias, to give the team that distinctive character or flavour with which its members can identify.

It would seem particularly advantageous to have the bias in a direction such that it suited the environment within which the team worked. It is logical to suppose, for instance, that biases in different areas would suit respectively a research oriented company, a company within a fast moving consumer industry, one with a particularly technical orientation and so on.... The precise definitions of such biases or business climates has been little researched so far, although it is certainly possible to surmise the orientations that might be best suited to various situations; e.g. 'Attention' orientation for the research organization, 'Commitment' orientation for the competitive fast moving consumer industry, etc.

However, this may well be an oversimplification. For a start, a distinction has to be made between a team (be it 'top team' or whatever) as a functioning unit within the company and with a particular role to play, and a team, perhaps particularly the top team, as representative of the company as a whole. Consider, for instance, the top team of the company in the fast moving consumer industry. As a representative of the company as a whole it would seem that the top team should have a commitment oriented style; i.e. the predominant motivation should be toward opportunist exploitation of current trends, with a strong competitive inclination. As a functioning unit within the company, however, the top team has the role predominantly of policy and strategy formation. This function, however, requires a pretty solid orientation toward the opposite-attention end of the scale.

An example might serve to clarify this. L. T. Cleaver Ltd. is a company in just such a fast moving consumer industry. It is at present highly successful, having made record profits three years running. The business climate created by the top team is very well balanced but with a slight weighting toward the attention-intention areas, particularly in the interaction areas *communicating* and *presenting* with least emphasis going to *deciding* and *operating*.

However, there is some evidence that the 'company business climate' as a whole is differently oriented. A study of forty-five middle managers was carried out in order to ascertain whether there was a discernible pattern within the action profiles which correlated with 'success' within that company. 'Success' was defined as effectiveness as judged by a jury of six senior managers. It was found that the following pattern predicted success with just one exception.

1 A score of 2·0 or more on:

      Investigating   *Operating*
      Determining   *Dynamism*
                      Deciding

But With

2 A score of between 1·0 and 2·0 allowable on:

                  Investigating or *Deciding*
providing there was alternatively a score of 2·0 or more on:
                       Communicating

This seems to indicate that to be considered 'successful' within this company it is an absolute necessity for a manager to be strong in *determining, operating* and *dynamism*.

Investigating and *deciding* are slightly less important. For whilst *deciding* is already covered by the requirement of *operating*, the interaction mode that draws *deciding* activity from other people, the need for *investigating* is also less crucial providing its corresponding interaction mode *communicating* is strong.

This is, of course, a useful piece of information for this company to know and would obviously be a useful kind of criteria for any company to possess. However, it also indicates something about the business climate created by the company as a whole.

If it is true that successful men make a successful company (and this company is highly successful), then it would seem logical to ascertain that a business climate created by a style that was weighted strongly toward *determining, operating* with a spread of high *dynamism* and well backed up by motivation toward *investigating, deciding* and *communicating* would enable L. T. Cleaver to operate most effectively within its particular environment. It must be stressed, however, that the bias toward the above components should never be allowed to rise above a certain level. If the weighting on strengths in the less emphasized of the first six action requirements should fall below say 14 per cent or 13 per cent as they did in Kale & Co. Ltd. (see page 187) particularly in the assertion factors *investigating, determining* and *deciding*, then the company would be in danger of creating a business climate too specialized to cope in a fast changing world.

Thus whilst we cannot as yet provide totally positive answers to questions concerning the matching of company climate to the broader industrial-commercial climate, there are certainly some guidelines appearing. At least the methods by which such information can be gained are becoming more apparent.

NEED TO IDENTIFY WITH THE TEAM STYLE

The importance of team style in providing a distinctive character with which its members can identify, was illustrated well by a recent study. The team had over a relatively short space of time received a new Managing Director, and four additional new members. This inrush of new blood had very evidently caused considerable dislocation and distress within the team.

Analysis of the action profiles showed that the new Managing Director, who had a strong personal style quite different from the former Managing Director, had recruited men close to his own style. In effect he was promoting a different image, hence upsetting the team's well established sense of identity. Many of the executives, particularly the longer standing ones, were worried about this and expressed concern that a split was appearing in a previously united team. Analsyis of team style in terms of the two groups—the 'old' members and the 'new' members—revealed the following differences: (The analysis shown here is performed according to spread of predominant strengths (score 3·0 or more). This gives an indication as to the direction in which the strongest joint motivation is pushing. Consequently differences are thrown up more clearly.)

The feelings that people have in such a situation vary of course from individual to individual, and are expressed in many different ways with various emotional overtones. If a summary can be made of the predominant feelings

Comparison of Groups within a Team

	New Members = 5		Old Members = 7		
	No. of Strengths (3·0 or greater)	% of Group	No. of Strengths (3·0 or greater)	% of Group	Difference
1 Investigating	3	60%	7	71%	11
2 Exploring	4	80%	1	14%	(66)
3 Determining	2	40%	2	29%	11
4 Confronting	3	60%	5	71%	11
5 Deciding	4	80%	3	43%	(37)
6 Anticipating	3	60%	6	88%	(28)
7 Communicating	3	60%	2	29%	(31)
8 Presenting	2	40%	4	57%	17
9 Operating	1	20%	2	29%	9
10 Dynamism	5	100%	7	100%	0
11 Adaptability	2	40%	3	43%	3
12 Identifying	5	100%	6	88%	12

Table 16. Team style of 'old' and 'new' members compared—Dall Overton Ltd.
Strength is defined as: Score of 3·0 or greater as measured on 4 point scale.
Areas of greatest difference are circled.

evident within each group it would be that whilst on the one hand the 'old group' felt the 'new group' was aggressively eager to make changes without due consideration for the roots of the company, the 'new members' felt that the 'old group' was narrow in outlook and outmoded in its approach to management.

The differences were naturally explained often in terms of background and experience. The Managing Director, Production Director, and Finance Director had all recently come from large public companies and this was seen to be an influencing factor in their approach, which no doubt it was. This led to the criticism understandably that they didn't allow for the 'personal' nature of a smaller private company. They were schooled in the tough depersonalized style of so called professional management and insensitive to the 'spirit' of this company. Most of the old members had spent a large part of their career at the one company. Hence they were somewhat written off as stick in the mud, old fogeys. However, it could equally be argued that all of the new members had spent as long at their various other companies at various stages during their career.

Our contention is that whilst people certainly are pawns to their environment, influenced by their various experiences, susceptible to prevailing attitudes; each person incorporates the fruits of his experiences according to the enduring dictates of his own personality. Two people may emerge from the same moulding experience with a similar attitude, yet the way that attitude is later retained, discarded, expressed, implemented will depend upon factors inherent in each person's personality pattern.

Hence an analysis of more fundamental behavioural differences is a more solid basis for promoting clarity than any amount of history comparing. Even pointing to a single difference such as between the *exploratory* and *anticipatory* approach has been found to cast a considerable light over the otherwise confused mass of supposition, inference and emotion.

It can be seen from Table 16 that the greatest differences between the two groups appear in *exploring, deciding, anticipating* and *communicating.* The old members are much stronger in *anticipating* (88 per cent of the old group show positive strengths whereas only 60 per cent of the new group do). The new members are stronger in *exploring* (80 per cent versus 43 per cent) and *deciding* (80 per cent versus 43 per cent) backed up by *communicating* (100 per cent versus 71 per cent).

Except in the *exploring* area, where the old members are definitely weak, it is not so much a comparison of strong versus weak but a comparison of emphasis. For the old members the emphasis is very much on *anticipating* a prospect on the basis of detailed analysis of the situation in front of them. For the new members the emphasis is more upon throwing up all the possibilities available—to seek for new ideas, not just to *investigate* what happens to come up, but with much less emphasis on projecting toward an objective or end result. Their *communicational* strength would enhance still further the tendency to stay longer in the initial review and *exploratory* stage. On the other hand, their emphasis on *deciding* lends a much greater urgency to their approach than is the case with the older members.

Such differences are important because they are fundamental to the way in which the two groups are interacting and the way in which they feel about each other. These differences were discussed as follows:

The team as a whole is characterized by a high overall level of *dynamism* and *identification.* This gives rise to a high level of activity in terms of sheer exertion plus the possibility of strong sense of team unity. The qualification is made because some have expressed the feeling that at present there exists a 'split', a degree of difference of interest and feeling amongst the team as it is now constituted, which did not exist before the appointment of the new

Managing Director, Mr. Story. This has caused considerable anxiety to some of the longstanding members of the team. Thus it may sound a contradiction to state that the quality of *identification* which makes for a sense of participation and team cohesiveness is still strongly evident in all members of the team.

The seriousness of the breakdown in team unity may have been somewhat over-exaggerated. Precisely the fact that there is a strong need for involvement and *identification* will mean that any degree of disunity will be felt more intensely. Were there a higher degree of aloofness or detachment within the team, lack of unity could be tolerated with much less concern. The trend appears to be toward improvement in the situation. There is evidence of a great readiness on the part of the older members of the team to accept the Managing Director and recognize the benefits that he can bring about. It would improve the situation if there were a similar readiness on the part of the Managing Director to recognize that a bigger contribution could be drawn from the older members of the team.

Reasons given to explain the 'split' have been various, but there is an underlying feeling amongst some that there has been a somewhat aggressive advocacy of the need for change from the newer members without the slightest recognition of the successes in the past. There is a general agreement that change is for the good and a strong willingness to accept and further it, yet it would be inhuman if there were not a feeling that every time a change is proposed, there is an implied criticism of the way things were done before. These are very human feelings, but there is another fundamental reason why the addition of three new members to the board should be felt so keenly.

Many have recognized that, in general, there has been a lack of readiness to *explore* amongst the group and from the behavioural studies this is certainly borne out. Of the twelve people studied only five are strongly *exploratory*. Four of these are new members. The three additions to the main board are all strongly *exploratory*. Of the existing members only Mr. Skate (the Company Secretary) is strongly *exploratory*.

The approach evidenced by the three new main board members (and Mr. Sawyer, the Personnel Manager, when he participates) is therefore fundamentally different from the style portrayed by the older members. Amongst the newer members there is a spontaneous readiness to continuously question the way things are done. There is never just one way, always there are six alternative ways. Nothing can be accepted simply because it is there, but every possible alternative must be *explored*. Before any decision can be made there are many possibilities to be reviewed. This is a spontaneous approach. It does not happen so much in a formal or studied way.

Amongst the older members of the team there is a much greater weighting in favour of the *anticipatory* approach. Here the motivation is toward being in tune with the trends, to see where events are leading, with much less concern for the details of the present. There is a far greater ability to set objectives which are flexibly in tune with the way events are moving. This is not necessarily manifest in the drawing up of formal forward plans.

It is interesting to note that where there is a spontaneous behavioural readiness there is often less tendency to apply formalized methods or techniques. Hence those naturally strong in *anticipating* (i.e. the older members) will be more likely to institute formal methods of survey and review; i.e. *exploration*. In comparison those naturally strong in *exploring* (the newer members) will be more likely to want to institute formalized methods of outlining forward plans and objectives. Each can play a useful part—both the formal techniques and spontaneous behaviour stemming from the different approaches.

It may be beneficial to highlight the kinds of misunderstanding that can arise from such differences of approach in a more colourful way.

The Anticipatory Approach

On the part of people more *anticipatory* in approach there is an inbuilt confidence that their sense for the way events are leading toward a future prospect is perceptively accurate. There is also a tendency to cope with various problems by preventing their occurrence by means of *anticipation* of how events are going. They cope by means of insightful prevention rather than resourcefulness in finding a cure after the event.

The Exploratory Approach

People who are more *exploratory* in approach may simply not foresee a possible problem. However, they in their turn have an inbuilt confidence that whatever problems do turn up, they will have a sufficient fund of resource, alternatives, ideas to draw upon in order to cope with any eventuality. They cope by means of resourceful cure rather than relying on foresight.

The misunderstandings that may arise are that whilst on the one hand the more *anticipatory* group may have no faith in the resourcefulness of the more *exploratory* group, the *exploratory* group will distrust the foresight of the more *anticipatory* group. Such a fundamental difference can underlie many of the surface differences that occur. The problem is, of course, that disagreements will be seen in the form of the details of various discussions and differences that arise and the basic reason can remain undiscovered. Although there has been an influx of people strong in the *exploratory* motivation, there is still an overall weakness here, compared to the good spread of strengths in other areas. Thus it is essential to make the best use of what there is available.

The fact that there is in addition amongst the newer members a greater readiness to relate in the *communicative* manner (60 per cent versus 29 per cent) which is the manner of relating to encourage the activity of *exploring* and *investigating*, must render the *exploratory* approach even more obvious.

They are ready not only to contribute the fruits of their individual *exploration,* but in the process of their interaction ideas will escalate and there will be a gathering of momentum in this way.

In addition the greater motivation within the newer members to actually get to a stage of commitment (80 per cent versus 43 per cent on *deciding*) must be felt by the older members. This may be felt as unnecessary urgency by the older members, whilst the newer members will feel frustration at the apparent lack of willingness to start off the process of implementation.

The answer must lie in greater understanding of the special contribution that each approach can make. However, there is perhaps a slightly greater need for the particular contribution made by the *exploratory* approach to be recognized and understood. It is making a big difference to the style of the team, but a beneficial difference.

Meanwhile there is evidence that the trend is positive. Such differences as there are, are becoming less if anything rather than more. Bearing in mind that there is a strong participatory readiness evident amongst the team there is certainly little need for concern that the team spirit will be destroyed. It may change in nature, but certainly it won't disappear.

PART IV

Results

CHAPTER 15

Criteria

It must be apparent from the previous accounts, that the influence upon a company as a result of a 'Top Team Planning' study must vary considerably. The extent of that influence must vary, the nature of that influence must vary and so too must the benefits gained. A case has already been made for the usefulness of the action profile information, apart from its accuracy. But how can such usefulness be measured? What are the positive benefits to be gained from the application of the action profile assessment and, more to the point, its extension to a 'Top Team Planning' study? Indication of benefits have already been given in various places, but there must ultimately be a concerted effort to evaluate the 'Top Team Planning' exercise as concretely and usefully as possible.

In order to measure the success and effectiveness of anything, a criterion has to be set up. To measure the effectiveness of a new machine the criterion might be increase in production, or decrease in breakdowns, or improvement in quality. The criterion will depend upon the type of machine and the reason for its installation and will be relatively easy to define. If improvement in quality is required, a machine is installed which is likely to obtain that improvement and its effectiveness is measured accordingly.

The commissioning of a 'Top Team Planning' assignment is obviously a much more complex process, and many more variables are involved. Of the managers who have been responsible for commissioning a 'Top Team Planning' assignment, their reasons for doing so have been various and so too have their expectations of the benefits to be gained. It is usually possible to point to a central need, such as a succession problem or conflict, but beyond that the range of expected benefits and actual benefits is wide.

It is possible to categorize the kinds of benefits that can result from a 'Top Team Planning' study:

1 In the case of the individual managers studied it will result in increased self-awareness and a more accurate perception of individual style.

2 It may result in an increased awareness of others, enabling a different approach and more effective interaction.

3 This may extend to a whole group or team, which will result in more effective team work.

4 There may also be an increased awareness of team style in all its aspects, i.e. as company identity, reflection of leadership, an inbuilt criterion for success within that company, and a powerful force in the creation of the company business climate.

5 There will be a clearer understanding of individual development needs in terms of how the individual sees himself and how the company (as represented by superior, training officer or whatever) sees him.

We have to assume that all the above are beneficial, i.e. that it leads to greater managerial effectiveness. Some may dispute this. It is difficult to prove conclusively that greater awareness and understanding of people in management does lead to greater efficiency, and increased profits. But it seems a logical assumption to say that if people work better together with fewer crossed wires, greater effectiveness will result, and the evidence does point in that direction.

More straightforward benefits accruing from the use of action profile information in a 'Top Team Planning' study are:

1 Appropriate new appointments where identified as needed.

2 Appropriate dismissals where identified as needed.

3 Beneficial job changes where relevant and possible.

4 Organizational change and improvement where needed.

In practice not all the above apply to the results of any one particular 'Top Team Planning' study and the degree to which any occur will vary according to the personality and needs of the client. The needs of the client vary in complexity and range. However, in each case it is possible to identify a primary need.

One of the most straightforward ways of judging the effectiveness of a 'Top Team Planning' study then is to isolate the primary need as indicated by the client and then to ascertain whether that need has been achieved. This procedure will be applied to eight 'Top Team Planning' assignments. The results are discussed in the next chapter.

CHAPTER 16

Follow-up

1962 *Ferrier A.E. Ltd.*

The Need: To set up a marketing department.

In 1962 the board had decided on the recommendation of another group of consultants that a marketing department should be set up. Mr. Selman, who was to head the department, had to recruit his own staff, and determined to use the action profile information to assist him. The task included picking a team which would have to start from scratch and introduce marketing techniques. This team was to be the first professional managerial team outside the production side.

A team of five, excluding Selman, was established. Under Selman there was a marketing planning manager and three brand managers which were newly created functions. Market research, product development and advertising were moved from other departments into the new marketing department.

Gradually the department became operationally sophisticated and began to show profits. It has been reputed to have saved the company £30,000 in the first year.

Selman found that the reports made on the men who were to make up his marketing team were good guides. However, he saw the reports as being valid only while a carefully constructed team remained. In such instances they were 'on the whole, very effective'. When one member was removed, however, the effectiveness of the whole team was likely to decrease, and the man who had been removed might also be found to function less effectively in another team.

The above team, as it was set up by Selman and Warren Lamb, worked well for two years. However, in 1967 the company merged with another and a further reorganization took place, and Selman moved to sales, away from marketing.

SUCCESSION AND FULL UTILIZATION OF STRENGTHS

1964 *Trailer Evans & Co.*

This is a company in the construction business which at the time of the study had four separate operating divisions.

The Need:

    (i) To solve a succession problem.

    (ii) To ease communications and to see that men were in positions where their strengths could be applied and their weaknesses were not crucial.

The study was commissioned by the then Chairman of the company who was contemplating retirement in the near future and was concerned to leave his house in order. His son was a manager at that time and the father was concerned as to whether he could take on the responsibility of the company.

The eight most senior managers in the company were studied. It was confirmed that the son was indeed capable of greater responsibility. He is now a successful Chairman. Action profile information showed that two of the eight did not fit in with the team style and were constituting a serious barrier to the successful team work potentially available amongst the others. One of these men was persuaded to leave soon after the study had been done. The son was able to take over his division and improve the existing low state of morale considerably. The other manager identified as prohibiting efficient team work was allowed, however, to remain for another two years. He finally retired a year early, leaving a factory in a disastrous state and running at a loss.

The following suggestions were made toward a reallocation of abilities:

    1 The manager strongest in the 'intention' area with the most pioneering aptitude and the ability to persevere with a badly run down situation, and who had founded a division from scratch in Scotland, it was suggested could take on a problem division which was in a very bad state.

This was not carried out. The Scottish division was running smoothly and the son did not feel he could take the risk. (Although the father had been in agreement.) Subsequently they had to close down the problem division. The manager concerned did not know of this proposal at the time, but commented later: 'I've certainly had a fair amount of experience in the company of going into the sticky bits and trying to put it right, so that had I gone to Hellmay, I would certainly have enjoyed it and probably had some success, but I don't think it would have had any material effect on the final disposing of the business.' Who's to know?

The son did comment at about the same time that retrospectively some of the traps they had fallen into would have been avoided if they had stuck more closely to what had been suggested as a result of the study.

Further suggestions were made as follows:

    2 The manager who at the time of the study was under the son at one of the divisions, would be capable of running it on his own

allowing the son to take on greater overall responsibility. He subsequently did this very successfully and then proceeded to take over the loss making division from the manager who had been retired early. He has gradually improved the situation till now in his third year he is expected to make a profit of £110,000 a turn around from a loss of £40,000.

3 It was suggested that the son could form a particularly efficient team with a relatively new member of the team. This happened as the new member was moved to the son's division and the son recognized that it was indeed true that they made a compatible working team.

The company has, since the study, continued to increase its profits. An overall comment made by the present Chairman is that:

'This method has helped partly as a means of placing people correctly relative to strengths and weaknesses.' He did not know if the method had any real validity. 'It may be a load of rubbish but he is getting good results because of his (Warren Lamb's) own perception.' Considering the short time Warren Lamb was with Trailer Evans & Co., he felt the reports were accurate and helpful.

A CONFLICT SITUATION

1968 R. N. Sniper Ltd.

The Need: To resolve an entrenched conflict situation.

The company had been built up over the years by Lawrence whose entrepreneurial flair, tempered by the discrimination of his brother David, made it a profitable concern. Company activities were divided into two main areas. The largest was the machinery and contracting section which represented the core of the company's trading activities, the other was comprised of various interests including horticultural and retail businesses.

The family controlled the company, and problems had arisen when Lawrence's son, Stephen, was appointed Managing Director. He had grown up with the company and was over-shadowed by the dominant character of his father, and to a lesser extent by David, who represented the older generation. The conflict generated by these relationships emerged at board level where, because of the tension, policy making became frozen and the company began to lose profits.

More specific factors leading to the conflict included the failure of the company to retain outsiders who had recently joined, either because Stephen the son felt his control challenged or because the company did not offer the organizational framework within which new members could operate. Some of the businesses belonging to the second area of activity were running at a loss and this was used to support those who wished to retain only the tradi-

tional interests of the company. Stephen felt that one possible solution to
the problems was to merge or be taken over by another company, and had
made tentative steps in this direction. Further difficulties arose because of
the extent to which the directors' shareholdings were locked in the company,
and any selling of these was regarded as a traitorous action. Stephen claimed
to be frustrated by the lack of progressiveness in the company and had handed
in his resignation by August 1969.

The terms of reference drawn up for the study included recommended
action for an organization framework that would encourage more effective
policy formulation. This would involve renewing the present structure and
method of policy formulation, an investigation of the roles of executive
directors, a survey of the execution of director responsibilities and information
necessary to plan effective leadership. Alongside this, suggestions for the
development of senior management abilities and planning for succession
would be made. The establishment of current senior manpower requirements
consistent with business objectives would be necessary. Finally, definitions
would be required to outline directors' distinctive individual contributions,
senior management responsibilities and the principal senior management
activities.

The subjects of the survey were:

> Lawrence—Chairman and Founder
> David—Lawrence's brother
> Stephen—(Lawrence's son)—Managing Director
> Michael—(David's son)

and three other executive directors, the Company Secretary and a
Director Designate. Behavioural studies of the men involved were
made and analysed against the yardstick of action requirements for
management.

Stephen, David and Lawrence (and the director designate, now head of
administration) were asked how they felt about the survey two years after it
had been completed:

The now head of administration	'Warren Lamb's intervention, while it didn't bring about all the right solutions, certainly brought things up with a jerk, pointed out some possible solutions and paved the way to Lawrence's leaving the company' and 'I give him a lot of credit for what happened, but not all.'
Stephen now Managing Director	'We saw the survey as an agent of change. It had redirected the family conflict and provided a basis for re-thinking.'
David	'The survey was helpful in that it guided us towards better organization.'

Since the survey took place the company has overcome the heavy price that had to be paid for the conflict, and profits have risen appreciably.

Whereas one possible solution might earlier have been a takeover or merger, R. N. Sniper itself has now taken over one firm and plans further takeovers. It is true that another company wants to take the company over, but they have been able to withstand the pressure. Recently additional capital has been made available to the company—a sign that they are more favourably viewed by the city.

THE INHERITED TEAM

February 1970: *Stelion Wilmott Ltd.*

The Need: That of a new Managing Director to understand his people better and how best to work through them.

The company is a small subsidiary of a large group. Just prior to the 'Top Team Planning' survey, a new Managing Director had been appointed. There had been serious production problems and the Production Director had left. The company had just broken through to profitability after a difficult period but was again undergoing retrenchment because certain environmental conditions had reduced anticipated sales. The group as a whole was experiencing a difficult period with inevitably some backwash on Stelion Wilmott Ltd.

A stated objective was to achieve a certain turnover, more than three times the current turnover, and to increase the turnover considerably from new products. The overall need for diversification, because of the present reliance on weather conditions, had still not been satisfactorily met. Whilst the record of the existing 'top team' of senior executives had been good, it had been mainly in the climate of a recovery situation and the team could not claim to have had any experience in working together to meet ambitious business objectives.

The five senior executives were studied plus the new Managing Director.

The study prevented the Managing Director from making two precipitate dismissals. It gave him sufficient understanding of a man who at that time was fulfilling a technical design role, to give him the production position. This was a role for him which the Managing Director had not previously considered for a moment and which he was very much against at first. The appointment is proving highly successful. In general the study has given him increased awareness of his own style, that of his managers and his particular relationship to them. He has been able to alter his approach toward one manager, the Finance Director, which has resulted in greater effectiveness on his part. Previously he had been unwittingly pressurizing the poor man into a state of near paralysis. Amongst the other managers, the relationship between the Marketing and Finance Directors has improved visibly.

A by product of the study has been that the Group board has gained a greater appreciation of the Managing Director's way of working and have been able to utilize his particular *operational* talents more effectively.

TO BUILD A STRONGER TEAM

April 1970 *Kale & Co. Ltd.*

The Need: To enable a new Managing Director in an extremely difficult situation to decide which of his present team were good enough for their jobs and in general how he could use the management material he had.

Mr. Myer and Kale & Co. Ltd. have already been referred to in previous chapters. Kale & Co. is the run down Northern company, taken over by an American International corporation. Mr. Myer is the *unadaptable* manager who although successful in supposedly similar situations in other places all over the world, had great difficulty in getting this company to yield results in response to his leadership and was consistently making a loss.

At the time of the 'Top Team Planning' survey he had a team in which he placed little confidence. He was simply unable to identify which were the managers who should be given greater responsibility, which he could usefully move elsewhere and which, if any, would have to depart.

Now, three years later, there is a strong management team of seven at Kale & Co., four of which were already in the company at the time of the study and three of which have been recruited during the study, which took place in two stages. Both divisions of the company are now making a profit, though the smaller one is still struggling.

The work done at Kale & Co. has been the most extensive of any 'Top Team Planning' studies and the company has been influenced according to all the categories previously mentioned (pages 217–18).

1 Increased self awareness of individual managers.

Myer himself has had exhaustive discussions on his own style of management. On moving from this company he is proposing to base decisions about future situations upon this information.

Apart from the normal counselling sessions, the thirty-two managers who have been studied have attended a 'teach-in' for further education on the action profile concepts, with group discussions on specific problems.

Three of the senior managers, the Financial Director, Personnel Manager and Deputy Managing Director, have undergone individual courses, varying from ten half day sessions to four full day sessions. These courses were based directly upon the action profile information.

2 The extension of increased awareness of own style to that of others, enabling a different approach and more effective interaction.

Evidence of this happening tends to come from the comments of individual managers. The Sales Manager of the largest division, for instance, had been having trouble with his office manager. His morale seemed to be low. He had plenty of ideas but never seemed to do anything about them and was being reprimanded regularly by the Managing Director for making errors in calculations and other routine matters.

The Sales Manager had diagnosed the problem as lack of 'commitment'. The action profile study showed him to be very weak in 'intention' with almost no *determining*. It was advised that he needed support here, almost to the extent of morale boosting. The man needed to be given the basic confidence that he could do his job.

The Sales Manager has been approaching him in this way and he has shown remarkable improvement. He is now fully in control of the job and taking initiative in relevant areas beyond his immediate concern.

3 Awareness of interaction in terms of the action profile enabling more effective team work.

The sales team has had a half day seminar based upon their own profiles, interaction and team style.

Five senior managers defined as holding the 'key' positions underwent a five day training course, a great deal of which has already been described (page 161). The aim of this course was precisely to acquaint each manager in detail with the effects of his behaviour in terms of the action profile and to give guidelines as to more effective team interaction.

All the senior managers reported improvement in their relationships with Myer after being able to compare their own action profile with his.

4 Increased awareness of team style.

This can only be said to apply to the five managers who took part in the training course. They learnt to recognize their *operational* style and to realize its strengths and limitations.

5 Understanding of development needs.

Apart from the normal counselling sessions, discussions have taken place with superiors with particular reference to the development needs of their subordinates. The Personnel Manager has been trained to interpret the action profile and has incorpor-

H

ated the terms into a development programme and appraisal scheme.

According to the last three categories of influence:

(a) New appointments.

Two new appointments have been successfully made according to the action profile assessment.

(b) Dismissals.

One manager was immediately asked to leave on the results of the survey and is now more happily placed with his own small business.

Of the ten originally studied, four were seen as possible growth prospects but with a question mark. Of these, one (a Sales Manager) has been returned to straight selling (much to his relief), one has been fired and two are presently considered to be making satisfactory progress.

(c) Organizational change.

This has occurred only in terms of individual roles and based rather upon action profile information (and other factors of course) than on direct recommendation.

The head of design of the larger division was made first, technical manager of that division then production and technical manager and is proving highly successful. The former technical manager, for whom a contraction of role was recommended, was made Deputy Managing Director but is still considered only a moderate success, although he has a profound knowledge of the industry.

TO ENCOURAGE INITIATIVE

June 1970 *Pennsylvania Industries*

The Need: To find out why the senior management team was taking considerably less initiative than the Managing Director expected.

Mr. Lexington is the Managing Director concerned. He has been described at length on pages 48–54. As already discussed, the question was answered primarily in terms of the distinctive style of his management team, the rather flamboyant characteristics displayed by Mr. Lexington himself and the interaction between the two.

It took a long hard battle to persuade him of this. With accusations of the consultants' alleged onesidedness and naivety, he disappeared without trace for six months. Six months later he reappeared, asserted that the intervening period had proved the assessments 'brilliant' much to his chagrin, as he had been looking for inconsistencies. He claimed to have a better understanding now of his executives and requested three more assessments.

Mr. Lexington now has a reasonable understanding of the action profile terms and uses the assessments in his own way, and entirely for his own purposes. The executives in the first group were given counselling sessions. Mr. Lexington considered this to have been useless in some cases and harmful in others. Hence no more contact is now allowed with any of his executives.

AN ORGANIZATION PROBLEM

March 1970 *Fellows Acre Ltd.*

The Need: To clarify functions, and delineate roles more clearly to prevent overlapping according to the strengths of managers.

This survey has also been described to some extent in previous chapters˙ The idea of the survey of the organization structure came from the Managing Director as a service which would help him to plan improvements both to meet and encourage company growth. The company was (and is) profitable and although open to some criticisms could be claimed to be successful. The survey was therefore conducted in a healthy context and free from pressure to meet any sort of crisis.

The survey took place in two stages. The company was divided geographically, as mentioned earlier, with divisions in Nottingham, Bristol and Manchester. The Managing Director was located at Bristol, the Chairman at Nottingham, whilst the works were at Manchester. The Chairman was at first sceptical of the survey so it was confined to the Bristol division. After the presentation of the first stage report, the Chairman insisted that the rest of the company was studied. Overall, thirty managers were studied, including the Chairman and the Managing Director and the General Works Manager who comprised the board of directors.

At the time of the survey the structure was loosely organized around three divisions and an export division. The structure was as shown in Chart 3.

The Managing Director was concerned as to whether he could effectively operate a structure with so many departments directly responsible to him. He had several possibilities in mind such as amalgamating divisions 2 and 3 and moving the export clerical staff under the home office manager. However, any organizational change was clearly understood to depend upon the strengths of the people and to be governed by that consideration.

A matching process was carried out between the needs (as defined by the Managing Director and the consultants) and managerial potential, in the light of information thrown up by the survey.

FELLOWS ACRE LTD.

ORGANIZATION STRUCTURE BEFORE SURVEY

Division 1 (Bristol)
M.D.
Chief Engineer
Sales Manager
Marketing Manager
Office Manager
Research and Development Manager
Service Manager

Division 2 (Nottingham)
M.D.
Sales Director (Chairman)
Sales Manager
Office Manager (Bristol)

Division 3 (Bristol)
M.D.
Chief Engineer
Sales Manager
Office Manager

Export Division (Bristol
  all divisions)
M.D.
Manager
Shipping—Sales

Accounts and Secretarial

M.D.
Company Secretary
Accountant
Cashier—credit control

General Admin
M.D.
General Manager
Female Supervisor

Works (Manchester)
M.D.
General Manager
Factory managers (2)
R & D Engineer
Accountant
Buyer

Chart 3

The Needs

1 Clarification of an untidy organization structure at Bristol causing overlapping and duplication, particularly in respect to administration.

2 Simplification of the lines of authority from the Managing Director.

3 More effective organizing of development effort, more directly related to an adequately performed marketing function.

4 Provision of corporate planning against the Board's ambitious growth targets.

In ability to meet these needs, it was apparent that as the team was presently structured and in terms of the predominant team style (pages 194–206), there were some gaps, or rather mismatches of motivation, in relation to function.

The behavioural requirements to fill the gaps were defined and matched against the characteristics shown by the managers. On the basis of this and in conference with the Managing Director, the structure in Chart 4 was defined.

The most significant point about this structure is that it makes the distinction between the operational function and advisory more policy forming oriented function and distinguishes people who are BEHAVIOURALLY more suited to carry out these functions.

The marketing planner, head of administration services and technical adviser (at that time chief engineer of Division 1) were considered three people who could become a management 'brainbox' to which the Managing Director could refer problems singly and as a group. The instigation of this arrangement came:

(a) From the need for the review, advisory, questioning function to be emphasized due to the predominantly commitment, *operational* team style and:

(b) From the fact that these three men all have a strong weighting in the attention area according to their action profiles (at least stronger than other members of the team: see chart).

For the operational function, the Division 2 and 3 man was identified as having good all round managerial ability. The Division 1 man was seen as not so strong but the only person available. According to the Managing Director this structure is working excellently. He finds the advisory group a great assistance.

In terms of the other areas of influence the following are apparent:

1 Self awareness:

The Managing Director himself reports that he is now more aware of his behaviour in terms of the action profile.

One of his major problems, due to equal stress on each of the three assertion factors, is a circularity in action (going back to *investigation* as soon as a *decision* is about to be made typified by constant changes in priority).

He says that he is aware of this and constantly questions himself as to whether a *re-investigation* is really necessary. He admits truthfully that it is hard not to fool himself.

Other problem areas were a lack of *confrontation* and *presentation* (inability to challenge subordinates) and a tendency to precipitate them into activity without first *communicating* the reasons why.

Fellows Acre Ltd.: Organization structure after Top Team Planning

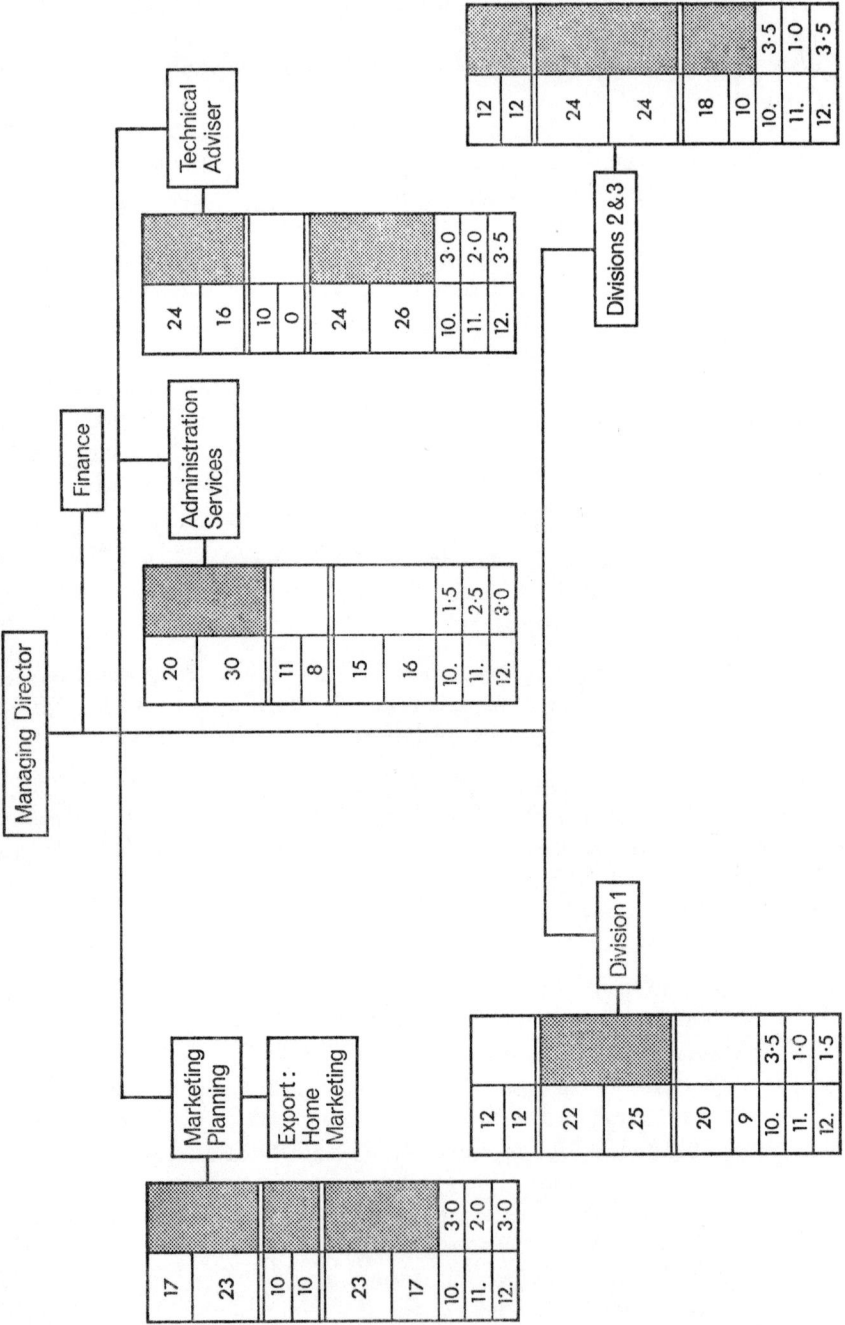

Chart 4

He is attempting to rectify this, but finds it hard to know if he's successful or not. The main thing is that he's aware of it and prepared to cope with the possible consequences.

2 Awareness of others:

The Managing Director for example has been able to approach people differently. The head of administration for instance, who is weak in *determining,* he feels he has been able to supply him with resolve (see page 149). Under this treatment he has improved considerably.

The action profile material has been used in considering job changes made after the survey was done.

The general works manager has used the action profiles in preparing for a reorganization of the factories.

3 Team Style:

As well as the three directors the advisory team have all had access to this analysis and have given it considerable thought. The analyses of the two teams, Bristol (sales oriented) and Manchester (production oriented), has enabled a better co-ordination of the two:

'Manchester have altered quite a lot in their outlook. Probably as traditionally it was two separate things (production and sales) nobody wanted to change the status quo. But we are co-ordinating more smoothly now.'

In considering a streamlining of the staff at the works the team style information influenced the choice in making one of two men redundant. The one with the 'attention' weighted balancing characteristics was retained. See the account of Laver (page 126). In general as the Managing Director said:

'Now we realize you have to ask questions. My own role has been comparatively decisive in making them ask questions—to say let's be more selective, contract into situations we're really good at.'

5 Awareness of Development Needs:

Apart from the individual awareness generated through counselling sessions, little co-ordinated effort has as yet been attempted. The Managing Director has felt it necessary to wait until the team has stabilized after the various restructurings before a development programme is put in hand. It is projected that the head of administration, has the aptitude to take this on.

6 Appointments:

None have been made.

7 Dismissals:
   Two have been judged necessary due to unfavourable trade
   conditions. Decisions as to who, were influenced by action
   profile information.

8 Organization change:
   The primary need—dealt with above.

L. T. Cleaver Ltd.

The Need: To keep a continuous account of the available managerial
          strengths.

L. T. Cleaver is a fast growing company, with a multi-million pounds
turnover in the pharmaceuticals industry. They have been using action profile
information for 20 years. Over that time more than two hundred studies have
been made of managers largely at senior level for appointment and promotion,
in answer to particular problems and in consideration of possible team com-
positions and organization changes. The action profiles are being used more
and more now in planning induction and development measures.

This company has seen the development of the action profile approach
right from the beginning. At first there was a great deal of scepticism and
lack of understanding of the theory underlying the method (not surprisingly
as it was still in the process of being formulated). With the distillation of the
twelve factor framework six years ago, there has been rapid progress both in
acceptance and understanding of the method.

There is now a library of over a hundred action profiles of managers in the
company including all the senior managers and an increasing number of
middle and junior executives. The action profiles are presented both in chart
form as used in this book and score form to allow easier comparison of
individuals and groups.

The twenty most senior managers have undergone a fairly concentrated
programme of education on the action profile concepts. This culminated (for
the 'top team') in a day meeting where the action profiles of the participants
were openly displayed and used as a basis for discussion of individual ways of
working, possibilities for greater use of action motivations and possibilities
of various groupings for various functions. Specific exercises used were an
attempt at solving the mystery of a problem team using action profile information and analysis of videotaped discussions of specially composed groups (as
in the five-day group course, see page 244). A two-day course with similar
objectives to the five-day course was conducted for the next level.

One of the most significant indications of the usefulness of the action profile
approach which was clearly evident at these meetings was the use of the terms
as a systematic language. The managers were all able to use the framework

of management action precisely, accurately and fluently as a medium for discussion of people characteristics which allowed much greater clarity and mutual understanding than would ever be achieved otherwise.

The managing director has been able to devote a considerable amount of time to special projects concerning the action profile assessments. (He has his top team so well organized that he has time for such diversions!) One such project was the investigation into the action profile pattern of the 'successful' L. T. Cleaver manager (see page 208). As mentioned before, a clear pattern did emerge.

To be able to identify a measurable criteria which will predict with almost 100 per cent accuracy whether a manager is likely to be considered effective within a company, is obviously a great advance in the use of behavioural study. But such a criteria, at this stage, obviously cannot be used carte blanche. There are still too many unknown factors. The managing director of L. T. Cleaver approached the problem in this fashion:

> 'It is difficult to be clear about what should be done about the results of this survey. On the one hand there is reasonably clear evidence that there is a means of predicting likely effectiveness within the LTC organization. On the other hand these managers seem to be effective, but may be being effective because of attributes of other managers who are not being seen to be effective. One must approach the problem rather cautiously. However, it may be worthwhile considering that new entrants should be checked against the criteria listed above, and if they fail to meet them *significantly* then they should not be appointed. However, one should tend to think that in this experimental stage if a particular applicant's experience and success pattern seems particularly appropriate for us, although he marginally fails to meet the criteria, one should feel free to recruit him.
>
> Similarly, if on any internal promotions or transfers where the managers involved are not too clear as to whether the person will be successful or not in the new role, checking the action profile assessment might help in confirming a decision, but it is important to think very carefully about a person's actual behaviour pattern if the action profile criteria indicate a potential failure. One needs to think about whether in fact the action profile assessment on the particular action requirement is correct or not, and it is possible for an observant manager who has worked with a person for a year or more to have a clear view over most of these important action requirements.'

A further project on which the managing director is embarking is an empirical definition of the particular action motivation pattern required for a particular function in L. T. Cleaver. The method for doing this will be to

I

study the action profiles of managers who have fulfilled the role and look for differences between those who were effective and those who were not, so as to isolate the main requirements for effectiveness in that job. The action requirements for a job can obviously be determined via questioning managers, but only to a certain level of accuracy. Mistakes will always creep in because consultants and managers have preconceptions about what a job should entail, very often prejudiced by their own action motivations and of course the actual content of a function, though it may be called the same thing, will vary over time within one organization and between organizations. An empirical definition such as is being attempted by the managing director of L. T. Cleaver will give a far higher level of accuracy to the isolation of the pattern of action requirements for particular jobs.

CHAPTER 17

Prospects

So far as the practice of the action profile approach as applied in the 'Top Team Planning' study goes and as the follow-up chapter has indicated, the 'Top Team Planning' study is becoming an increasingly useful form of behavioural study in management. Although the extent of the study and the extent of application of the action profile principles vary considerably, in each case the primary need of the client at least has been met. Mr. Lexington of Pennsylvania Industries is perhaps a minor exception as there is little evidence that he has as yet overcome his problem of lack of initiative from senior executives, but he certainly now has a more systematic and disciplined understanding of their strengths and limitations. In the case of the other studies the primary need was met in a more straightforward way. In the Ferrier A. E. Ltd. study, the need was to set up a marketing department and a very successful marketing department was set up. For Trailer Evans & Co. the need was to solve a succession problem and use managerial strengths to greatest advantage. The first need was met absolutely and the second to a high degree. Even in a highly emotionally charged situation as in R. N. Sniper Ltd. the problem of an entrenched conflict situation was solved. The need of the new managing director of Stelion Wilmott Ltd. to understand his inherited team better and how best to work through them was also met. The changes he made based on the action profile assessments were still working two years after the study. Of Kale & Co. Ltd., Mr. Myer's primary need was to build a stronger team and this he was certainly able to do. The managing director of Fellows Acre Ltd. was able to effect a reorganization to his complete satisfaction.

Of course in taking such a blunt criteria of the effectiveness of a 'Top Team Planning' study as we have here; i.e. the fulfilment of a primary need, one is open to the criticism that the 'Top Team Planning' study may just have coincided with an improvement in the situation and not actually been the cause of it and secondly that there is no evidence that as good or better results would not have been achieved without the study. Such criticisms are relevant and also pretty well unanswerable. However, if time after time the primary need is met or the problem is solved and if the 'Top Team Planning' study continues to coincide with improvements in utilization of managerial strengths and greater understanding of individual managers' ways of working, if managers continue to show evidence that they would prefer the aid of the action profile information to their own intuition or luck, then one begins to feel more confidence in assuming that there is some causal relationship between improvement in understanding and utilization of managerial potential and use of the action profile approach in a 'Top Team Planning' study.

It is significant that of the last five companies in which studies have been carried out, four have become continuous employers of the action profile method. The other is satisfied but has found no further need yet for this kind of information. Forty-four other companies have been continuous employers of the action profile method at various times for several years. Since the distillation of the twelve action requirements factor and the consequent possibility of educating managers in the principles underlying the action profile study, the trend has been increasingly for managers to continue to make use of the assessments and to extend the use of the concepts into other areas.

In consideration of the more recent studies, where the work has not stopped at just a team report or individual assessment reports but has continued in various ways, the prospects for greater and greater use being made of the action profile material become very encouraging. Kale & Co. and L. T. Cleaver are examples of the extent to which the action profile approach can be used, and indicate that it can be developed even further. In both Kale & Co. and L. T. Cleaver there is now a library of systematically organized information on the spontaneous strengths and limitations of a large proportion of the executive personnel. There is, in addition, a common understanding of a language about managerial behaviour. There are development programmes on the basis of action profiles.

Individual and group training have been based upon action profile principles (concentratedly so in the Kale & Co. individual and five day courses). Teams and special project groups have been set up on the basis of action profiles. Appointments, transferences and promotions and, in some cases, dismissals have been made with reference to action profile information. For a totally 'people-centred' approach to the study of managerial behaviour this is indeed a widespread and comprehensive application within a company. The action profile approach as it now stands has considerable weaknesses and is as yet under-researched and underdeveloped. It obviously has, however, great potential as a tool for studying managerial behaviour and providing a framework to allow the application of the knowledge gained to practical day to day management functioning.

So far as the theory behind the action profile method is concerned, for further confirmation it must await further research. The studies carried out so far have obviously been inadequate, but not so inadequate as to give no hope for improvement and greater accuracy. The whole system still needs to be investigated at many different levels. First there is the straight movement observation level. There is a need for inter-observer reliability studies. Some work has been done in this direction but not enough (see page 92). There is a need for more investigation into the movement phenomenon itself. There is some work being carried out in California upon the physiological components of the activation of the various movement elements and its relationship with cortical activity which looks interesting, but it is still in infant stages. Secondly there is still the link between the activation of movement elements (tension states) and psychological or motivational states to be studied further. Thirdly there is the application of action profile information in management to training, development, study of team style, study of the creation of business climates, etc., etc., to be researched in greater depth.

The action profile method has reached a stage already however, both in theory and practice, where it is capable of revealing some very interesting features about managerial behaviour which of course this book has been relating. The most significant feature brought to light is the compelling nature of certain behavioural characteristics; i.e. the action motivations. That if a manager is to be self motivated (hence satisfied and effective) then he must be able to act in accordance with his action profile. That if a manager has a certain degree of freedom of action and has a reasonably stable sense of identity he will act in accordance with his action profile and will thereby create a certain kind of business climate. It is very revealing to talk to managers about their pattern of action motivation.

A manager who is strong in *determining* and weak in *exploring* for instance will so often say: 'But the situation here demands persistence and determination. I recognize I don't do much *exploring* but there's never time. I would like to concentrate more on that side of things but the pressure at present is just too great.' (You can be sure he'll never find the time!) The man who is strong in *exploring* and weak in *determining* in exactly the same situation will say: 'Well I never do push things much. There's no need really. There's always a way round a problem. If you once stop looking for alternatives in this kind of business you've had it.'

The manager who is a strong *presenter* and strong in *determining* and *confronting* will say: 'Of course in this kind of set up you have to make things clear. People don't know where they are if you don't take a firm stand. I assure you it's absolutely essential to talk straight to people, then they'll get on with it.' The strong *communicator — investigator — explorer* in the same situation will say: 'Well I just think it's pretty important to involve people from the beginning. I always try to get my subordinates to contribute to any plan. I find you get much greater co-operation if you just talk to them on their own level and ask for suggestions. Once they're involved they tend to get on with it much better. Of course, you do have to vary your approach for different people though. People are all so different.' The strong *operator—*

decider—anticipator in the same situation again may pay elaborate lip service to whatever's going, but in fact he'll just get on with it. He'll just organize people into action.

Two managers were asked to define the action requirements for a job which was to head up a project for planning the installation of a computer system. One was a straight *operator*. He said the job was straightforward organization and required no particular surveying or research work just *operating*. The other manager was strongly *investigatory* and *determined*. He said the job required the ability first to *investigate* the situation and devise the best method of application and second it required the *determination* to sell the plan (i.e. *presenting* as well as *determining*) and to stick to it against all the vying opposition and counter suggestions.

Managers see their function in terms of their action motivations to an extraordinary degree. With experience and education on a framework like the twelve action requirements they accept intellectually that there are different ways of approaching a job. They realize that a particular function may not actually require what they think it does in terms of their own action motivations. But they will still see their own function as requiring the action they are motivated to take. And this is right, for then they will be self motivated and effective. But it is all the more necessary then to know what these action motivations are, both for oneself and for the other members of a team. Not only so that you can ensure there is opportunity for their maximum and most suitable expression but so that you know what kind of business climate will be created. Then you will discover you are not only employing management practice—you are acting out *your* individual motivations and, in so doing, actually creating the management context.

The Interaction Value of Posture and Gesture

Aim: To discover whether:

1 Posture-Gesture Merging (PGM) expression in interaction is interpreted as a genuine and wholehearted and sincere expression of meaning.
2 Gestural expression in interaction is interpreted as an insincere, conventionalized or somewhat empty apology for a true expression of meaning.

The following detailed hypotheses were set up:

Hypotheses

1 Verbal communication backed up by PGM movement will be experienced as a convincing and sincere expression of the verbal message.
2 Verbal communication supported by gestural movement will be experienced as insincere, unconvincing.

Subjects were 30 students at a teacher training college: 3 males, 27 females average age 22 years.

Method

To test each hypothesis there was a 'performance' of a simple message, individually by five trained 'interactors'. For each of the two performances the interactors were taken away for $\frac{1}{4}$ hour and trained:

1 For the first performance, to repeat a simple message such as 'I'm pleased to see you' backed up with a PGM movement expression. In this instance it was simply a handshake.
2 For the second performance the interactors were trained to repeat the same message as for the first performance but this time accompanied by a gesture—again a handshake but with the movement strictly confined to the arm and hand only.

The verbal messages were:

> 1 I'm pleased to see you.
> 2 It's a privilege to meet you.
> 3 Come in you're welcome.
> 4 Goodbye you can rely upon me to help.

Each interactor chose his own message and style of movement accompaniment according to how comfortable he felt with it.

After the ¼ hour training the interactors (I1–I5) went back to the room where the other 25 'respondents' were waiting. They were situated in five groups of five (R1–R5) around the room, each in front of a screen (S1–S5).

> C = Communicator
> R = Respondent Group (of 5)
> S = Screen

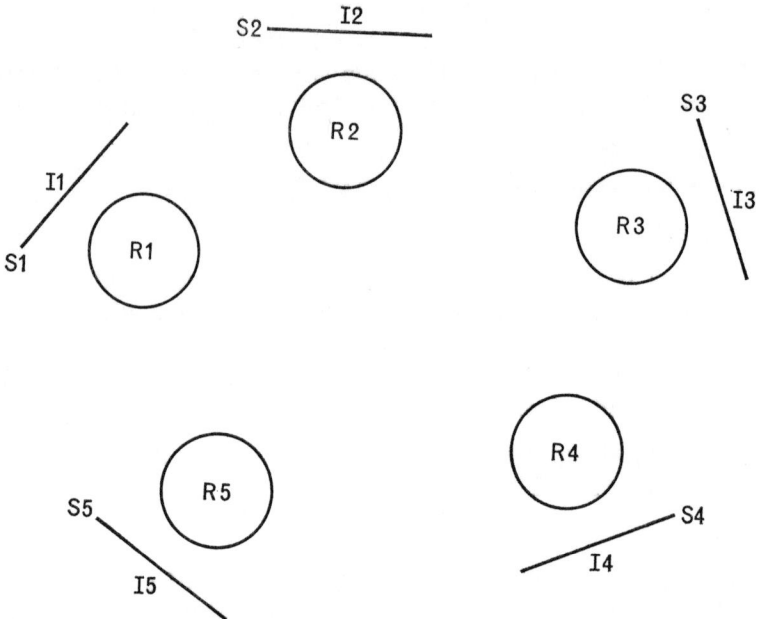

The interactors (I1–I5) each went behind a screen. The respondents went behind the screen one at a time and received their respective messages. They then filled in a report sheet (see page 241) whilst the interactors were taken off and trained for the second performance. On their return they each rotated one screen. I1 went to the second screen S2 and received respondent group R2, I2 to S3 and received respondent group R3, etc.

This was done to reduce any bias occurring due to the characteristics of any particular interactor. (The design of the experiment was in fact more complex than so far explained. There were six hypotheses to be tested and a corresponding six performances. The rotation ensured that each group of respondents met each interactor at least once.)

An example of the report sheet filled in after each performance by each respondent is below.

REPORT SHEET 1

Name...................................

Meeting No. ....

Interactor Name...

Group No. ....

Of the following words tick which you think to be *relevant* to the interactor you have just experienced.

Sincere	Unrewarding	Seriously Intended
Unpleasant	Convincing	Unconvincing
Laughable	Insincere	Rewarding
	Pleasant	

Write here the word you think *best* describes the message you received

....

As can be seen the respondents were asked:

1 To choose from ten words (five pairs of opposites) which they considered to be a 'relevant' description of the message they had just received. They could mark as many or few as they wished.
2 To write a word which they considered to be the 'best' description of the message. A verbal instruction was given that it could be a sentence or paragraph, whatever they felt they needed to express their opinion.

Performance 1: PGM Movement Back-up

The table would seem to indicate that there is some consensus of opinion that to the first performance where the verbal message was backed up by PGM movement, that the words, *sincere, unconvincing* and *pleasant* are most relevant.

The application of *unconvincing* is something of a contradiction but it is significant that the judgements of *unconvincing* were concentrated on two only out of the five interactors and not scattered across the whole line. It was apparent at the time that these two interactors were not responding as well to the training as the others.

The words used to give the 'best' description of the message conveyed are also revealing in this respect. The message conveyed by the first of the above mentioned interactors was described by four of the respondents as *seriously intended,* and by one as *unconvincing.* The other had received a mixed

Results

Table showing comparison of the total number of times each word was marked as 'relevant' for Performance 1 (PGM) and Performance 2 (Gesture)

	Performance 1 PGM	Performance 2 Gesture
Sincere	13	5
Convincing	7	2
Seriously Intended	7	6
Pleasant	14	4
Rewarding	0	1
Insincere	3	5
Unconvincing	8	6
Laughable	3	12
Unpleasant	2	1
Unrewarding	0	1

Table 17

reaction—*insincere* (2), *pleasant* (1), *laughable* (1) and *convincing* (1). It is probable that she was in fact putting across a rather conflicting message for it is quite possible to express all kinds of inconsistency both in non-verbal expression itself and in the relation between the verbal and non-verbal expression.

The message conveyed by the other three interactors were described variously as *genuine, sincere, convincing* and *pleasant* and for each there was considerable uniformity of judgement within each group of respondents even though they filled in the report forms without reference to each other.

Performance 2: Gesture Back-up

For performance 2 where the verbal message was accompanied by gestural movement, the strongest consensus was that the word *laughable* was relevant. Apart from that there is a pretty mixed opinion.

The words used for the best description are again perhaps more revealing. Positive words like *convincing, sincere* and *pleasant* are used with reference to one interactor only and every one of her group of five respondents used one of these words to describe the message conveyed by her.

The reports upon all the other interactors are a great mixture. *Laughable* is used four times, *unconvincing* twice, *seriously intended* once and *unrewarding* once. Examples of other comments are: *Pleasant but automatic; without much significance; good, strong and welcoming but overdone; I felt like a stooge in a comedy; I felt ridiculed; so false; felt sent up; fairly pleasant but sincerity uncertain; very strong but a little too harsh; trying to be sincere but unconvincing; trying not to 'colour' the words.*

Discussion

Hypothesis 1: Verbal communication backed up by PGM movement will be experienced as a convincing and sincere expression of the verbal message.

There does seem to be some measure of support for this hypothesis, but the evidence is not completely conclusive.

Hypothesis 2: Verbal communication supported by gestural movement will be experienced as insincere, unconvincing.

The hypothesis is not supported to the letter but there is indication that a modification would prove realistic.

It can certainly be said, as a result of this experiment, that people do seem to be sensitive to the difference between a verbal expression backed up by PGM movement and one accompanied by gestural movement. There is a tendency for the verbal message accompanied by a total bodily expression or PGM movement to be interpreted as a consistent expression, i.e. where the message is one of welcome, there is a tendency for it to be interpreted in terms such as *pleasant*, as well as *sincere*, and *convincing*. When, however, the verbal message is accompanied by gestural movement there is a greater tendency for inconsistencies to appear in the interpretations. The verbal message was clearly one of welcome, but the accompanying gestural movement expression caused people to be confused as to the 'real' or intended meaning of the message. The written opinions do indicate that there was a considerable amount of feeling that the message itself was inconsistent or just plain insincere—or a mockery of a real expression of meaning.

Conclusion

It is not surprising that there were variations in the interpretations of both types of expression. People obviously vary in the sensitivity to the subtleties of non-verbal expression. In addition, the interactors obviously varied in their ability to alter the bodily expression to order. However, there was enough uniformity of interpretation to indicate that there is a perceivable difference in the interaction value of the PGM expression and the gestural expression if not exactly as predicted at least along the lines that were indicated.

Videotape Pilot Study

A brief résumé of this study was given in the section on research into the action profile as a valid description of behaviour (page 112). In full it is as follows:

Aims

1 To find out if the action motivation definitions could be used to analyse the contributions made by individual managers in carrying out a group task.
2 To find out whether these categories were useful and meaningful to a group of observers relatively untrained in these concepts in order to describe the progress of the group interaction.
3 To ascertain whether the assessments made by the observers of the managers in the action motivation terms corresponded at all with our own assessments made on the basis of movement patterns.

Procedure

1 Four people were invited to come as observers. These were associates who knew of our work, but had no first hand experience of it.
2 Paisley, Child and Travers were given two brief case studies to work on. They were given three-quarters of an hour on each one.
3 Whilst they were working, the meeting was videotaped and the observers watched it on a monitor T.V. in another room. Previously they had been given a half hour explanation of the first nine action motivations.
   (i) During the first session they were asked to classify each manager's behaviour according to the action motivation classification, considering only the first six factors. They were given tabulated recording sheets on which they attempted to tally the incidence of behaviour for each manager according to the action classification.
   (ii) During the second session they were required to tally or observe the incidence of behaviour according to the three interaction modes.

The action profiles of the three subjects are as follows:

Paisley, Child, Travers, first six action requirements only

Key		Paisley	Child	Travers
		% of activity	% of activity	% of activity
ATTENTION	Investigating	25	15	10
	Exploring		6	10
				12
INTENTION	Determining	30	31	10
	Confronting	12	24	28
COMMITMENT	Deciding	15	9	30
	Anticipating	8 / 10	15	

Action Profile 26 VIDEOTAPE PILOT STUDY

||||| Shading indicates areas of greatest emphasis

As can be seen, Paisley's activity is strongly weighted toward the attention stage. As much as 35 per cent of his application will be concentrated in this way. Of Child's activity, 56 per cent is concentrated particularly in the intention phase of the sequence whereas Travers' activity to complete the picture is primarily located in the commitment stage 58 per cent. They all show a fairly even weighting between the assertion and perspective factors particularly in their strongest area. In each case the area of greatest activity is shaded in for easy reference.

Results

1 The observers reported in a discussion after the observation sessions, that they had found the classification reasonably easy to use and had found it applicable to the behaviour that occurred. However, not surprisingly it

was revealed in the discussion that misunderstandings of the definitions had occurred and this, of course, reduced the accuracy of the observations made.

2 Analysis of the observers' scoring sheets gave a total for each manager of the incidences of behaviour observed under each of the six classifications. This was calculated as a percentage of the total incidence of behaviour recorded for each manager. The results are presented in the table below.

For each manager the first column represents the distribution of activity as judged by the observers, and next to it is the assessment according to the movement pattern.

Comparison of action patterns derived respectively from observations of group behaviour and observations of movement

	Paisley		Child		Travers	
	% of activity		% of activity		% of activity	
	Observers' assessment	Move- ment assess- ment	Observers' assessment	Move- ment assess- ment	Observers' assessment	Move- ment assess- ment
Investigating	15	20	15	15	9	10
Exploring	55	35	14	6	13	10
Determining	8	12	32	31	17	12
Confronting	9	15	19	24	46	10
Deciding	10	8	13	9	9	28
Anticipating	3	10	7	15	6	30
	100%	100%	100%	100%	100%	100%

Table 18

As can be seen there is a reasonably close correlation between the observers' judgement and the movement pattern of analysis for Paisley and Child, particularly where the area of predominant emphasis was concerned. The observers were able to see fairly clearly that Paisley concentrated most of his activity in the attention area, with a weighting on the perspective side, *exploring*, and that Child placed most emphasis on the intention stage with a weighting toward the assertion or *determining* side. Travers, however, would appear to have been mistakenly assessed, or was acting decidedly out of character.

A calculation of the degree of correspondence between the observer's assessments and the movement assessment, for each subject, over the six factors revealed that for Child the correspondence was significant, there being less than a 1 per cent probability that the same results could occur by chance. For Paisley, however, the probability for the same results occurring by chance was 15 per cent, for Travers 25 per cent.

Here one has to take into consideration the nature of the tasks set. They were both case studies requiring primarily consideration, survey, review, questioning. The aim of the first exercise, for instance, is expressed as follows: 'to establish what consensus of opinion exists among you prior to meeting with him' (the Managing Director).

It is a primarily attention—intention oriented situation, therefore the expression of commitment is bound to be somewhat reduced. It is interesting to note in this connection that the Managing Director of Travers' company was told about the proposed experiment in considerable detail. He has had close experience of the action profile assessment concepts over a number of years and has become quite skilled in categorizing and recognizing the behaviour of his managers in these terms. His comment on the experiment was: 'I don't expect they [the observers] will have much trouble in identifying the attention and intention weighted chaps, but I bet they won't pick the commitment bloke. It's difficult to see a "committer" in action in a meeting'.

Since then, more and more experience has been gathered with this type of material. It has become apparent that the commitment oriented manager 'bides his time' in discussions and meetings. He is expert at seizing upon other people's ideas, projecting the implications and either dropping them or encouraging their progress toward a concrete plan of action. Our own detailed analysis of Travers' contribution revealed this kind of pattern. He showed constant concern with the actual implementation of any suggested course of action accompanied always by a consideration of the likely consequences. He was concerned with the sequential or programming aspects of a suggested plan, even before it was accepted. He suggested few ideas of his own, but exploited and developed those of the other managers if he saw the prospect of a concrete plan of action coming out of them.

To return to the experiment with the three managers, Paisley, Child and Travers, during the second exercise the observers were asked to classify the managers, this time according to the three interaction modes *communicating, presenting* and *operating*. The results were as in Table 19.

Again Travers has caused the most disagreement. The complete action profiles of the three are on page 249.

The *dynamism* has been included as this is the comparative measure that puts the pattern of the first six action characteristics in context. As the *dynamism* is measured on a four point scale Travers is pretty high in comparison to other managers, whereas Paisley is fairly low. The *dynamism* measure can be used as an index for accurate comparison. If Paisley's

Assessment of interaction strengths derived from observations of group behaviour

	Paisley	Child	Travers
Observer 1	Predominantly a *communicator*	Predominantly a *presenter*	Predominantly a *presenter*
Observer 2	Predominantly a *communicator*	Predominantly a *presenter* but with strong signs of *operating*	A *communicator* or a *presenter*
Observer 3	Predominantly a *communicator*	Predominantly a *presenter* with most *operating* of the three	A *presenter*
Observer 4	Predominantly a *communicator*	Predominantly a *presenter*	Predominantly an *operator*

Table 19

percentages are multiplied by 2, Child's by 3 and Travers' by 4, a true comparison can be made.

The interaction capacities are shown by the extent to which the area is shaded in. An interaction ability can be as great as the extent of the 'ingredients' or action components, but no greater. Paisley places greater emphasis upon the *communicating* mode of relating than Child not because there is any greater harmony in his 'manner' or non-verbal expression of *communicating*, but because he has more to *communicate* with; i.e. his *investigating* and *exploring*, the components of *communicating* are more strongly evident. If according to the *dynamism* weighting, however, one makes a strict comparison, Child is closer to Paisley in his *communicating* ability than would at first sight appear. The profiles weighted according to the *dynamism* measure appear on page 250.

The adjustments to enable true comparison have been made because this exercise drew from the observers comments of a comparative nature. Just looking at the interaction factors now it can be seen that:

(a) Paisley is still the strongest *communicator*
(b) Child is still the strongest *presenter*
(c) Travers is obviously the strongest *operator*
    but
(d) Now Travers appears as the second strongest in the *presenting* mode whereas on the previous chart it appears to be Paisley.

Reference to the observers' comments shows that Paisley was unanimously seen to be the most predominant in relating in the *communicating* mode. One

Key	Paisley		Child		Travers	
	% of activity	Inter-action	% of activity	Inter-action	% of activity	Inter-action
ATTENTION	25		15		10	
Investigating						
Communicating			6		10	
Exploring					12	
INTENTION	30		31			
Determining					10	
Presenting						
Confronting	12		24		28	
COMMITMENT	15					
Deciding			9			
Operating	8				30	
Anticipating	10		15			
Dynamism	2·0		3·0		3·9	
Adaptability	3·9		2·0		0·0	
Identification (N.B.)	3·0		1·0		2·5	

Action Profile 27 VIDEOTAPE PILOT STUDY

of the observers commented in fact that he seemed primarily concerned to preserve harmony within the group—not surprising as according to the definition of *communicating* it is primarily the promoting of an environment where mutual understanding and a reciprocal interchange of information can flourish. The observers' assessment of Paisley corroborates the action profile, based upon the movement pattern.

Child was considered by all to be predominantly a *presenter* in manner of relating. Two of the observers saw some sign of the *operational* mode, which

Action Profiles weighted according to *dynamism* measure

Key	Paisley % of 200	Inter-action	Child % of 300	Inter-action	Travers % of 400	Inter-action
ATTENTION					40	
Investigating					40	
Communicating						
Exploring			45		48	
INTENTION			18		40	
Determining						
Presenting	50		93		112	
Confronting	60					
COMMITMENT			72			
Deciding	24					
	30		27		120	
Operating	16					
Anticipating	20		45			
Dynamism	2·0		3·0		4·0	

Action Profile 28   VIDEOTAPE PILOT STUDY

we too have indicated, none observed any evidence of *communicating*. This again corroborates our view as in our assessment *communicating* is Child's least emphasized mode of relating.

Travers was considered by all except one observer to be predominantly a *presenter*. As the comparative profiles show, he is indeed strong in the *presenting* mode. A later detailed analysis of the interaction revealed that Travers did display a great deal of *presenting* behaviour, but that his *operational* tendencies were still strongly evident. Again the nature of the task which was like the first primarily rooted in the attention — intention stages may have caused the overshadowing of the *operational* mode. Another factor to be borne in mind was that during the second exercise Child became very firmly fixed upon one particular idea. He persisted in *presenting* this one idea with enormous conviction over and over again. Travers didn't see this as an idea leading to a practicable programme of action. Hence before he could get to the implementation stage, he had to match Child's *presentation*. This naturally cast a spotlight upon the *presentational* interaction between the two men and much of the second exercise was taken up with this conflict of intention.

Observer 4 recognized, however, the *operational* leanings in Travers' manner of relating. She commented that he seemed 'more calculating, more far-sighted, more ready to think of the future than the others', that he seemed to be 'working through other people's ideas in order to achieve an end result'. She added, 'I got the idea that he'd already committed himself, but was just going through a process.'

Text References and Further Reading

1. FINKLE, R. F. and JONES, S. W., *Assessing Corporate Talent*, Wiley Interscience, New York 1970.

2. McCLELLAND, David, *New Society*.

3. ARGYLE, Michael, *Social Interaction*, Methuen & Co. Ltd., London 1969, p. 135.

4. SMITH, P. B., 'The T Group in Industry', *New Society*, 6 August, 1964.

5. CAMPBELL, J. P. and DUNRETTE, M. D., 'Effectiveness of T Group Experiences in Managerial Training and Development', *Psycholog. Bulletin* 70, 1968, pp. 73–104.

6. BLAKE, R. R., MOUTON, J. S., BARNES, J. S. and GREINER, L. E., 'Breakthrough in Organisation Development', *Harvard Business Review*, 43, 1964, pp. 133–155.

7. BLAKE, R. R., MOUTON, J. S. and BLANSFIELD, M. G., 'How Executive Team Training Can Help You', *Journal of American Society for Training and Development*, iv (i), 1962.

8. RACKHAM, N. with COLBERT, M., HONEY, P., MORGAN, T., *et al.*, *DIS*, *Interactive Skills, Commercial and Industrial Training*, April–December 1971.

9. MASLOW, Abraham, *Motivation and Personality*, Harper & Row Inc., N.Y. 1954.

10. HERZBERG, Frederick, *et al.*, *The Motivation to Work*, John Wiley & Son, New York 1959.

11. SECORD, P. F., 'The Role of Facial Features in Interpersonal Perception', in R. TAGUIRI and L. PETRULLI (eds), *Person Perception and Interpersonal Behaviour*, Staford U.P., 1958.

12. BRUNSWICK, E., 'Social Perception of Traits from Photographs', *Psycholog. Bulletin* 42, pp. 535–536, 1945.

13. ARGYLE, M., SALTER, T., BURGESS, P., NICHOLSON, H. and WILLIAMS, M. (1969), 'The Effects of Verbal and Non-Verbal Signals'—roneoed—See *Argyle Social Interaction* (3).

14. MEHRABIAN, A. and FERRIS, S. R., 'Inferences of Attitudes from Non-Verbal Communication in Two Channels', *Journal Consult. Psychol.*, 31, 248–252.

15. BIRDWHISTELL, R. L., *Kinesics in Context*, Allen Lane the Penguin Press, London 1971; Univ. Pennsylvania Press, Phil., 1970. *Description of Birdwhistell's Mother*, p. 52.

16. HARRISON, R. P., 'Dictic Analysis towards a vocabulary and syntax for the pictorial code, with research on facial communication', *Diss. Abs.* 26, 519.

17. KESTENBERG, Judith, 'The Role of Movement Patterns in Development, II. The Flow of Tension and Effort', in *Psychoanal. Quarterly*, Vol. xxxvl, No. 4, 1965.

18. LABAN, Rudolf and LAWRENCE, F. C., *Effort*, Macdonald and Evans, London 1947.

   Rudolf Laban, born 1879 in Bratislava, then part of the Austro-Hungarian Empire, became interested at an early age in the theatre, studied architecture at the Ecole de Beaux Arts in Paris, then branched out into stage, design, drama and dance. His basic interest was the architectural aspects of human movement and the nature of the effort which produced the movement. He developed theories which were to have influence way beyond the sphere of the theatre. The elements of movement analysis which he laid down have been the basis for developments in several spheres: education (known as modern educational dance); therapy; personality assessment; child development and interaction study.

19. KESTENBERG, Judith, MARCUS, H., ROBBINS, E., BERLOWE, J. and BUELTE, A., *Development of the Young Child as Expressed Through Bodily Movement I*, Sands Point BNY—roneoed.

20. KESTENBERG, Judith, 'The Role of Movement Patterns in Development I Rhythms of Movement', in *Psychoanal. Quarterly*, Vol. xxxiv, No. 1, 1965.

21. LAMB, Warren and TURNER, David, *Management Behaviour*, Gerald Duckworth & Co., London 1969.

22. DELL, Cecily, *A Primer for Movement Description*, D.N.B. Inc. 1970, to be obtained from D.N.B. (Center for Movement Research and Analysis), 8 East 12th Street, New York, 10003.

Index

Page references in italic indicate a table or a diagram